# Nation and National Identity in South Asia



Edited by

**S.L. Sharma**

and

**T.K. Oommen**

**Orient Longman**

The papers included in this volume, except for the Introduction, were originally published in the *Sociological Bulletin,* Journal of the Indian Sociological Society, 48 (1 & 2) 1999.

The map on the cover of this book is not to scale. The external boundaries and coastline of India as depicted are neither authentic nor correct.

NATION AND NATIONAL IDENTITY IN SOUTH ASIA

**ORIENT LONGMAN PRIVATE LIMITED**

*Registered Office*
3-6-272 Himayatnagar, Hyderabad 500 029 (A.P.), INDIA

*Other Offices*
Bangalore, Bhopal, Bhubaneshwar, Chandigarh, Chennai, Ernakulam, Guwahati, Hyderabad, Jaipur, Kolkata, Lucknow, Mumbai, New Delhi, Patna



First published 2000
Reprinted 2002

ISBN 81 250 1924 3

*Typeset at*
Bukprint
Delhi

*Printed in India at*
Baba Barkha Nath Printers
New Delhi

*Published by*
Orient Longman Private Limited
1/24 Asaf Ali Road
New Delhi 110 002

# Contents

# Contents

# Nation and National Identity in South Asia

# Foreword

It gives me great pleasure in associating myself with the publication of this volume on *Nation and National Identity in South Asia* edited by S.L. Sharma and T.K. Oommen. With this publication, the Indian Sociological Society (ISS) has opened a new chapter in its history.

The ISS is the only national level professional association of sociologists in India, with nearly 2000 life members from all parts of the country. Since its inception in December 1951, the ISS has been publishing, without interruption, a bi-annual journal, *Sociological Bulletin*, which occupies a respected place among the Social Science journals in India and abroad.

In the combined issue (1 and 2) of volume 48, the ISS published a bunch of high quality papers addressing the theme of *Nation and National Identity in South Asia.* Following a spontaneous and positive response from the reader, the ISS decided to publish it as a book for wider circulation of the ideas and arguments contained in the issue. Orient Longman readily agreed to the proposal and brought all their expertise and resources to bring out the volume on time without sacrificing their traditions of high publishing standards.

This is indeed a moment of pride for all of us in the ISS coming as it does close to its Golden Jubilee year. Having taken the first successful step, I am sure the ISS will be able to launch several such publications in the future.

The major credit for accomplishing this great but difficult task goes to Prof. T.K. Oommen. As the then President of the ISS, he conceived the whole project, persuaded colleagues to contribute seminal papers, and saw to its successful execution. Prof. S.L. Sharma, Managing Editor, *Sociological Bulletin*, who edited the papers, initially for the journal and later for this volume, also wrote the useful Introduction. I would like to thank both these colleagues for initiating a pioneering enterprise, which will serve as a model for their successors.

I also wish to thank all the contributors for making this historic event possible.

**B.S. Baviskar**
*President*
Indian Sociological Society

Delhi
28 July 2000

# The Discourse on the National Question in South Asia

*S.L. Sharma*

It is well known that much of our received knowledge about the concepts of nation and nation-state is derived from the West and is based on the Western experience. The experience of the rest of the world, particularly of South Asia, is different from that of the West. For the same reason, South Asia provides a fascinating laboratory for the study of the national question, for testing the formulations derived from the west, and also for generating new formulations. A preserve of political scientists until recently, sociologists have now begun to make forays into this field. While the first major sociological work on Indian nationalism by A.R. Desai appeared as far back as 1948, more recently, the Indian Sociological Society gave a new impetus to sociological discourse on the theme by choosing it as the main theme of its 25th All India Sociological Conference. The present book is a compendium of select papers presented at the conference and subsequently featured in the *Sociological Bulletin* (Vol. 48, 1999).

The intent of this introductory essay is not just to provide an overview of the contributions but to identify and analyse the issues thrown up by them. The idea is to make theoretical sense of the discourse and try and understand its distinctiveness vis-a-vis Western thinking on the subject. A brief digest of the papers is, nevertheless, necessary even for the purpose of analytical enterprise.

The contributions included in the book seek to conceptualise the experience of nation formation and de-formation in South Asia, particularly India, Pakistan, Bangladesh and Sri Lanka. Oommen, whose work on the theme of nation and state has exercised a major influence on South Asian studies in one way or another, focuses on the modes of conceptualising nation and nationality in the Indian subcontinent. He identifies and interrogates the following seven ways in which nation has been defined in the Indian subcontinent: as ancient civilisational entity, composite culture, political entity, religious entity, geographical/territorial entity with a specific cultural ethos, a collection of linguistic entities, and a unity of great and little nations. Of these seven he finds the sixth, that is the collectivity of linguistic groups proximate to 'our social reality' (p. 15), with the remaining ones suffering from ambiguity and ambivalence.

Without necessarily following the order in the list of contents, the other papers are abstracted here in terms of the following thematic scheme: a) the genesis of the nation-state in the West; b) the problematics of nation-building in India in relation to language, region, tribe, religion, caste and gender; c) the issues of nation-making and nationality in other parts of South Asia, such as Pakistan, Bangladesh and Sri Lanka; and d) the concept of civil society and the relationship between the state and civil society in India.

### The rise of the nation-state

About the rise of the nation state first. Reviewing the two prevailing views on the rise of the nation-state in the West—the ethnic drive argument and the capitalist engine argument—Gupta finds both of these indaequate to explain the emergence of the nation-state. In respect of the capitalist engine argument, he rejects both the structuralist and the conspiracy positions. Yet, he notes that 'capitalism and nationalism have been coevals' (p. 60). He also notes that capitalism undermined the old systems of stratification which were closed and ascriptive and replaced them with open systems of stratification. Given its universalistic orientation and its stress on the breakdown of closed systems of stratification, Gupta asks, 'Where is it in capitalism, with its open class structure, that nation-states are made essential?' He attributes it to capitalism's search for commitment. According to him, the old systems of stratification were marked by discrete units, the principle of repulsion and the potential of a viable basis of identity formation. But not so the open systems of stratification which are distinguished by continuous hierarchies that provide no bases for exclusivist identity formation. This creates structural pressures on capitalism to generate a new exclusivist identity in the form of a supra-local community called nation-state. It enables capitalism to disparage and undermine the primordial localised loyalties of kin, caste, religion and the like, on the one hand, and on the other, power capitalism with the 'politics of commitment' in place of the 'politics of responsibility'.

### The problematic of nation formation in India

Turning to the problematic of nation formation, Karna analyses the role of language and region in the formation of national identity and in shaping the pattern of the state-nation relationship in India. He also sheds light on the historic significance of the linguistic reorganisation of states in India and the consequences for nation formation. He finds the European model of nation-state unsuitable for a proper understanding of nation and nationality in India and pleads for adopting an alternative model of a multi-national state. In a similar vein, Pathy criticises the Indian state for following the Western model of nation-state and undermining tribal identities and pauperising the tribal peoples. Providing a systematic profile of the regional distribution of tribes in India, he offers a sensitive account of how the Indian state has conducted itself more in the manner of a nation-state in spite of its multi-national character, and how it has deprived the tribals of much of their land, livehood, language, religion and culture.

Surveying the visions of nationhood and religiosity among a select group of freedom fighters in India, Nandi shows how a secularist ideology permeated the speeches and writings of the founding fathers of modern India from Mahadev Govind Ranade to Jawaharlal Nehru. He locates the source of this secularist ideology in the assimilative, all-encompassing and eclectic religious tradition in India and accords to it the credit for the triumph of forces of integration over disintegration.

Given the vital place of caste in Indian social structure, it is only to be expected that caste would get implicated with the project of nation formation in India. Aloysius attempts to explain the ways in which caste has come to be implicated with nation and religion in modern India. He argues that the agency of nationalism here has continued to be more or less exclusively dominated by the communities accustomed to the wielding of power within the caste-varna mode since the beginning to the present. Endorsing the lower caste evaluation of nationalism as a brahmanic/upper caste obsession, he observes: 'Every effort was made by nationalists to ignore the existence of those who ought not to, according to tradition, venture into the public realm; when this was not possible their attempt at emergence was ridiculed as job-hunting or as tailor-parliamentarian and when this too would not suffice, their bid for power was confronted with plain violence' (p. 167). Referring to Gandhi's candid declaration in favour of the varna ideal and Ambedkar's opposition to it, he shows how the debate was settled mostly in favour of the caste forces represented by Gandhi (p. 168). Not surprisingly, secularism has been appropriated by the nationalists to mean equal regard for all religions. Thus, 'the traditional socio-religious practice of the dominant has reincarnated with no change in essentials as the new civil religion in modernity and secularism' (p.170).

Chaudhuri turns the spotlight on gender and provides a broad mapping of the manner in which women have been addressed both in the making of the Indian nation, and in the running of the Indian state. She argues that the Indian state has perceived women primarily in three ways: as agents and recipients of development, as citizens with equal rights, and finally, as cultural emblems. Her lament, however, is that the state betrays what it professes in what it practises. She attributes this to the inherent contradictions of a liberal state which is wedded to equality on the one hand, and to patriarchal private property on the other, to individual rights of women on the one hand, and to rights of cultural and religious practices on the other.

## Nation formation in South Asia

Moving to the other parts of South Asia, Fazal highlights the role of religion in the genesis of Pakistan and language and territory in that of Bangladesh. Born out of the idea of Muslim nationalism, Pakistan could not sustain the tempo of religious nationalism. In a matter of a few decades, the problem of ethno-nationalism gained stridency in the form of the Muhajir movement to contest the hegemonic project of the Pakistani state. However, the most decisive blow came from Bengali nationalism which was based on the edifice of cultural specificity, linguistic identity and territorial integrity, leading to the emergence of Bangladesh in 1971. Not much impressed with the role of religion and language in view of the flexibility in conceiving nation, Fazal, in the final analysis underlines the crucial importance of the 'subjective will' of the political actors as the only viable attribute of nation.

The problem of national identity in Sri Lanka engages the attention of Silva who explains it in terms of the dialectical interaction between caste and ethnicity. In the light of the available evidence, he maintains that certain caste grievances and skirmishes preceded the rise of ethnicity among northern Tamils in Sri Lanka. The weakening of the hierarchical ideology of caste, in his view, was perhaps necessary for the rise of a strong ethnic ideology of 'a deep horizontal comradeship', to use Anderson's phrase (Anderson 1983). Silva, further, traces the rise of Sinhala-Buddhist nationalism to the caste dynamics among the Sinhalese. However, the real boost to ethno-nationalist conflict in Sri Lanka, according to him, came from the hegemonic turn in Sinhala-Buddhist nationalism with its 'Sinhala only' official language policy. In conclusion, he observes: 'Since ethnicity in parts of South Asia may have some continuity with the traditional caste system, it may be qualitatively different from ethnicity in the rest of the world' (p. 214), and for the same reason, it may pose a more serious challenge to nation-building in south Asia.

### The state and civil society

Finally, the contributions on the theme of civil society. Reflecting on the concept of civil society, Uberoi says that 'the question of civil society can be approached from either of two opposed aspects, the question of culture and the question of power'... (p.19). From the cultural aspect, civil society can be viewed as 'a natural and universal development of intermediary institutions between the priest and the prince'... (p.19). Viewed from the power aspect, he finds civil society represented by intermediary institutions between the family and the state. Advancing his own position, Uberoi argues that 'civil society is a category of universal human society, or of historical civilisation as against pre-history, and not only a category of bourgeois society, or of modern capitalism, for example, as in the tradition from Hegal to Habermas' (p.19). He contends that civil society is 'often established on the life and death of the martyr rather than of the hero (or the victim)', it therefore, also requires 'new forms and concepts of pluralism, mediation of the one and the many, and of the common usage or custom of the people (vernacularism) to sustain it, whether in general amity or enmity, solidarity and reciprocity, conformity or transgression' (p. 19). In the light of the above hypothesis, Uberoi traces the struggle of civil society in India to 'the rise and recognition of the vernaculars and vernacularism everywhere in language, labour and culture'... (p. 29). He adds that 'it is the story of religion and politics proceeding from Kabir (1440-1518) to Mahatma Gandhi. Its political culmination, if we may call it that, is the movement for the linguistic reorganisation of the states of the Union after 1950...' (p. 29).

Pandey cautions us against the received understanding of the relationship between the state and civil society as mutually exclusive and hostile. Treating such an understanding as fallacious, he argues that 'state and/or society are interwined concepts denoting a dynamic discourse, each affecting and getting affected by the other, and neither of them being socially frozen identities/entities' (p. 42). He criticises both liberals and culturalists alike for raising the bogey of anti-statism and celebration of civil society. While the liberals have (mis)appropriated the term democracy to legitimise social inequalities under the banner of civil society, the culturalists have joined the bandwagon of civil society to find legitimacy for the religious, linguistic and ethnic movements against the 'homogenising Indian state' (p. 49). However, 'a weak state does not mean a strong civil society' argues Pandey (45). The prevailing ideology of anti-statism (or trans-nationalism, a more respectable term for globalisation and multinational corporatism), he apprehends, is problematic on account of the forces of cultural fundamentalism, on the one hand, and the celebration of free market and civil society, on the other (p. 56).

## Conceptual, substantive and theoretical issues

Having provided a gist of the papers, it is time to reflect on the issues — conceptual, substantive and theoretical — emerging from the contributions. On the conceptual front, the most important is the idea of nation and its conceptual constituents. Almost every article in the book addresses the concept of nation in one way or another. Leaving aside its varied conceptualisations in the West, in both liberal and Marxist historiography, in the context of the Indian subcontinent itself, Oommen distinguishes, as indicated earlier, seven ways in which nation has been interpreted. After reviewing the diverse interpretations, he settles for a definition of nation as a 'fusion between territory and culture' (p.15). In short, he views nation primarily as a 'territorial cultural entity'. Several contributors, including Karna and Fazal seem to subscribe to this view.

A few observations will be in order here. First, their particularistic nuances apart, the seven conceptions of nation identified by Oommen may broadly be subsumed into three categories: nation as a civilisational entity, as a cultural entity and as a political entity. While Oommen's assessment of the Indian nation as a civilisational entity is well taken, the fact remains that this is the way many Indians perceive the Indian nation, irrespective of the fact that several scholars find it objectively untenable. Myths perhaps are more real than objective realities as far as the constitution of social phenomena are concerned. Further, the civilisational notion of nation is important to recognise and reckon with in the Indian subcontinent, if we as social scientists wish to understand how the idea of nation in South Asia is historically different from that in the West. To say this, is not to commend the civilisational notion of the Indian nation, but to take notice of the historical specificity of the concept of nation in Indian thought. There is ample evidence to suggest that India was envisaged as a nation in terms of its civilisational thrust by seers and intellectuals long before the colonial encounter. Denying this goes against the grain of India's history and culture. Second, conceptualisation of nation as a culturally distinct territorial entity leaves something to be desired. It misses out on the political element of nation. Once again, it is a question of taking cognisance of peoples' perceptions. The term nation carries a political import in peoples' minds. Viewed in terms of peoples' perceptions, Anderson's (1983) definition of nation as a culturally grounded *imagined political* community makes better sense. Important points to note in this definition are the words *imagined political,* which imply two things : a) that it may or may not be an accomplished political community, but it certainly is an imagined community; b) that it is a political community, for though based on a sense of cultural distinction devoid of political element, Oommen's definition of nation sounds more like that of an ethnic community. For the same reason, perhaps, Mukherji observes: 'What is *ethnic* to Smith, is *nation* to Oommen' (1999 : 58).

At this point, it is pertinent to note that the term nation has been used in so many different senses by both intellectuals and laymen alike that it is extremely difficult to encapsulate it in a general definition. For the present purposes, however, it is essential to distinguish between two broad referents of nation: nation as a supra-local entity and nation as a culturally distinct locational entity. The term nation is in use in both the senses in the Indian subcontinent. In terms of a civilisational category, it signifies a supra-local entity. Notably, the civilisational notion of nation is open to both interpretations; communal and secular. Used in terms of Hindu civilisation or Hindutva, it takes on a communal character, while used as composite culture or as a plurality of cultural entities it takes on a secular character. These usages pertain to macro-level conceptualisations of nation. At the micro level, again the term nation is amenable to two interpretations — as a culturally distinct territorial entity and as a culturally grounded imagined political community. It thus all depends on the context. Any attempt at reducing it to one single definition is bound to leave out some of its other important conceptual constituents.

As for the constituents of nation, the existing literature generally lists common history, territory, language, religion and culture, apart from the 'subjective will' of the people. The papers in the volume, however, largely specify two main constituents, that is territory and language. Addressing his concern for identifying viable constituents of nation, Oommen, in particular, rejects religion in the light of the South Asian experience and foregrounds territory and language as the key constituents of nation. Stated in his own words: 'All available facts and experiences suggest that the two most critical elements in nation-formation are territory and language' (p. 8). In his earlier writings Oommen defines nation as 'a territorial entity to which the people have an emotional attachment and in which they have invested a moral meaning.... [A] nation is a community in communication in its homeland' (1997:33). Several other contributers including Karna, Pathy, Fazal and Uberoi also hold the same view.

Two observations may be in order here. First, it is hardly a tenable proposition to inject any essentialism into what constitutes a nation. That is so because the constituents of nation tend to vary from case to case. In one case, language may be the basis of nation-formation. In another instance it could be religion, and in a third, historical forces and circumstances. The South Asian example as analysed in this volume provides ample illustration of this.

Second, it is necessary to distinguish between two levels of conceptual constituents of nation: operative and normative. It is one thing to identify the operative constituents of nation and another to specify its normative constituents. Oommen as well as other contributors are right in specifying territory and language as *viable* constituents of nation. The use of the adjective *viable*, however, speaks volumes about the normative orientation on the part of the author/s. In simple words, the implicit message is that it is not religion but language that is the right basis of nation formation. Clearly an element of normativeness is involved in this position. At the operational level, however, social reality does not always follow the logic of normativeness; it works according to its own logic of exigencies, expediencies and contingencies, apart from the vested interests and motivated moves of the social actors. In effect, the operative reality cannot always be explained through normative parameters.

Viewed from the perspective of operative reality, religion emerges as an important constituent of nation in several cases. Juergensmeyer in his book *Religious Nationalism Confronts the Secular State* (1994) cites a number of case studies from various parts of the world, including South Asia, apart from the Middle East and Central Asia, and parts of the former Soviet Union. He also points out that with a few exceptions, such as that of Algeria, Afghanistan, Iran and Tajikistan, the religious nationalist movements have been controlled and directed by the laity. In South Asia, the emergence of Pakistan represents a sterling example of how religion can serve as a basis of nation-formation. Secession of Bangladesh from Pakistan does not mean the end of Pakistan as a nation based on religion.

From India he cites the rise of militant Hindu nationalism of the Bharatiya Janata Party (BJP) and the recent Sikh nationalism of Bhindrawale as telling illustrations of the power of religion as a competing constituent of nation. In view of these facts, it is hard to ignore the role of religion as an operative constituent of nation. The real challenge before social scientists is to study and understand how and under what conditions religion becomes a constituent of nation.

From this discussion on the concept of nation and its constituents, it follows that the term nation has been used to designate different phenomena by different scholars. Some have deployed it to refer to a culturally distinct territorial entity, others, to a culturally grounded imagined political community, and still others, to a political entity embodied in state. Similarly, in respect of the constituents of nation, some have underlined the centrality of region and still others of the subjective will of the people or of the political actors. In view of this diversity of perspectives, the following observation of Nazir rings true: 'there is not, and there cannot be, a general definition or universal definition or a general theory of nation, nationality or nationalism' (1986:494). Under the circumstances, we would do well to respect the diverse conceptual paradigms as well as refine, revise and reformulate them in the light of the study of how nations are constructed and imagined in historically variable and *place-specific* forms, to borrow the term from Jackson and Penrose (1993).

Whether nation is an entity independent of the state or congruent with it is another debate on the nation and its linkage with the state. There are two opposite positions on this: one that regards nation as independent of the state, and the other that regards nation as congruent with the state. Both positions are reflected in the volume. For example, while Oommen as well as Karna argue that nation is independent of the state and that India should be viewed as a multi-national state, Nandi subscribes to the idea of conflation between nation and state in his study of the Indian freedom fighters' visions of nationhood. Similarly, Fazal views Pakistan as a multi-national state comprising several nations, including Punjab, Baluchistan, Pashtun and Sindh.

It is essential to point out that unlike the concept of nation, which remains a contested terrain, the concept of state evokes no controversy. This is evident from the fact that while almost every paper uses it, none feels the need to define it. From the references, however, it emerges that 'state is generally taken to mean a political apparatus with sovereignty as its distinctive mark, along with a demarcated territory and a legal and administrative mechanism.

The debate, however, focuses on the linkage between nation and state. By and large, the contributers to this volume directly or indirectly maintain that nation is independent of state. They observe that a state may be multi-national, and that a nation may be divided between two or more states. Oommen for example reiterates: 'It should be underlined here that I clearly distinguish between citizenship and nationality. The former alludes to membership in a politico-legal entity, that is, the state and the entitlements thereof. The latter refers to membership in a cultural entity, that is, nation, and the identity that it implies' (p. 16).

Several scholars, though none of the contributors to the volume, have contested this position of Oommen. Mukherji, for example, contends:

> The concept of the *state-independent nation* does not appeal as a powerful analytical tool. In the burgeoning body of literature in this field no clear distinction between the ethnic group, ethnicity, nation, etc., is visible.... Each of these concepts pales into each other in different hands, so much so that one is left wondering as to whether or not the single most important consideration that lies behind endowing cultural groups with nation and nationalism, is the manifest or latent anxiety that the steam-rolling nation-state in its homogenising operation will crush their identities. But contemporary history bears testimony to the fact that the modern nation-state has in fact facilitated the proliferation of ever-new cultural groups rather than stifling them (1999:58-59).

In my view, the relationship between nation and state can be understood better if nation is viewed as an artifact; nation in fact, represents a legitimising ideology of the state. A nationalist ideology is fabricated, designed and created by intellectuals to legitimise the formation of a state as well as its substances. More often than not, it is fabricated in terms of culture or some particular element of culture.

To me, therefore, this debate does not help us comprehend the complexity of the linkages between nation and state. For, it erronously assumes both nation and state to be fixed entities or frozen categories which they are not. Both of them are formative/dynamic entities, and this is especially true of nation. A nation is always in the process of making or unmaking itself. It is never a static entity. It may, therefore, be revealing to focus on the process of nation formation.

In order to understand the process of nation formation in South Asia, it is a important to examine the linkages between ethnicity and nationalism as those between nation and state. For the same reason, the concept of ethnicity and the meaning one attaches to it is of crucial importance. In its anthropological usage, the term ethnic stands for a cultural group having some specific signifiers in terms of which it constructs its distinctiveness in comparison with other groups (Barth 1969). More recently, Brass has defined it as a subjectively self-conscious cultural community (1991:19) Elsewhere, in his earlier work Oommen defined the term ethnic as 'a people who share a common history, tradition, language and life style, but are uprooted from and/or unattached to a homeland' (1990:10). Oommen's definition of ethnic is clearly at variance with the received and widely held notion of ethnic in the current literature. While Oommen insists on viewing ethnicity as a cultural entity without a home, others view it as a cultural entity with or without a homeland. In defining ethnicity in this limited way, Oommen has denied himself a fascinating area of inquiry, i.e., the processual linkages between ethnicity and nationalism and the role of ethnicity in nation formation in India and other parts of South Asia. Other scholars, including Phadnis (1990), Brass (1991) and Mukherji (1999), have made valuable contributions in this field, and I have also written in this regard (1992, 1996).

It is widely acknowledged that modernisation, along with its attendant feature of the modern nation-state, has stimulated ethnic consciousness all over the world. In one of my earlier publications (1990) I had advanced substantial evidence on this from India. This sharpening of ethnic consciousness has led to the transformation of ethnicity from ethnicity-in-itself to ethnicity-for-itself, to use the Marxist phraseology pertaining to the concept of class (Sharma 1992: 2). In other words, this has drawn ethnicity into the arena of politics where it tends to take either of the two forms, as delineated by Brass: a) an interest group, and b) a self-conscious political entity (1991:20). In its latter form, it may demand either autonomy within the given federal framework of nation-state or full sovereignty outside it. Viewed in this manner, an ethnic community qualifies as an ethnicity when it acquires subjective self-consciousness in terms of a sense of cultural distinction, grows into an ethno-nationalist entity when it takes on a political aspiration and gets mobilised for political autonomy or sovereignty, and becomes a nation when it attains sovereignty.

## Ethnicity and nation formation

For the past some years, India has witnessed the spectre of ethno-nationalist movements, leading to the study of such movements in its various parts, including Punjab, Kashmir and the North-East. Such studies have revealed that non-ethnic factors such as the commissions and omissions on the part of the state, politics of the ruling classes, and distortions of the capitalist part of development play a more important role than ethnic factors such as demographic, religious and cultural factors in generating ethno-nationalist movements. I have also observed this elsewhere (1996).

The above, of course, is one of the two trajectories of nation formation, which Oommen recognises, although on his own terms. He observes that 'It is a combination of *instrumental ethnicity* emanating out of material deprivation and *symbolic ethnicity* based on the anxiety to preserve one's cultural identity, which gives birth to the motive force for state formation'. He hastens to add, however, that this 'is plausible only if the ethnic group can constitute itself into a nation, the pre-requisites of which are territory and language' (1997:21). This implies that Oommen views ethnic moments as movements for state formation rather than nation formation.

There is, however, another trajectory of nation formation which Brass identifies as a *state-centred nationalist project* (1991:20). This is directly linked with the integrative imperatives of the modern nation-state. the state-sponsored nationalist project owes its origins to the rise of the modern nation-state as an agency of cultural homogenisation. It may take the form of nation as a civilisational entity, or as a melting pot entity leading to a homogenous national culture, or as a composite culture entity, or even as a civic-secular entity. In most cases, it is likely to easily activate the suspicions of the local ethnic communities or of cultural minorities about the designs of the nation-state to annihilate their cultural identity. This volume is replete with such suspicions of absorption, marginalisation, discrimination, suppression, and the like as perceived by culturally aggrieved communities. Such suspicions tend to heighten the resentment of several ethnic communities or minorities against national governments and make them vulnerable to the designs of foreign powers.

Out of the cesspool of mutual suspicion harboured about each other, the ethno-nationalists and state-nationalists look upon each other's moves in different ways. While the ethno-nationalists perceive in the state-sponsored nationalist project a threat to their cultural identity, the state-nationalists view ethno-nationalist movements as a challenge to national integrity.

It is this dialecties between the state-led project of nation-building and the ethnic-led project of nation formation in contemporary India as also in other countries of South Asia like Pakistan and Sri Lanka that, renders the

South Asia experience distinctive in some ways.

It matters little whether we call India a multi-national or a multi-ethnic nation-state, for what is 'nation' to Oommen is 'ethnic' to Mukherji. 'The difference lies in the different paradigms through which the same problematique has been viewed', as observed by Mukherji (1999:65). The important point is the message of the volume, which is that the state should foster the policy of cultural pluralism.

## The policy of pluralism

The policy of pluralism brings the state in harmony with civil society. There are of course, several convential conceptions of civil society such as a civilised society, or a society which functions as an intermediary between the households and the state, or a bourgeois society, or a society beyond particularistic loyalties but below the state. Then there are the current conceptions of civil society as a secular society, or as a watch-dog society led by the third sector, i.e. the voluntary sector. Above all, we have the latest conceptions of civil society as 'a category of universal human society' with pluralism, equality and vernacularism as its constitutive elements, as postulated by Uberoi. It is this latest conception of civil society with its stress on the principle of pluralism, that is the principle of equality with a difference, that overcomes the problem of dualism between the state and civil society. Given such a conceptualisation of civil society in terms of pluralism, the concept of nation can well be redefined as a civil society, according to Uberoi (p. 37). However, Pandey's caution in this regard needs to be taken seriously. Pluralism should not be construed to mean 'a contested process for regional, religious, ethnic, linguistic and other bases of electoral support and yet hide social inequality by forwarding the illusion of expanding 'civil society' against the state' (p. 45). He also warns against the prevailing tendency of projecting the state as essentially the villain of the piece. (p. 49).

## An alternative paradigm

All in all, the papers in the volume bring out in a pronounced manner the perspective of the cultural pluralities on the conceptualisation of nation and articulate the linkage between the nation and the state in South Asia. Whether or not one agrees with the authors' formulation of nation as a cultural community with a homeland and the characterisation of the state as multi-national state in most parts of South Asia, their problematisation of the relationship between the cultural communities and the nation-state remains illuminating. They offer an alternative paradigm, which is theoretically articulate and distinct, to comprehend the complexity of nation and nationality in South Asia. The paradigm also seeks to effectively convey the concerns and issues of nation building from the end-point of the cultural pluralities. It calls into question the Western perspective of the hegemonic model of nation-state and seeks to conceptualise the South Asian experience in terms of the ground realities of South Asia, while also offering glimpses of the other perspectives upheld by the protagonists of the nation-state.

## References

Anderson, B. 1983. *Imagined communities*. London: Verso

Barth, F. 1969. *Ethnic groups and boundaries*. London: George Allen and Unwin

Brass, Paul. 1991. *Ethnicity and nationalism: Theory and comparison.* New Delhi: Saga Publications

Desai, A.R. 1948. *The social background of Indian nationalism.* Mumbai: Popular Prakashan

Jackson, Peter and Jan Penrose. 1993. *Constructions of race, place, and nation*. London: University College London Press

Juergensmeyer, Mark. 1994. *Religious nationalism confronts the secular state.* Delhi: Oxford University Press

Mukherji, Partha N. 1999. 'Nation-state reformulated: Interrogating received wisdom'. *Man and Development*, December: 51-68

Nazir, P. 1986. 'Marxism and the national question', *Journal of Contemporary Asia*, Vol. 16, 4:491-508

Oommen, T.K. 1990. *State and society in India: Studies in nation building.* New Delhi: Sage Publications

__________. 1997. *Citizenship and national identity: From colonialism to globalism.* New Delhi: Sage Publications

Phadnis, Urmila. 1989. *Ethnicity and nation-building in South Asia.* New Delhi: Sage Publications

Sharma, S.L. 1990. 'The salience of ethnicity in modernisation: Evidence from India', *Sociological Bulletin*, 39 (1&2): 33-51

__________. 1992. 'Ethnic challenge to Indian identity: Rethinking culture-polity interface', *Social Science Research Journal*, 1(1-2) Mar-Jul: 1-16

__________. 1996. 'Ethnic surge for political autonomy: A case for a culture-responsive polity', in A.R. Momin(ed). *The legacy of G.S. Ghurye: A centennial festschrift.* Mumbai: Popular Prakashan.

# 1

# Conceptualising Nation and Nationality in South Asia

*T. K. Oommen*

There have been several attempts to conceptualise 'nation' and 'nationality' in South Asia, given the multiplicity of cultural identities in the region. The present effort is *not* to review all such attempts but to locate the different *modes* of conceptualising nation and national identity and to understand their rationale. In this process the ambiguity, the ambivalence and the consequent inadequacy of these conceptualisations will hopefully be exposed.

## I

The compulsion for conceptualising an Indian nation was largely the outcome of British colonial presence and its articulations. In the pre-independence period, the use of the term 'nation' for India was applicable to colonial India, which consisted of present-day India, Pakistan and Bangladesh. The British were attuned to the European situation in which people belonging to one civilisation were not only divided on the basis of language, religion and denomination, but were also involved in protracted wars and continuous violence to establish nations and states. It should therefore surprise none that the colonial administrators did not view the Indian subcontinent as one nation. Strachey (1888: 5) wrote '. . . there is not and never was an India . . . no Indian nation, no people of India.' In the same vein Seeley (1883: 255) commented: 'India is . . . only a geographical expression like Europe or Africa. It does not make the territory of a nation and a language, but the territory of many nations and languages.' Understandably, therefore the earlier efforts to conceptualise India were meant to counter this orientation, and gradually different modes of conceptualising emerged in response to unfolding realities.

Broadly speaking, one can identify seven ways in which nation has been defined in the Indian subcontinent. These are: (1) ancient civilisational entity, (2) composite culture, (3) political entity, (4) religious entity, (5) geographical/

territorial entity, with a specific cultural ethos, (6) a collection of linguistic entities, and (7) unity of great and little nations. The first three of these are specifically pre-partition conceptualisations. The fourth initiated the impulse of partition, achieved that objective, and has continued to provide a source of legitimacy. The fifth, sixth and seventh conceptualisations largely belong to the post-partition period. However, it is important to note that these conceptualisations did not always surface in the order in which they are listed; some of these co-existed and competed for legitimacy.

The attempt to conceptualise India as an ancient civilisation gave emphasis to the wholeness of India due to its *geography* and its preponderantly *Hindu culture*. Radhakumud Mookerji (1914) had asserted the essential unity of India based on natural geography, an ancient pan-Indian Hindu culture, economic self-sufficiency and the inter-dependence of her constituent regions. Further, he had alluded to the 'national' consciousness, which had become a 'settled habit of thought' since ancient times. In the same vein, a quarter of a century later Beni Prasad (1941) referred to India's 'geographical wholeness' and her '. . . urge to political unification in defiance of vast distances and immense difficulties of transport and communication'.

The reasons invoked to justify the essential unity of an Indian 'nation' indeed are disparate: natural geography, ancient Hindu culture, and the urge for political unification, among others. If geography had been the basis of constituting nations, there would have been only a handful of them in the world and quite a few would not have emerged at all. The reference to Hindu culture as the element which provides the essential unity implies (a) that the time-referent is prior to Muslim and British intrusion/intervention, (b) and that the contributions of the Muslims and the British are completely ignored and/or they are treated as aliens, (c) that they indirectly 'disturbed' the unity of India that was provided by Hindu culture, and (d) that religion is a necessary element in the conceptualisation of nation and national identity. The reference to the 'urge for political unification' implies that a nation is a united political entity, comprising cultural multiplicity.

The points I want to make for the moment are the following. The two writers, Mookerji and Prasad, are mistaking civilisations for nations although the former is a much broader entity as compared to the latter. Generally speaking several nations and/or states co-exist within a civilisational region. Second, 'natural geography' or religion are both not necessary conditions for a nation to emerge and exist. Third, a nation is essentially a cultural entity and it is not natural for a nation to establish its own state, as is widely believed. Such theories and experiences are European and do not fit the reality of South Asia.

Those who describe India as a composite culture emphasize the fusion of Hinduism and Islam, as against the distinctiveness of Hindu culture. This *fusion*, a product of conflict and synthesis, although an ancient tendency, is believed to have intensified with the Muslim conquest. 'As soon as the first waves of conquest, plunder and desecration had spent themselves, there began the operation of the forces, inherent in human nature, which interknit contacts into conational wholes and transform plurality into community' (Beni Prasad 1941: 8). Tarachand (1963) graphically described the efforts of Kabir, the saint-poet, to fuse Hinduism and Islam; Humayun Kabir (1955) referred to Emperor Akbar's effort at creating a syncretic religion as the first conscious attempt to establish a 'secular state'. Nehru was more explicit: 'Akbar became the great representative of the old Indian ideal of a synthesis of differing elements and their fusion into a common nationality. He identified himself with India, and India took to him although he was a *newcomer*' (Nehru 1961: 146, italics mine).

The Muslim 'conquest' provides the cut-off point in Indian history to those describing India as a composite culture. In contrast, those who describe India as an ancient Hindu culture and civilisation consider the Aryans to be its original inhabitants, with the Aryan 'advent' marking the beginning of Indian history, in their view. For both, *pre-Aryan* culture either did not exist, or if it did, it was a 'low culture' contributing nothing to 'Indian culture'. Thus, this conceptualisation ignores the pre- and non-Aryan peoples–the Dravidians, scheduled castes and scheduled tribes–who together constitute nearly 50 per cent of the population of India. If Hinduism provides the essential content of Indian nationalism, as per the first of the seven modes of conceptualising India, then, according to the second mode it is the *fusion* of Hinduism and Islam that provides content to Indian nationalism.

There are other difficulties and contradictions in the 'synthetic' view. If conflict and synthesis are inherent in human nature, as Beni Prasad suggests, then it should happen everywhere and we cannot anchor Indian specificity to that process. The transformation of plurality into community is an assumption and not a fact. The belief that Hinduism and Islam had fused, as Tarachand assumes, is not only contrary to facts but probably also denies the possibility of the two co-existing without fusing. Humayun Kabir's notion of a secular state or Jawaharlal Nehru's idea of 'nationality' does not fit into any of the accepted conceptualisations. The use of the adjective 'newcomer' to refer to Akbar points to his being regarded as an outsider; it exposes the persisting tension between insiders and outsiders and is contrary to the spirit of an evolving composite culture.

Those who characterise the fundamental unity of the Indian 'nation' in terms of composite culture invariably recall the examples of emperors like Chandragupta Maurya (a Hindu), Asoka (a Buddhist) and Akbar (a Muslim) as shining examples of statesmen who nurtured this idea. But it is often forgotten that in empires there are elites, subjects and slaves and therefore the adjective 'composite' connotes different layers of a hierarchy. In contrast, by definition the people-at-large constitute a nation, a community in which they share a common culture, notwithstanding class differences. Apart from this, one notices a glaring omission in regard to the contribution made by Jainism and Sikhism to the composite character of Indian culture. This omission 'takes-for-granted' religions of Indian origin other than Hinduism (Oommen 1990 [a]: 43-66) and denies autonomy to them. Take the example of Buddhism which was the main proselytising religion of India and which was practically banished from India, instead of being retained, nurtured and assimilated into the composite whole. In retrospect it would seem that the very characterisation of Indian culture as composite was a political project intended to mollify both Hindus and Muslims and to avert the partition of India. Despite the nobility of intention, the project failed and in the process an erroneous conceptualisation, namely, the 'two-nation theory' got wide currency. Compositeness implies assimilation and fusion, and hence is the very antithesis of pluralism, which instead is the celebration of diversity in order to facilitate the co-existence of cultures, in spite of their distinctiveness.

The 'synthetic' view had its predictable consequences; the Indian 'nation' came to be viewed as a political entity; state and nation became interchangeable. In characterising the Indian 'nation' as a fusion of Hindu and Muslim cultures the reference was to a civilisational entity, a vast continent inhabited by one-fourth of humanity. Viewed in terms of the context in which the notion crystallised this is understandable. During the colonial era the nationalist expectancy was visualised primarily in political terms. The 'nation'-to-be was conceived as a community of would-be citizens; the thrust of the anti-colonial struggle was to transform subjects into citizens. But as the dismantling of colonialism became imminent, this disjuncture between state and nation should have been squarely recognised and an appropriate re-orientation in conceptualisation should have been effected. But this was not to be. Consequently, in independent India state and nation became synonymous notions.

Even Indian Marxists, who conceptualise India as a multi-national state, do not maintain a clear distinction between state and nation. For A.R. Desai a nation is an entity consisting of economic, political and cultural elements. He writes:

> The national culture exposes, or kindles emotions of indignation or hostility towards all forces that thwart the development of national society, such as feudal remnants of a pre-national historical period or foreign domination. It cries lyrically, or through ratiocination, against all obstacles to the free material and cultural advance of the nation (1948: 27).

Almost everything, from the development of agriculture, religious reforms to the emancipation of women is viewed as the expression of 'nationalism' (see Desai 1948: 382-87). While the existence of nationalities, that is, linguistic collectivities, is recognised, some of them are seen as 'dormant', others 'wakened' and yet others moving from the dormant to the wakened stage (ibid.: 387-90). Such a characterisation of the Indian 'nation' and 'nationality' is problematic because it postulates a hierarchy among Indian nationalities.

Although the 'two-nation' theory was the one to gain wide currency, in fact three religious communities Hindus, Muslims and Sikhs—had explicitly invoked religion as the basis of nation, although admittedly for different reasons. In 1940, M.A. Jinnah, the then president of the Muslim League observed: 'The history of 1,200 years has failed to achieve unity and has witnessed, during the ages, India always divided into Hindu India and Muslim India' (1960: 161). Basing himself on this view he asserted that Hindus and Muslims were two separate nations and demanded a separate 'homeland' for the Muslim 'nation'. The fact that the majority of Indian Muslims were converts from Hindu castes and tribes did not improve the standing of the neo-convert Muslims in the Hindu social structure.

> … a Muslim, when he is converted … becomes an outcaste … a malecha (untouchable) and the Hindus cease to have anything to do with him socially, religiously and culturally or any other way… It is more than a thousand years that the bulk of the Muslims have lived in a different world, in a different society, in a different philosophy and a different faith (ibid. 1960: 230).

Viewed in this perspective the movement for Pakistan was aimed at equality for Muslims in the subcontinent and indeed it overshot its target.

Those invoking Hinduism as the basis of the Indian nation were more explicit in their advocacy. The statements of Golwalkar were the clearest and sharpest in this regard. For him the basic divide was between believers in the religions of Indian origin—Hinduism, Jainism, Buddhism and Sikhism—and believers in religions that had originated outside India, like Islam, Christianity, Judaism, Zoroastrianism and the Baha'i faith. Those professing religions of Indian origin were insiders and nationals while all others were outsiders and aliens, expected to reconcile themselves to a subordinate position or agree to be assimilated.

> The non-Hindu people in Hindustan must learn to either adopt the Hindu culture and language, must learn to respect and hold in reverence Hindu religion, must entertain no idea but those of glorification of the Hindu race and culture . . . may stay in the country, wholly subordinated to the Hindu nation, claiming nothing, deserving no privileges not even citizens rights. In this country, Hindus alone are national, and Muslims and others, if not actually anti-national, are at least outside the body of the nation (Golwalkar 1939: 55-56).

There are several difficulties with this position. Let me list just three. First, there is no Hindu language; Hindus are drawn from several speech communities. Second, there is no Hindu race. Third, this position is utterly undemocratic.

For both Jinnah and Golwalkar national reconstruction meant reappropriation of an appropriate past. For the Hindus this meant ancient Indian culture and civilisation, with the Gupta Age being regarded as the golden age of India and Chandra Gupta Maurya as the ideal emperor. For the Muslims the golden age was the medieval period when they had been the rulers of India. Both the Hindus and the Muslims had to invent and construct tradition and history. However, it is clear that these remain mere inventions. Why?

First, in such a conceptualisation of nation one of the religious collectivities gets rehabilitated at the 'centre' as the hegemonic collectivity, relegating others to the periphery and marginalising them. This surely represents an untenable exercise in a multi-religious democratic polity. Second, the beginning of 'national' history gets relocated following the entry of the hegemon: hence we may hear of the 'Aryan advent' or 'Muslim conquest', as the case may be, conveniently forgetting that the same territory had been inhabited prior to the Aryan intrusion, and that prior to the Muslim invasion there had existed a sprawling civilisation in this region. Third, the untenability of this conceptualisation is demonstrated by the fact that: (a) Pakistan could not be held together solely on the basis of common religious bonds and came to be divided into two within 25 years of its creation; (b) despite the biggest transfer of human population known in history—that is, during partition when nine million Hindus and Sikhs moved to India and six million Muslims moved to Pakistan—India continues to be the second biggest Muslim country in the world with more than the population of either Bangladesh or Pakistan; and (c) the Muslims who migrated from India—the Bihari Muslims who went to Bangladesh and those who settled in Pakistan as the Mohajirs—are not accepted as 'nationals' but treated as 'outsiders'.

The third religious collectivity in India that defines itself as a nation is the Sikhs. The demand for a separate Sikh 'nation' was first articulated in 1946, but a majority of the Sikhs preferred to stay with India. Sikh demands were not feasible because in the Indian Punjab, where they are concentrated, the Sikhs constituted a mere 33 per cent. In spite of the fact that the Hindu-Sikh interaction was intense and included inter-marriages, an essential wedge existed between them. The popular belief that the Hindu-Sikh divide is recent, and is the handiwork of a handful of crafty politicians, militants and terrorists, is not exactly correct. Khushwant Singh, an acknowledged 'secularist', writes: 'The only chance of survival of the Sikhs as a separate community is to create a state in which they form a compact group, where the teaching of Gurumukhi and the Sikh religion is compulsory, and where there is an atmosphere of respect for the traditions of their Khalsa forefathers' (1966: 305; the reference to 'a state' is not to a sovereign state but to a province within a federal set up).

The untenability of conceptualising India (which at the time included the Pakistan and Bangladesh of today) as a nation by invoking religion was understood only by a select few. Pursuantly, they sought to define nation essentially as the homeland of all religious communities who belonged to it. Thus Pandit Madan Mohan Malviya wrote in 1905:

> It is not the Hindus alone who *now* live in Hindustan. Hindustan is *no longer* exclusively their country. Just as Hindustan is the beloved birthplace of the Hindus, so it is of the Muslims too. Both these communities now live here and will always live here . . .To establish real affection and brotherly love among these communities and all the communities of India–Hindu, Muslim, Christian, Parsi–is the greatest duty before us all (quoted in Pandey 1990: 212; italics mine).

According to this conceptualisation Hindus do not have the monopoly of claiming Hindustan as their exclusive 'beloved birthplace' because non-Hindus too live here *now*. The unstated assumption is that Hindustan was essentially and originally the homeland of Hindus. But this raises several questions. First, what about the pre-Aryan people of India? Were they Hindus? Second, the fact that a majority of Indian Muslims and Christians are converts from lower castes and tribes would mean that they too are pre-Aryan people. Does one lose one's nativity/nationality if one changes one's religion? If yes, does this apply also to those who embrace Buddhism, Jainism or Sikhism? Third, there is no distinction made between a migrant religious collectivity, which has maintained both its cultural and physical purity (e.g. the Zoroastrians), and those who are converts from local groups. The point to be noted is that it is not territorial affinity but religious affiliation that is taken as the critical marker in defining nationality even by Malviya. Consequently, the presumed rupture between people who profess religious faiths that have originated in India and those who are believers in 'alien religions' influences his definition of nation and nationality, as in most other cases.

Lala Lajpat Rai articulated his idea of Indian nationhood without any ambiguity thus in 1920: 'The Indian nation, such as it is or such as we intend to build, neither is nor will be exclusively Hindu, Muslim, Sikh or Christian. It will be each and all. That is my goal of nationhood' (quoted in Nagar 1977: 175). Accordingly, India is the homeland of a plurality of religious collectivities and hence the Indian nation encapsulates all of them. Mohandas Karamchand Gandhi articulated it with greater clarity:

> If the Hindus believe that only Hindus should people India, they are living in dreamland. The Hindus, the Mohammedans, the Parsis and the Christians who have made India their country are fellow countrymen . . . In no part of the world are one nationality and one religion synonymous terms; nor has it ever been so in India (1938: 49).

If religion is not a necessary element in nation formation, what are the essential attributes of a nation? All available facts and experiences suggest that the two most critical elements in nation formation are territory and language. These could be ancestral or adopted. Adoption is a voluntary act. Thus if a people have a common homeland and if they adopt a common language they could become a nation. Such an effort was made and is being pursued in India.

It is instructive to recall the trajectory of this pursuit. First, Hindi was adopted as the 'national' language despite a virulent controversy over this issue. As Ambedkar noted '... there was no article which proved more controversial than Article 115, which deals with the [Hindi] question. Hindi won its place as national language by one vote' (1955:14). Second, Hindi was constructed as the national language by labelling several languages—Bhojpuri, Awadhi, Braj Bhasha, Chattisgarhi, Rajasthani, Maithili—as its dialects. Third, some of these languages/dialects are closer to other Indian languages (for example, linguists consider Maithili to be closer to Bengali than Hindi) and yet were aligned to Hindi to bolster up its numerical superiority. Even then, Hindi as defined officially is spoken by only 38 per cent of the people of India. Fourth, the procedure prescribed in Article 351 of the Constitution to develop Hindi as the national language smacks of deep cultural prejudice. Article 351 reads:

> It shall be the duty of the Union to promote the spread of the Hindi language, to develop it so that it may serve as a medium of expression for all elements of the composite culture of India and to secure its enrichment by assimilating without interfering with its genius, the forms, style and expressions, used in Hindustani and in the other languages of India specified in the Eighth Schedule, and by drawing, wherever necessary or desirable, for its vocabulary, primarily on Sanskrit and secondarily on other languages.

Of the numerous problems raised by this article let me mention just two: (1) Hindustani is not listed in the Eighth Schedule of the Indian Constitution; one cannot develop a non-existent language or a language to which no legal status is attached as the 'national' (read official) language of a country; (ii) if Hindustani is the language to be developed as the national language, Persian may be as much, if not more, relevant than Sanskrit. Admittedly, we encounter the distinction between Sanskrit, a 'native' language, and Persian, an 'alien' language. In fact, the expression 'composite culture' used in the article stands in substance for cultural hegemony rather than synthesis.

The Indian practice, however, clearly indicates that all major linguistic collectivities with a territorial base are deemed to be culturally distinct entities, that is, nations/nationalities. The Indian National Congress endorsed the idea of creating administrative units based on linguistic homogeneity as early as 1921. In 1928 the Nehru Report acknowledged the desirability of creating linguistic provinces. Although Prime Minister Nehru accepted the principle underlying linguistic provinces on 27 November 1947 in the Constituent Assembly, the mobilisation by linguistic collectivities was cognised as a threat to the 'nation' (that is, to the state) and was labelled as chauvinist, parochial and anti-national. After this initial resistance and ambivalence, the States Reorganisation Commission was appointed in 1955. The commission did by and large uphold the principle of a language-based administrative reorganisation of India. As of today 18 languages are listed in the Constitution as national languages. This in effect is a vindication of the definition of nation as a linguistic collectivity with a territorial base. The Indian experience also demonstrates that if nations are conceded a certain level of politico-administrative autonomy within a federal set up they may not demand separate sovereign states; the co-terminality between nation and state is not axiomatic. In fact, most Indian nations have renounced the idea of having their own sovereign states.

There is a tendency among some authors to refer to tribal and linguistic collectivities as sub-nations or 'little' nations. In this strand of thinking, the little nations and their nationalism are juxtaposed to the great Indian nation and its nationalism. Thus 'great nationalism' according to Guha emerged in the colonial context as the ideology of the pan-Indian big bourgeoisie which was eager to capture an appropriate share of the growing market in India. The bourgeoisie perceived an Indian state more conducive to meeting its aspirations and establishing the hegemony of Indian capitalism. On the other hand, the 'little nationalism' emerged as the ideology of the regional small bourgeoisie, the regional middle classes, who feared competition not only from the middle classes of other regions but also from the pan-Indian big bourgeoisie. Thus, the ideology of little nationalism is oriented to the exclusive control of regional markets by the respective middle classes (see, Guha 1979: 455-58; 1982: 2-12).

N.K. Bose (1941: 188-94) discussed what he terms sub-national movements among tribes, which are according to him typically characteristic of economically backward communities in new nations, initiated by the emerging elite to subserve their interests and aspirations. Roy Burman (1971: 25-33; 1979: 101-22) goes a step further and distinguishes between proto-national and sub-national movements among tribes. Proto-national movements emerge when tribes experience a transformation from 'tribalism' to nationalism; it transcends tribalism. In contrast, sub-nationalism is initiated by an acculturated tribal elite to cope with the disparities of development. In sub-nationalism the ultimate sanction is the coercive power of the community; in proto-nationalism it is primarily the moral consensus of the community which is the motive force. All the authors who refer to sub- or little nationalism endorse the view that India is a nation but what they mean by the word nationalism varies according to individual perceptions. For Guha, the battle between the two nationalisms—great and little—is motivated by economic considerations. However, no nation or nationalism can emerge and exist exclusively on this basis. In contrast, proto-nationalism is trans-tribal whereas sub-nationalism is intra-tribal, both being anchored to the problematic of identity; the first in transcending and the second in reinforcing it. But there are several movements which are inter-tribal (e.g. the Jharkhand movement) and geared simultaneously to economic development, political autonomy and cultural identity. Bose's contention that sub-nationalism is a characteristic feature of backward groups and a mere manifestation of manipulations by an elite is too rash an evaluation.

The fact is that several nations are vivisected across South Asian states: the Tamils between India and Sri Lanka, the Bengalis between India and Bangladesh, the Nagas between India and Mynmar, the Punjabis and the Kashmiris between India and Pakistan. While these collectivities have a common nationality their citizenship differs. Similarly, subaltern peoples are divided and allocated across politico-administrative units within India. Just to cite two examples, the Bhils are divided between Gujarat, Rajasthan and Madhya Pradesh; the Santals between Bihar, Orissa and West Bengal. Mobilisations by these collectivities for their political and cultural consolidation are national movements. But these attempts are designated as sub-national, proto-national or even anti-national because of the threat they pose to the state and/or government. Unless we transcend this state-centrism anchored to the notion of terminal loyalty, which instantly installs a hierarchy of loyalty, we will not achieve the required clarity. In reality there is no hierarchy of loyalty but only contexts of identity.

## II

Having briefly reviewed the different modes of conceptualising the 'nation' in South Asia, it is necessary to indicate which of these conceptualisations are proximate, if not entirely isomorphic, with our social reality. While there has existed and perhaps there continues to exist a South Asian civilisation, the territory that this civilisation encapsulates now hosts several states. The frame of reference of those who refer to India as a civilisational entity is the Indian sub-continent. Admittedly, independent India constitutes only a part of this civilisational region. We cannot and should not substitute the part, even if it is a substantial and significant part, for the whole.

The effort to equate South Asian civilisation with Hindu civilisation is unsustainable because it ignores the nativity of non-Hindu groups and underestimates their contribution to this civilisation. It may be noted here that the biggest congregation of Muslims in the world is in South Asia. Independent India has the second biggest Muslim population in the world. Similarly, 75 per cent of Zoroastrians and a substantial proportion of Baha'is in the world have adopted India as their homeland. The persisting tendency to stigmatise Islam and Christianity as products of conquest and colonisation is historically incorrect as both Islam and Christianity were present in India prior to the Islamic conquest and British colonisation. Further, the overwhelming majority of Muslims and Christians in India are converts from lower castes and tribes who are drawn from the pre-Aryan population. Admittedly then, South Asian civilisation cannot be equated with Hindu civilisation.

Can it be that the followers of a multiplicity of religious faiths co-existing in India have given birth to a composite culture? The characterisation of Indian culture as a composite culture is only partially correct in that while the different religious collectivities of India do share a common layer of culture they also have certain elements of culture specific to them. The product of this sharing process is not a composite but a plural culture. The notion of composite culture smacks of a melting-pot syndrome and it ultimately implies assimilation into an imagined mainstream which in the final analysis is hegemonic in its thrust. In contrast, pluralism implies the very celebration of cultural diversity.

Following Ralph Linton (1936) one may distinguish between cultural universals, specialities and alternatives. Cultural universals are common to the entire humanity. But within this universe one can speak of cultural specialities across civilisations and societies. All societies permit variations at the individual level in regard to dress, food, and style of life in general. Cultural alternatives indicate the individual variations in cultural practices within cultural specialities. If a sufficient number of individuals followed similar alternatives they came to constitute a cultural sub-group.

Cultural specialities are identity markers of cultural groups—religious, linguistic, or tribal. Cultural specialities of religious groups are their beliefs and rituals. Rituals in turn are of two types: social and canonical. Social rituals are shared by those who belong to the same linguistic community, that is, nation, irrespective of their religions. There is hardly any social ritual shared by the entire Indian population. That is, the cultural groups which adhere to the same social ritual are linguistic groups and not religious groups. The latter share only canonical rituals but with their co-religionists all over the world. It is of particular relevance here that the citizens of a polity too share a set of common rituals but these are political rituals linked to the state, such as

Independence Day, Republic Day, and the like in the case of India. Due to the conflation of state and nation, political rituals are wrongly perceived as 'national'.

To invoke canonical rituals as the sole identity markers of religious groups, ignoring all other aspects of their life—social, economic, political—is to misrepresent social reality and to do violence to the cultural integrity of these groups. And yet this is precisely what religious nationalists are trying to do. This is deliberate, false and mischievous and should be questioned and exposed through sociological analyses.

Cultural integration of a polity should be measured in terms of the intensity of cultural specialities of the communities which constitute it. The proportion of cultural speciality practised by religious communities in India is very limited and increasingly diminishing, particularly among the younger generation. In fact, cultural specialities across linguistic communities (i.e. nations) are more elaborate and persistent than those of religious communities in India. But the irony is that religion-based cultural specialities are magnified and utilised to mark out some of the religious minorities.

From the early part of this century till 1947 the salient variable for defining nation and nationality in South Asia was religion, an irrelevant variable. To link nation, which necessarily implies territory, with religion is clearly untenable. None of the followers of any of the world religions are confined to the territory in which their religion originated. The Jewish Diaspora and the consequent dissociation between religion and territory is too well known. The Zionist movement and the creation of Israel as the Jewish homeland is a response to genocide and persecution of the Jews. It is a response to an abnormal situation. Both Islam and Christianity, instead, are deeply entrenched, often in regions *other than* those of their origin. This is also true of one of the religions of Indian origin, that is, Buddhism. There are several Buddhist majority countries in the world, although in India, Buddhism's original homeland, Buddhists are less than one per cent. Similarly, the Indian diaspora has transformed several countries—Mauritius, Surinam, Fiji—into Hindu majority countries. Clearly, the tendency to assume that a nation's territory is the sacred land of the followers of a particular religion and to define the content of nationalism in terms of religion is factually incorrect and existentially incongruous.

To conceptualise India as a 'great nation' composed of several 'little' nations or 'sub-nations' expresses both ambivalence and fear. The ambivalence is implicit in the recognition accorded to the specificity of little nations or nationalities accompanied by an unwillingness to accept their specificity completely. This seems to be buttressed by an unstated assumption that if these little nationalities are recognised as nations they would necessarily clamour for their exclusive sovereign states; a fear based on the European experience but not supported by South Asian history.

This ambiguity and fear is generally evident in South Asia, particularly in India and Pakistan. As a consequence language and tribe have been accepted as the bases to constitute administrative units, thereby investing them with a degree of legitimacy. This in effect means that linguistic and/or tribal collectivities with a firm territorial base are recognised as 'nations'. However, some of the linguistic collectivities and tribes which are viable nations are denied the possibility of maintaining their cultural identity because of state policy and the hegemonic tendencies of the bigger nations.

The completion of this unfinished task, namely, according recognition to these neglected and marginalised subaltern nations will go a long way in accelerating the process of democratisation and promoting cultural pluralism. Such a step will not weaken, as is popularly believed, but strengthen and enrich South Asian states. Conceptualising nation as a cultural entity, according legitimacy to cultural nationalism and refusing to endorse the unsustainable doctrine that state and nation should always be co-terminus (see Oommen 1990 [b]: 163-182) are necessary prerequisites in this endeavour.

All seven modes of conceptualising the nation that I have listed have receded into the background of late. Today national identity is widely but wrongly believed to be surfacing either during games of soccer or cricket played by state teams, when states engage in wars, when bombs are exploded or when cross border migrations occur. To locate expressions of national identity through the route of competition in sports and games is at best puerile. Such fierce expressions of loyalty also surface when competitions between several teams *within* the state and/or nation occur. Wars are waged between states and not nations. The explosion of nuclear devices are undertaken for reasons of state and are exercises in statecraft. Issues relating to interstate migration concern citizens entitlements and are not matters of national identity. That is, conflation of state and nation inevitably leads to the confusion between patriotism and nationalism.

Contrary to what many think and theorise, the partition of British India did not create two 'nations', even if religion is accepted as the basis of nation formation. (There are more Muslims in India than in Pakistan or Bangladesh.) But partition did mutilate South Asian civilisation, and divided several nations—Bengal, Punjab, Nagaland. Indeed, partition created two states to begin with and a third one subsequently out of which two invoke religion, explicitly or implicitly, for their legitimacy.

In the case of the third one, namely India, while the state explicitly disapproves this approach, some political parties attest it. That is why the aggressive display of religious symbols, invocation of gods or goddesses belonging to one or another religion, demolition or construction of places of worship, persecution of religious minorities and the glorification of the assassination of 'the religious other' have become accredited expressions of nationalism in South Asia today. These are clear indications of the route to 'fascism' and 'fundamentalism', which are negative and narcissistic constructions of the nation and repressive expressions of nationalism which will eventually destroy democracy and humanism. What we need is a positive and emancipatory construction of nation and national identity.

The utility of a concept depends on its ability to come to grips with the empirical reality it intends to capture. A meaningful conceptualisation of nation and national identity in South Asia should combine several elements identified in the different modes of conceptualisations that I have listed. First, South Asia is home to a long and enduring civilisation, which was earlier referred to as the Indian civilisation. Second, this civilisational region now hosts several states and some of these states are divided into administrative units with a certain level of cultural specificity and political autonomy. Third, the states have jurisdiction over clearly demarcated territories; disputes, if there are, will have to be settled satisfactorily on the basis of principles. In turn, some of these states–India, Pakistan and Sri Lanka—should be viewed as *collectives* of linguistic groups, quite a few of which are large and firmly anchored to specific territories. The people of these linguistic collectivities cognise the territory to which they are attached as their ancestral homelands. That is, they are nations—products of fusion between territory and culture. Even though nations, most of them do not aspire to become sovereign states; they only insist on having a certain level of administrative and fiscal autonomy. In the final analysis, *South Asian states should be viewed as collectives of nations co-existing within federal states*.

I find support for this mode of conceptualising in the articulations of a statesman and of a scholar. I quote extensively from both without apology:

> It is fascinating to find how the Bengalis, the Marathas, the Gujarathis, the Tamils, the Andhras, the Oriyas, the Assamese, the Canarese, the Malayalis, the Sindhis, the Punjabis, the Pathans, the Kashmiris, the Rajputs and the great central block comprising the Hindustani-speaking people, have retained their peculiar characteristics

> for hundreds of years, have still more or less the same virtues and failings of which old tradition or record tells us and yet have been throughout these ages distinctly Indian, with the same national heritage and the same set of moral and mental qualities (Nehru 1961: 61).

In the same vein Mukerji (1958: 268-9) had written:

> Cultural symbiosis is the outstanding feature of India's cultural reconstruction. It is to be clearly noticed in the specific culture patterns of the *Arya Bhumi* and the *Anarya Pradesh* of Bengal, Maharashtra and Tamil Nadu. We submit that these symbiotic patterns are the true significance of the terms 'nationalities' in India. Our nationalism in the political sense may be the gift of industrial capitalism . . . but the student of Indian history with the proper approach will find the meaning of nationalism in every case in the formation of cultural patterns.

A few comments are in order here. First the expression 'India' stands for South Asia in both these articulations. Second, Nehru confuses between caste collectivities (e.g. the Marathas, the Rajputs) and national collectivities (e.g. the Tamils, the Punjabis). Third, within independent India the difference between those linguistic collectivities without a specific homeland (e.g. Sindhis) and those which clearly identify a specific part of India as their homeland needs to be recognised; the former are ethnies and the latter are nations. Finally, Mukerji views nations as essentially cultural entities; that is, the linguistic and tribal collectivities of India are nations. While these nations have their cultural specificities they have a common civilisational thrust and orientation which they share with the whole of South Asia.

It should be underlined here that I clearly distinguish between citizenship and nationality. The former alludes to membership in a politico-legal entity, that is, the state and the entitlements thereof. The latter refers to membership in a cultural entity, that is, nation, and the identity that it implies (Oommen 1997). South Asia's polities include different religious communities and a multiplicity of castes, none of which can legitimately lay an exclusive claim to the whole or specific parts of the territory as both these socio-cultural categories are territorially intermingled. The persisting effort to define some of these religious communities as 'outsiders' to the soil and others as 'insiders' is to perpetuate falsehood and distort history. Similarly, the tendency to perpetuate the age-old discrimination and oppression based on caste and tribe is to undermine the cardinal principles of democratic citizenship.

## III

I must conclude by indicating the domain assumptions and the rationale which inform the arguments presented. The assumptions are: (1) even in the most homogenous societies class distinctions would emerge and persist and are perhaps unavoidable. In contrast, discrimination, oppression and exploitation based on race, language, religion, gender, and so on, are avoidable; (2) the dignified co-existence of a plurality of nations *within* a federal state is possible and even desirable; (3) a democratic polity can be constituted only if the people participate in the decision-making process, for which their mother tongue should be fostered. In a multi-lingual state this can be achieved only by constituting language-based administrative units to effect substantial decentralisation of the decision-making process; (4) a nation does not necessarily aspire for a state of its own.

Now for the rationale. Although a wide variety of factors provide the bases for constituting polities, the most frequent ones are race, religion and language, or often a combination of two or more factors. While races or physical types and geographical spaces were originally closely linked, conquests, colonisation and immigration have drastically changed the situation. Today, a large number of polities are multi-racial. Similarly, notwithstanding the fact that particular religions had their origin in specific parts of the world due to conquest, proselytisation and immigration, the original association between religion and territory has become irrelevant except as a symbolic association.

Generally speaking, there is a close association between language and territory. When groups migrate and settle in new linguistic regions they may have to learn the language of the new habitat, whereas they need not change their religion and, of course, they cannot change their race. That is, the reshuffling of populations does not go counter to the need for developing a common language, an imperative for communication. This, however, does not imply that each linguistic group (nation) should have an exclusive sovereign state for itself. One can visualise several substantial linguistic groups co-existing within the territory of a state.

In the light of these considerations I suggest that when states are multi-national, they should consciously and systematically foster the policy of linguistic pluralism. This is the essential first step for avoiding the rupture between state and nation and the only sane option for multi-national states. This advocacy is in tune with the currently approved and widely accepted notion of cultural rights for groups and communities.

## References


Ambedkar, B.R. 1955. *Thoughts on linguistic states.* Bombay: Ram Krishna Press.

Beni Prasad, 1941. *The Hindu-Muslim question.* Allahabad: Indian Press.

Bose, N.K. 1941. 'The Hindu method of tribal absorption', *Science and Culture,* 7(2).

Desai, A.R. 1948. *The social background of Indian nationalism.* Bombay: Popular Prakashan.

Gandhi, M.K. 1938. *Hind swaraj.* Ahmedabad: Navjivan Publishers.

Golwalkar, M.S. 1939. *We or our nationhood defined.* Nagpur: Bharat Prakashan.

Guha, Amalendu. 1979. 'Great nationalism, little nationalism and problems of integration: A tentative view.' *Economic and Political Weekly,* 14 (7&8): 455-58.

________. 1982. 'The Indian national question: A conceptual frame,' *Economic and Political Weekly,* 17 (31): 2-12.

Jinnah, M.A. 1960. *Speeches and writings,* Vol.1 (ed. by Ahmed, Jamilud-Din). Lahore: Shaik Muhammad Ashraf.

Kabir, Humayun. 1955. *The Indian heritage.* Bombay: Asia Publishing House.

Linton, Ralph. 1936. *The study of man.* New York: D. Appleton Century Co.

Mookerji, Radhakumud. 1914. *The fundamental unity of India.* London: Macmillan.

Mukerji, D. P. 1958. *Diversities.* New Delhi: People's Publishing House.

Nagar, P. 1977. *Lala Lajpat Rai: The man and his ideas.* Delhi: Manohar.

Nehru, Jawaharlal. 1961. *Discovery of India.* Bombay: Asia Publishing House.

Oommen, T.K. 1990(a). *State and society in India: Studies in nation-building.* New Delhi: Sage Publications.

________. 1990(b). *Protest and change: Studies in social movements.* New Delhi: Sage Publications.

________. 1997. *Citizenship, nationality and ethnicity: Reconciling competing identities.* Cambridge: Polity Press.

Pandey, Gyanendra. 1990. *The construction of communalism in colonial north India.* Delhi: Oxford University Press.

Roy Burman, B.K. 1971. 'National movements among tribes', *Secular Democracy,* 4(3&4).

Seeley, R. Sir John. 1883. *The expansion of England.* London: Macmillan.

Singh, Khushwant. 1966. *History of the Sikhs,* Vol. 2. Princeton: Princeton University Press.

Strachey, Sir John. 1888. *India: Its administration and progress.* London: Macmillan.

Tarachand. 1963. *Influence of Islam on Indian culture.* Allahabad: Indian Press.

# 2

# On Civil Society

*J. P. S. Uberoi*

## God, Man and Nature

The question of civil society can be approached from either of two opposed aspects, the question of culture and the question of power, on both of which sociology as well as social anthropology have something to say. One may approach the question first from the one side and then from the other in order to arrive at a better definition of the field in terms of the possible mediation as well as opposition of the two perspectives, although it may not amount to a synthesis. This definition will enable us to explain the history of civil society, its origin, meaning and effect in Europe as well as India, specially in thc modern period. Finally, we shall propose an hypothesis to the effect that civil society, since it is often established on the life and death of the martyr rather than of the hero (or the victim), also requires new forms and concepts of pluralism, mediation of the one and the many, and of the common usage or custom of the people (vernacularism) to sustain it, whether in general amity or enmity, solidarity and reciprocity, conformity or transgression. In this sense, civil society is here supposed a category of universal human society, or of historical civilisation as against pre-history, and not only a category of bourgeois society or of modern capitalism, for example, as in the tradition from Hegel to Habermas.

From the one side, civil society is a natural and universal development of intermediary institutions between the priest and the prince or between the household and the state. If we divide the history of mankind into five periods, (a) pre-historic, (b) ancient, (c) medieval, (d) modern and (e) post-modern, one can say that the history of civil society begins only when the institution of the sacred or the divine kingship begins to dissolve into two differentiated institutions at the dawn of the ancient, or at the very latest the medieval period out of the past. It was Frazer of Britain who placed the fascinating institution of the divine kingship, in which the king is also simultaneously the 'chief priest of the state', at the centre of social anthropology, where it threatens to remain even now. Its modern secular version continues to exercise an implicit baneful influence, for example, on the sociology of totalitarianism and its varieties, Oriental despotism, Fascism and Communism.

Frazer believed himself to have proved through the accumulation of a mass of evidence that the 'combination of spiritual and temporal power, of which Graeco-Italian tradition preserved the memory, has actually existed in many places'. There was in fact a triple unity, the love of God, king and country, but Frazer, who saw only the first two terms, did see that later in 'some' countries, 'a partition is effected between the civil and the religious aspect of the kingship, the temporal power being committed to one man and the spiritual to another'. What he did not see is that only so would the love of country, the third party, come into its own and establish the institutions of civil society.

> This division of power between a sacred and a secular ruler is to be met with wherever the true Negro culture has been left unmolested, but where the Negro form of society has been disturbed, as in Dahomey and Ashanti, there is a tendency to consolidate the two powers in a single [priestly] king.

Thus by implication here the god-man of Christianity and the Oriental religions, instead of being the mediator in his life and death between religion and politics or between the people and the gods, is reduced by Frazer to a mere monstrous diversion and dead end in the rational evolution of human civil society. This implication is at once both the secret force and the fault of his great anthropological work; and it is still widely influential subconsciously.

> We have seen that in savage or barbarous society there are often found men to whom the superstition of their fellows ascribes a controlling influence over the general course of nature. Such men are accordingly adored and treated as gods ... [and] they are kings as well as gods .... Their supposed divinity is the essential [cultural] fact with which we have to deal. In virtue of it they are a pledge and guarantee to their worshippers of the continuance and orderly succession of those physical phenomena upon which mankind depends for subsistence. Naturally, therefore, the life and health of such a god-man are matters of anxious concern to the people whose welfare and even existence are bound up with his; naturally he is constrained by them to conform to such rules [of royal and priestly taboos and other magic] as the wit of early man has devised for averting the ills to which flesh is heir, including the last ill, death.... But while in the case of ordinary men the observance of the rules is

> left to the choice of the individual, in the case of the god-man it is [socially] enforced under penalty of dismissal from his high station, or even of death.
>
> [Far from being a despot in such early kingdoms] the sovereign in them exists only for his subjects; his life is only valuable so long as he discharges the duties of his position by ordering the course of nature for his people's benefit (Frazer 1950: 122, 198, 203, 305, 326, 414ff).

## Varieties of Mediation

This was an approach from what we may call the problem of the solidarity of God, man and nature, the foundation of faith, morals and a way of life, and of its representation and embodiment in institutions and custom or culture. The opposite approach is from the problem of power, authority or hierarchy and sovereignty, and the concomitant legitimate use of force in a given society and its territory. This aspect of the question of civil society has been best formulated by Hobbes and his followers who argue that the human species could not have emerged out of its supposed pre-social state of nature, where life was generally 'solitary, poor, nasty, brutish and short', without the surrender of liberty by self and the other to the law and the sovereign, Leviathan or the state and its organs. This single sovereignty, whether set up by the 'social contract' or otherwise, is indivisible in its power and scope; and it alone has brought mankind out of the primitive state of nature into the state of grace, where good order and progress are possible for all. 'The state of nature is the state of men without government. In the state of nature, men's [equal] rights [to life and liberty] are perfect, and they have no duties' (Jaffa 1968: 87).

The remedy for the state of nature, according to Locke and Hobbes, is the state of civil society, which is the same as the state of grace and good government, although not in the sense of Oriental despotism. It is established by the social contract, the twin premises of which are (a) to suppose that the many are in fact/value one, and (b) to let a part stand for the whole and be its sovereign. This liberal democratic tradition thus places civil society, like the concept of the nation or of the state, somewhere between the concrete reality of the single individual and the abstract reality of the human species. Such appears to be also the impression formed of the institutions of democracy other than the state that de Tocqueville (1835-) discovered in America, most recently updated under the name of civility, for example, by Shils (1997).

After the two modern revolutions *c.* 1800 of industry in Britain and democracy in France, the concept of civil society as representative of the general will and the common good was equally frequently associated with social democratic thought and the movement for industrial democracy, economic federalism, the trade unions and occupational representation or functional corporatism and guild socialism. For example, Durkheim's lectures of around 1900 before he went to Paris, *Professional ethics and civic morals*, are not so much to the glory of the state, private property or the law of contract as to the glory of the independent professions which stand between the state and the market.

> So that our political malaise is due to the same cause as our social malaise: that is, to the lack of secondary cadres to interpose between the individual and the State. We have seen that these secondary groups are essential if the State is not to oppress the individual: they are also necessary if the State is to be sufficiently free of the individual. ... There is therefore no reason to believe that it is this professional life that is destined to form the basis of our political structure ... [e.g.] the true electoral unit (Durkheim 1957: 96, 103).

It was left to the Marxist tradition, however, to elaborate what is in effect a critique as well as a defence of civil society–when it is not simply reduced to political economy or the market–as the arena of the class struggle, the project of hegemony and other conflicts, including the institutional conflict of the state and civil society itself. This last question has again come to the fore in order to help explain the fall of Communism in Russia and eastern Europe, *c.* 1990, where the institutions of civil society are believed to have been underdeveloped and/or had atrophied as compared to the Leviathan of the state.

Ever since Hegel, who first attributed religion to the human heart as well as the state to the agency of reason, European writers, whether liberal or Marxist by persuasion, have not had one good word to say about the relation of religion and civil society, with the single possible exception of Weber, although this has been a matter of the greatest practical concern throughout the modern period in Europe, America and Russia. The same absence is unfortunately true also of the concept of the nation as against the state, although it is clearly required as the empirical as well as the theoretical point of reference for that 'whole' society which includes family, civil society and the state or even simply the two powers of the prince and the priest. Although it is not the received view just now, both sentiments of religion and the nation may be important to support the life of institutions in a civil as against an uncivil society, for example, as when post-war prime minister Attlee said that British labour and the welfare state owed more to Methodism than to Marxism. Similarly, in Gandhi's explanation, 'Violent nationalism, otherwise known as imperialism, is the curse. Non-violent nationalism is a necessary condition of corporate or civilised life' (*Young India*, 27.xi.1924).

It is to his credit on the other hand that Hegel's *Philosophy of right* (1821) includes in relation to the study of civil society the world of work, business, public authority and civil law–as against military or ecclesiastical law–'but also morality, ethical life and world-history'. His English translator Knox has commented that what we watch in studying civil society is a process of mediation: I gain my ends first by your means and then by means of a generalised organisation (e.g. the corporation). Hegel himself writes that 'the whole sphere of civil society is the territory of mediation', we may say of the particular and the universal, self and other, and so on.

Hegel explained the trinity of family, civil society and the state as arranged in chronological as well as logical order, but he was mindful of the difference.

> Civil society is the [stage or phase of] difference which intervenes between the family and the state, even if its formation follows later in time than that of the state. ... The creation of civil society is the achievement of the modern world.

The organisation of civil society, the state and the modern world had of course its problems too:

> Against nature man can claim no right, but once society is established, poverty immediately takes the form of a wrong done to one class by another. The important question of how poverty is to be abolished is one of the most disturbing problems which agitate modern society (Hegel 1967: 233, 266f, 277, 354).

## Definition by Opposition

Though initially civil society was used with imprecision, the properties of the concept became clearer over time as a series of conceptual oppositions developed between what came to be seen as civil society and something else. [a] It was regarded as an attribute of 'polished' advanced nations as opposed to primitive and barbaric

> societies as in Adam Ferguson's *An essay on the history of civil society* (1767). Later Hegel, in a similar vein, was to remark that earlier societies did not possess civil societies. [b] To the [social] contractarians, Hobbes and Locke, civil society was opposed to the state of nature. [c] To Hegel, civil society was distinct from either the household or the state. It is in Hegelian theory that the concept comes to acquire specific connotations, since to the theorist, civil society was a property of modern bourgeois societies. In German, civil society is *burgerliche Gesellschaft,* thus to Hegel as to Marx, civil society is bourgeois society. However, the identification is by no means merely a literal translation; it refers to a particular kind of society that comes into prominence with the birth of capitalism. [d] To Marx, civil society is an autonomous arena of economic exchanges which is dominated by the commodity principle, it is distinct from earlier forms where political and economic power were collapsed. [e] To Gramsci it came to symbolize a space where the state constructed a project of hegemony, it was a property of sophisticated opaque states as opposed to transparent and openly coercive states. ... I have argued that civil society is a sphere which is flanked by the domain of particularistic loyalties [religious, linguistic and ethnic or caste and tribe in India] and the state (Chandhoke 1995: 113, 251).

This is the summary of a recent review of the concept of civil society by a political scientist, who is assuredly familiar with the aspect of power. She says nothing about the nation, but concludes that 'civil society is the public sphere where individuals come together for various purposes both for their self-interest and for the reproduction of an entity called society.' 'Society consists of the entirety of social practices [customs] both public and private which mark a collectivity', which we may surely call the national society (see also Oommen 1990a and 1990b). It is then possible to accept both her conclusions (a) that, 'as a mediation level between the private and the public, civil society is the site of expressed politics'; and (b) that 'the politics of civil society are polarized between those practices which affirm the project of the state [or of the family?], and those which contest it' (Chandhoke 1995: 72, 168f, 198).

In the dialectical logic of Hegel on the other hand the three terms, family, civil society and the state, form a set in which they are opposed to each other and at the same time each of them is a 'moment' that mediates the opposition of the other two. So Hegel writes (a) that 'as the family was the first, so the Corporation is the second ethical root of the state, the one planted in civil society', like the voluntary association, independent professions or the self-governing medieval craft guild; and also (b) that the state is the 'true ground' of both family and civil society, supporting the sanctity of the former and saving the latter from its own atomicity. Moreover, according to the dialectic, (c) there must be a further progressive transformation of the first term into the second and of the second into the third.

> The expansion of the family, as its transition into a new principle [from right to morality], is in the external world sometimes [a] its peaceful expansion until it becomes a people, i.e. a nation, which thus has a common natural origin, or sometimes [b] the federation of scattered groups of families under the influence of an overlord's power or [c] as a result of a voluntary association produced by the tie of needs and the reciprocity of their satisfaction.

Hegel's civil society might be the 'system of the ethical order' but it must properly give way to the universal human or rather divine reason of 'the rational state', 'the march of God in the world', 'the power of reason actualizing itself as will'. In the words of his commentator Knox,

> Civil society is the sphere of the particular as opposed to the universal.... In other words it is the sphere of the *concrete person*.... He differs from the subject in gradually coming to recognise himself as a member of society and to realise that to attain his own ends he must work in with others. Through working in with others, his particularity is mediated; he ceases to be a mere unit and eventually becomes so socially conscious, as a result of the educative force of the institutions of civil society, that he wills his own ends only in willing universal ends and so has passed beyond civil society into the state (Hegel 1967: 122f, 154, 279, 283f, 350, 353).

## Europe

If this civil society was the 'child of the modern world', even then it is the Christian society and its early modern reform that we may also have to consider and not only the bourgeois society of modern capitalism. By this definition, modern civil society was established or revived in Britain at any rate by the struggle of the Nonconformists, the new Christians, who together severed connection with the established Church of England when it accepted royal supremacy at the time of the Reformation. The Puritans and the dissenters, the Baptists, Independents, Presbyterians and Methodists, were all opposed to the union of the church and the state at the national level as initiated by Henry VIII, which readily passed in the modern period into the sovereignty of the nation-state as against God, 'the absolute power on earth' (Hegel 1967: 212, 356). The new Christians wanted what we may call salvation through religion-in-society instead, with pluralist freedom of conscience and worship for all. The project was wide, deep and strong enough to require its military defeat on the battlefield, leading to the fall of the short-lived Commonwealth, the restoration of the monarchy and then the Act of Uniformity, 1662. The subsequent Conventicle Acts of 1664 and 1670 were also designed to enforce public worship in England according to the officially standardised *Book of common prayer and liturgy* (1549-), and imposed severe penalties on all those citizens or subjects who met for other 'unauthorised' congregational worship in voluntary associations of five or more.

This was the picture of religion, civil society and the state in Britain at the height of what is known as the Scientific Revolution, *c.* 650, but the struggle had already begun when the Reformation and the Renaissance came together in western Europe, *c.* 1500. Nevertheless, another century and a half later, one can show that all the intellect of the Industrial Revolution, 1760 to 1840, was produced by the mechanical institutes and the so-called dissenting academies of the Nonconformists, that is, outside the two universities of England, Oxford and Cambridge, which had remained loyal to the church and the state in combination, and leaving aside what Cromwell had tried to start at Durham. The life and death struggle between the posited unity of the state and the church at the supreme national level *versus* the plurality of free religion-in-society as a principle of motion of history, which continues throughout the modern period in Europe and even in America and Russia, is made quite clear by the following dramatic scene, a narration from *Foxe's book of martyrs*. Incidentally the majority of English households have probably possessed copies of this popular book since it was first published four and a half centuries ago. Here then is the story of the martyrdom of John Lambert: the place is London and the time is 1538; 'the authority and name of the bishop of Rome being utterly abolished', the monasteries are being suppressed and dissolved; and Henry VIII is all set to represent the trinity of the state, the church and the nation or of God, king and country all in himself.

> Then came the king himself as judge of the [Eucharistic] controversy, with his body-guard clothed all in white. On his right hand sat the bishops, and behind them the celebrated lawyers, clothed in purple, according to the manner. On the left sat the peers

of the realm, justices, and other nobles in their order; behind whom were the gentlemen of the king's privy chamber. ... Being seated on his throne, he beheld Lambert with a stern countenance, and then turning himself to his counsellors, called forth Day, bishop of Chichester, and commanded him to declare to the people the cause of the present assembly and judgment [called against heresy].

The oration being concluded, the king rose, and leaning upon a cushion of white cloth of tissue, turned himself toward Lambert with his brow bent and ... said, -- 'Why standest thou still? Answer as touching the sacrament of the altar, -- whether dost thou say, that it is the body of Christ, or wilt deny it?'

Lambert said -- 'I answer with St. Augustine -- That it is the body of Christ, after a certain manner.' Then the king said -- 'Answer me neither out of St. Augustine, neither by the authority of any other man; but tell me plainly, whether thou sayest it is the body of Christ or no?' Then Lambert meekly replied -- 'I deny it to be the body of Christ.' The king on this said -- 'Mark well, for now thou shalt be condemned even by Christ's own words: Hoc est corpus meum [This is my body].' He then commanded [the archbishop] Cranmer to refute his assertion; who, first making a short preface to the hearers, began his disputation with Lambert....

Lambert answered, That there was no place of scripture wherein Christ doth at any time say, that he would change the bread into his body: and moreover, that there is no necessity why he should so do. But this is a figurative speech, everywhere used in the scripture, when as the name and appellation of the thing signified is attributed unto the sign. [In his earlier defence written to Henry, Lambert had said strictly in the style of Zwingli the Swiss reformer that Christ was only present in the spirit and that Hoc est corpus meum therefore meant only -- 'This signifies my body.'] By which figure of speech, circumcision is called the Covenant -- the lamb, the Passover, besides six hundred such instances. With great firmness he then said -- 'Now it remaineth to be marked, whether we shall judge all these after the [priestly or liturgical] words pronounced [to] be straightway changed into another nature [transubstantiation].'

At last when the day was passed, and torches began to be lighted, the king desiring to break up this pretended disputation, said to Lambert, 'What sayest thou now after all these great labours which thou hast taken upon thee, and all the reasons and instructions of these learned men? Art thou not yet satisfied? Wilt thou live or die? What sayest thou? Thou hast yet free choice.' Lambert answered, 'I yield and submit myself wholly unto the will of Your Majesty.'

'Then,' said the king, 'commit thyself unto the hand of God, and not unto mine.' To which he piously replied -- 'I commend my soul unto the hands of God, but my body I wholly yield and submit unto your clemency.' Then said the king, 'If you do commit yourself unto my judgment, you must die, for I will not be a patron unto heretics.'

Then sternly ... [was] here performed the condemnation of Lambert by no other ministers than [Protestant] reformers themselves, namely, Taylor, Barnes, Cranmer and [the lord] Cromwell, who afterwards in apparent judgment [of Providence], all suffered the like for the gospel's sake.

Upon the day appointed for this holy martyr of God to suffer, he was brought out of the prison at eight o'clock in the morning unto the house of the lord Cromwell, and ... sat down to breakfast with them, shewing no manner of sadness or fear. When breakfast was ended, he was carried straight to the place of execution at Smithfield. The manner of his death was dreadful; for after his legs were nearly consumed and burned, and that the wretched tormentors and enemies of God had withdrawn the fire from him, then two who stood on each side with their halberds, pitched him, from side to side as far as the chain would reach; while he, lifting up such hands as he had, cried unto the people in these words: -- 'None but Christ, none but Christ!' He was soon after let down again from their halberds, fell into the fire, and there ended his life (Milner and Cobbin N.D./1883: 350ff).

## India

The nature and pursuit of the national civil society in power and culture can be put in the form of four propositions. (a) Civil society is truly the locus of God-realisation or self-realisation as well as of the common usage or custom of the people, and not only of tradition and authority or what is handed down. (b) It is the sovereign arbiter of custom as against the priest, custodian of tradition, and the prince, maker and executor of the state and its law. (c) Inspired in the modern world by new religion, secularism or pluralism, civil society alone has the inherent power to find a people's principle of history and so to change the common usage, the 'custom of the country', as well as itself, as in the Gandhian view of self-rule and self-reform, the one being the condition of the other. (d) The prince and the priest, whenever the two rule together, either through a state-established religion or a religion-established state, are the enemies of civil society, its national autonomy, self-expression, political economy, customs and morality.

The struggle of civil society in India during the modern period runs parallel to the rise and recognition of the vernaculars and vernacularism everywhere in language, labour and culture; and it is the story of religion and politics proceeding from Kabir (1440-1518) to Mahatma Gandhi. Its political culmination, if we may call it that, is the movement for the linguistic reorganisation of the states of the Union after 1950, that is, as against the previous politico-administrative map of British Indian provinces and the states of the princes. Civil society was thus established in the Indian modernity by the 'separation of powers' of the priest and the prince, the Brahmin and the Rajput, followed by the introduction of a system of pluralism and vernacular democracy in the social space so opened for the nation and the people.

Gandhi wrote down his gospel of truth and non-violence for this civil society in the form of a dialogue with people like Savarkar, advocate of the Hindu nation-state, on his sea voyage from London to South Africa in 1908. Savarkar scratched the outline of his contrary *Hindutva* on the walls of his prison cell in the Andamans a few years later, but had already as a student met and hated Gandhi in London. Savarkar wrote that the strength, cohesion and progress of India depended in the last resort upon the sense and sentiment of Hindutva or Hinduness, relegating questions of social reform and Hindu-Muslim unity to merely side issues. Whether or not he was the inspiration of terrorists and assassins, Savarkar brought all his talent and energy to focus on the project expressed by the slogan that he coined on his birthday in 1941, 'Hinduise all politics and militarise Hindudom!' He was widely recognised as a hero of the national freedom movement; and for him the Hindus alone constituted 'the foundation, the bedrock, the reserved forces of the Indian state' (1923: 119-28).

Gandhi, on the other hand, who led the movement in civil society, was the martyr of *swaraj*, self-rule or home-rule. Even in his civil disobedience he was the supreme witness to the causes of pluralism and social reform, Hindu-Muslim unity, the removal of Untouchability, and of *swadeshi* (home-grown) as the love of one's neighbour and of his or her labour, putting the truth of God and civil society above the state and the transfer of power as well as above the tradition of the priestly *shastras*. Gandhi wanted the pluralist 'equality of all religions' (1930) as the foundation of modern Indian society, nationality and culture, whether politically organised as one independent state or as two (1947); and he consistently refused to subordinate means to ends or ends to means, either for himself and his own or for any other segment of humanity. Needless to say, his method and praxis of *satyagraha*, truth and non-violence, Savarkar rejected outright as sinful as well as suicidal.

In Gandhi's civil society the self would always look the other in the eye as its second self, and offer dialogue and non-violent conversation without fear of the possible consequences. For him the national freedom movement of *swaraj* meant essentially the self-reform and self-rule of civil society; and Ram Rajya was to bring the rule of salvation-in-society, a 'kingdom of Heaven' in politics viewed as self-management of the institutions of civil society rather than of the state. While telling the British as well as Tagore that 'our non-cooperation is a retirement within ourselves' (1921), he in fact produced out of tradition, or rather from the customs of the country, a modernity of India's own; and in order that India could come into its own in the world with a reformed tradition of pluralism and what I call vernacular democracy. In this way the path of national salvation in history was transformed from *dharmayuddha*, the classical just war of priests and princes, into the new *satyagraha*, the struggle for truth in any and every field by the methods of martyrdom, self-control and non-violence, whether it was for the achievement of independence, ending foreign domination and exploitation or for the regulation of relations among the different communities at home.

## Pluralism and Civil Society

If it is to represent the principles of solidarity as well as reciprocity and not be only the arena of the struggle for power or profit, civil society must next address the problem of pluralism defined as the mediation of the one and the many and not only as a synonym for diversity. Indeed one may go futher and suggest that, apart from or along with the hardy perennials of domination and exploitation, death and destitution, affliction and alienation, the problem for the (post-modern) world today is perhaps the reconciliation of difference with equality in civil society. This surely cannot be achieved within a framework (a) of the permanent majority and the minority, hierarchy, superordination and subordination or the centre versus the periphery and the margin, or alternatively (b) of a falsely imagined unity brought about by uniformity, homogeneity and centralisation. In this sense the Gandhian 'equality of all religions' means that all of them are equally true and truly equal as well as equally humanly imperfect, and therefore each of them is capable of self-rule and self-reform (*swaraj*) in the common light of God's truth and non-violence.

It is necessary to add that to this Gandhian attitude in religion there would correspond a true federalism in the state, even if imperfectly under the Mughals and the British, and real tolerance and purity in civil society, labour and the economy. This has been the modern Indian way of knowing when to combine and when to separate a multi-religious nation, a modern pluralist society and a federal secular state. The secular state, for example, is then ideally required by some to be the managing director of a secular civil society, but by others contrariwise as the pre-condition for the self-fulfilment of religion-in-society, and this is a possible and legitimate meaning of unity in variety.

We may now explain the background of the Indian modernity on the analogy of language, which is the people's system of custom or the common usage that is farthest removed from the influences of the priest and the prince, tradition and the state: it represents the country in the trinity of God, king and country.

> Linguistic diversity is an established way of life in India; ... which is, in fact, one aspect of cultural pluralism. People in a multilingual country develop ways of speaking in which they can maintain their own language and still communicate with speakers of other languages; they become bilingual or multilingual. Languages are not employed parallelly in all spheres of activity .... The patterns of use of languages in a [single] bilingual community are largely complementary.
>
> All languages are equal, but different languages have different roles in society, and have different positions in the education system .... That each speaker has [reciprocal] access to the other's variety (e.g. Hindi or Urdu) and also to the common variety (Hindustani) underscores the integrative aspect of such variations [v. uniformity]. The assertion and acceptance [of identities] are reciprocal and mutual. In this way, different social groups can maintain their separateness on the one hand and express their togetherness on the other. The face-to-face communication allows for more [strategies of] negotiation than any other context.
>
> [Pluralist] integration is thus different from [a] the 'melting pot' on the one hand and [b] segregation on the other. The melting pot results into complete assimilation with the dominant group, a merger of identity. Segregation results into isolation [or stratification] and the tensions thereof.
>
> Hindi and Urdu, in the language of structural linguistics, form one set of correlation; it is an opposition in which one can only be explained in the context of the other: Hindi and Urdu are two sides of the same coin: if you have one then you have to accept the other .... Urdu identity [for example] becomes more relevant only in the context of Hindi rather than in the context of any other language.
>
> Though the institutional affiliation of Urdu is with the Persian

> literary tradition and that of Hindi with the Sanskrit literary tradition, Hindi and Urdu literature have been developed by the same population in the same region -- Hindu and Muslim writers have contributed to both these varieties. As in various other spheres of creative arts, music, painting, dance and drama, so [also] in writing, there has been a remarkable reciprocity.... Persian scholarship flourished alongside the traditional Sanskrit scholarship for a long time in the Northern courts ... [and] for the first time in the history of Indian languages, a common *lingua franca* [Hindustani] becomes the language of the court, administration, law and order, though spread [and varied] over a vast territory .... Linguistically, Urdu and Hindi are recent [alternative] standardisations of a medieval [or an early modern] *lingua franca.*
>
> Our linguistic issues are not the multiplicity of languages, social variation and varieties, but of the gaps between the colloquial [or the vernacular] and the [elite] literary standards (Pandit 1977: 3f, 37, 47, 50, 56, 60).

The logic of national pluralism, therefore, makes the common usage of civil society prevail over or along with the authority of inherited tradition, and perhaps this is the normal and the proper condition of modernity. Multilingualism is thus inclined to keep its distribution of differences generally functional, contextual and domain-specific as well as group-specific, for example, in relation to the family, neighbourhood, bazar, formal education, including the laboratory, work, administration, worship and play, although there will be also degrees of overlap and competition. Several independent studies confirm that spoken and written languages live and develop, not by seeking purity or insulation or officially-sponsored standardisation, but by free on-going contact, interaction and exchange with other languages in a plural setting, national and international.

The European writers who could be quoted on the subject, e.g. Levi-Strauss and Lotman, have duly recognised but two tendencies at work in history and society, the centripetal and the centrifugal or homogeneity and heterogeneity, whereas the Indian experiment will show us a field of four possibilities to make up the logic of pluralism. The Europeans imagine any two things to be either (a) similar and together (equality or homogeneity) or (b) separate and different (inequality or heterogeneity). But this opposition completely ignores and excludes the other pair of possibilities that two things could be in the relation of competition, equivalence or correspondence, that is (c) separate but similar, or else of complementarity, that is (d) together but different; and all four empirical and theoretical relations can be shown simultaneously on two perpendicular axes of similarity/difference and togetherness, proximity or contiguity/separateness (Uberoi 1996: 106f).

Such a system of national pluralism, for example, multilingualism or multiculturism, classical and/or vernacular, is constantly sustained, made effective and integrated by the simultaneous operation of two social tendencies or principles: (a) the distribution of differences into complementary, and not only competitive, domains and contexts of situation; and (b) the convergence of underlying structures, not only their divergence, through the free human act of communication. (For example, the Saurashtri dialect of Gujarati emigrants who settled in Tamil Nadu from *c.* 1500 onward is Pandit's case in point. The similarities between Tamil and Gujarati can be seen as part of a larger framework of comparison of Dravidian and Indo-Aryan. There are certain significant differences also. In so far as Saurashtri shares these features with Tamil and not with Gujarati we are able to say that the linguistic structures of Tamil and Saurashtri are much more closely related to each other–indeed they are almost identical–than either of them is to the original parent Gujarati.)

The first principle is a kind of self-control on variation and differentiation within the system (synchrony), while the second is a self-control on variation or diversification between two or more systems in evolution (diachrony). We may therefore conclude that under the regime of pluralism all differences are negotiable in civil society because no one truth or reality falsifies another; and that the strategy and dialectics of negotiation, whether in harmony or conflict, amity or enmity, produce in effect neither homogeneity (or equality) nor heterogeneity (inequality) but a new non-dualist axis of mediation, that is, of equality with difference.

## The Concept of Custom

We may finally ask what is meant by the 'custom of the country' whether or not its 'country' is a separate territory: (a) as the unit and foundation of what we have termed vernacular democracy, and (b) in relation to the emergence of human history and civil society out of the primeval state of nature.

The recent review by an historian, Kelley 1990, offers perhaps the best documented summary of the concept of custom. In the form of second nature (*altera natura*) it has run through all departments of European life and thought, and the idea of culture as second nature underlies the history of modern social science. Beginning with the ancient Greek distinction between nature (*physis*) and man-made rules, law and conventions (*nomos*), one approach has continued the tradition from 'custom is king' (Pindar) to Bagehot's dictum in explaining Britain's constitution as both forming and formed by the 'cake of custom' (1867). Custom, in the sense of consensus and usage, was the ruler (*magister*) of human speech and so of human life in terms both collective (the common usage) and individual (the sense of habit).

During the Christian middle ages of Europe, the church as well as the state took a dim view of custom (*consuetudo*). Apologists for the supreme legislative authority of the state urged that making law was the exclusive monopoloy of the sovereign and it always superseded custom (which was already not included among the sources of classical Roman law); but some French and Italian jurists argued in the interest of civil society that on the contrary 'custom abolishes law'. The terms of this debate referred to natural law or man's universal reason, on the one hand, and to the law of nations (custom), on the other hand, this latter being the office of the people. The fathers of the Christian church, Augustine and Jerome, laying down the canonical foundation, rejected custom as being the corruption rather than the generation of human nature and of human law, thus regarding it as alienated from the sacred or the divine and the ecclesiastical law. Isidore of Seville had conceded only that 'custom is a sort of general law [*jus*] established by manners [*mores*], which is taken as a legal rule [*lex*] when legal rules [statute law and/or the canon law] are lacking'. The more generous view of the jurists, however, was that 'the power of custom is three-fold: it is the founder of law, the interpreter of law and the abrogator of law' (Paulus); custom therefore represents the will of the people and it also rules their conduct.

In early modern Europe, the movement of the Renaissance and the practising jurists, as Kelley says, took the latter view that in short 'custom, not natural instinct or universal reason, was the ruling force in civil society' (Connan), thus reinvoking the Greek *nomos basileus*, custom is king. The simultaneous evolution of the common law in England and the *droit commun* in France was wholly a matter of custom versus both state absolutism and the Roman church; and 'use', as Hamlet said at the time, 'almost can change the stamp of nature'. The official or the magisterial Reformation of Luther and Calvin, however, continued to insist that our second nature was even more corrupted than the first (after the Fall of man). Luther often repeated the gospel to the effect that Christ the lord had identified himself as being the truth and not as habit or custom (John 14: 6). The Puritans and the dissenters of the radical Reformation, as we have already discussed above, nevertheless stood up for a plural civil society in the form of freedom of conscience and worship in the history of the Protestant martyrs.

Habit and custom, individual and collective, were also dissolving in philosophy under the attacks of rationalism on the one side and of naturalism on the other, although Michaux still argued that 'customs are the true monuments of the nations of Europe, and the creation of these nations as a body'. 'We emerged into a social and political order', not by the Leviathan of the social contract, 'but rather as revealed in our customs', as we shall also conclude.

At the point of maturation of modernity, the French revolution of 1789 onwards attempted to deal a death blow to the concept of custom, replacing it some fifteen years later with the Civil code, the work of the state and its citizens. But it continued to lead a posthumous life in modern social science, including linguistics and psychology as well as sociology and anthropology, not to mention also in the politics of culture, nationality and identity until today. At the same time, on the other side of the Channel, the Industrial Revolution had split the unity of custom as the representation of the common usage and collective consciousness as well as conscience into a duality, the rule of technical reason versus merely tradition, habit or what is handed down, which duality Kelley does not discuss (1990: 85-100).

## Society without the State

The question of the order of power or the power of order in the sense of the first emergence of order out of anarchy—at the cost of setting up a system of sovereignty with a single authority and hierarchy, centralisation and stratification—has been settled by the mediation of a state of 'ordered anarchy' articulated by a system of alternate oppositions and solidarities ruled by custom versus the state of nature where prevailed the war of each against all. This is the seminal result of the theoretical and empirical work of the British school of political anthropology beginning in 1940 with *African political systems* edited by Fortes and Evans-Pritchard up to the synthesis of *Politics, law and ritual in tribal society* by Gluckman in Britain (1965) soon to be followed by Balandier's *Political anthropology* in France (1970). Its chief contribution to theory is that, against the supposed 'social contract' of Hobbes and his followers which envisaged a community or many communities living together under the empire of one law and sovereignty, which was supposed to be indivisible, it shows that the many may continue to practise their home-rule within a 'community of sovereignties' (pluralism), if the expression is allowed, which is the positive aspect of ordered anarchy relevant to both war and peace, for example, in the theory of international relations.

In many tribal societies without the state (or the church) there is found a simultaneous distribution of sovereignty and territory under the common law and general rule of 'balanced opposition' or segmentary systems of self-help, solidarity and reciprocity. The whole population, which may number tens of thousands or lakhs if not millions, and its territory are divided into two or more homologous sub-divisions, local communities or segments at a number of descending/ascending levels, such that the two systems are parallel and coordinated at each level. The ordering of segments is often socially reckoned on a pyramidal and unitary genealogy of generations of ancestors, in the male or more unusually in the female line, each of whom is identified with and invoked by the corresponding local community of a territorial section or sub-section. All local communities at each and every level of segmentation are reckoned as structurally equal (homologous), like two or more teams in a game of sport, and possess a degree of corporateness, such that internal conflict or dispute will be subject to mediation, arbitration and conciliation in the first as well as the last instance–as against the supposed tribal law of an eye for an 'eye and a tooth for a tooth'.

The series of unilineal descent groups that are homologous and are in a system of solidarity and opposition are also, by the rule of exogamy, interrelated by marriage, forming a network of affinal alliances as well as of matrilateral links called complementary filiation, which acts as a further brake on public delict and the spread of disorder. This does not apply of course to the Arabs whose lineages are non-exogamous and without cross-cutting ties, but their lineage system is nevertheless coordinated with their territorial system to form the segmentary political system. Apart from these two principles, descent/ kinship and territory, there are usually found also decentralised but uniform systems of age-sets or of rituals, including systems of the ceremonial exchange of gifts like the *kula* of Melanesia, which require or assume alternate competition and cooperation among the local communities at each level of segmentation, that s, by their situational aggregation/segregation. It is not necessary that such varied sub-systems within a tribal society should all correspond to each other, point by point, but there must exist some method of their correlation in order to call it one society and polity, though being without central government, the state or a single chief.

By the situational aggregation/segregation jointly called segmentation is meant primarily the social process of 'balanced opposition' of one tribe against its neighbouring tribes; of one primary section of a tribe against its other primary sections; of one secondary section against other secondary sections of the same primary section; and of one tertiary section against other tertiary sections within the same secondary section, this nesting political series necessarily stopping before the single family household and its territory.

The principle of relativity permeates segmentary systems almost by definition, so that the political meaning and effect of any event depends upon its context of situation. For example, the single offence of homicide or a dispute over land may lead respectively (a) to a kind of war when it occurs between men of two independent tribes; (b) to a raid of reprisal between the remote agnatic cousins of two primary sections of the one tribe; (c) to a long feud of reciprocal serial killings between the nearer agnatic cousins of two secondary sections; (d) to a quickly-settled vengeance or payment of blood-money when it occurs between two adjacent tertiary sections. (e) Within the small and close group of a single tertiary section it is a heinous crime and inexpiable sin for a brother to kill a brother, and there is no remedy. Such an event would be simply denied or blamed on their (assumed) different mothers; and patricide, if it is at all conceivable, would end in the self-administered punishment of suicide or a guilty exile.

Such principles of comparative politics, including the claim of civil society to its sacred or profane territory, have been revealed by the study of segmentary stateless societies, and they are not replaced but only somewhat muted by the emergence later of government and administration, nations, states and empires in history. Meanwhile the concept of custom and the common usage, including its consciousness as well as conscience or its sense and sensibility, remains the hallmark and the mainstay of human civil society or of civility, as indeed of its language and territory. The concept of the nation existing in a system of nations can be then redefined as that civil society whose sense of collective subjectivity and responsibility has determined to resolve within itself, with or without the state and its organs, the questions and problems of inequality as well as difference, of stratification as well as segmentation, which are common to the human species.

## Bibliographical Note

The references cited here are not comprehensive but minimal, selective, comparative, theoretical and ideological. The Indian references are limited to only new themes and approaches.

Although there is found no article or index entry under the heading of civil society, several key terms, definitions and articles relevant to issues of civil society can be readily located in a previous standard work of reference, *International encyclopaedia of the social sciences*, but they will need to be updated, interrelated and critically applied. Jaffa 1968 on the concept of natural rights is a case in point. On the other hand, Hegel 1967, first published by the Clarendon Press in 1952 translated from the German of 1821 which also bore the alternative title *Natural law and political science*, is the single definitive classic text, difficult but essential, on the morals and ethics of the state and civil society, if not also of the family.

Frazer 1950, first published in 1922, is by far the most influential study of politico-religious kingship, its associated personal charisma and magic, which left no room for a civil society.

Balandier 1970 is an excellent comparative review, critical and original, of the English and French sources. It bears on the continuities and discontinuities of politics and civil society in emerging from pre-history into history. Gluckman 1965, *Politics, law and ritual in tribal society,* as its title indicates, is a synthesis of the three dimensions of social anthropological theories of the state and conflict or strife in civil society, well-illustrated with detailed ethnographic examples. Fortes and Evans-Pritchard 1940 comprises eight monographic studies with two comparative chapters by Radcliffe-Brown and the editors that established the sociological theory of segmentary systems based on descent/kinship and territory, and so on, which could form the principles of civil society even without the state and the church.

Kelley 1990 is an excellent review of the literary sources of classical or ancient, medieval and early modern periods in Europe. It complements from an historical civilisation with church and state the anthropological perspective on law, custom and society. Milner and Cobbin's edition of *Foxe's book of martyrs* is sub-titled 'a complete and accurate account of the lives, sufferings and triumphant deaths of the primitive and Protestant martyrs, in all parts of the world'. It is a popular book of modern Britain that explains best how Christian witness, self-sacrifice and conscience make, open and reopen a free space between the state and the (established) church.

First published 1835, de Tocqueville 1945 is American liberal democracy's best defence, with intermediary institutions between the citizen and the state standing in for civil society. In the same tradition, Shils 1997 has nine selected essays on American liberalism, tradition and civil society, informed by sound (if conservative) sociological sense. On the other hand, Durkheim 1957 comprises lectures given at Bordeaux, 1890-1900, and in Paris, 1904, 1912, and so on, on the state, the individual and modern institutions of civil society and the economy in the tradition of social democracy.

Chandhoke 1995 is a review from political science, specially good for ready reference on the Hegel, Marx and Gramsci tradition. Pandit 1977, *Language in a plural society*, is an important definition of modern Indian pluralism from a sociolinguistic point of view. Oommen 1990a, and 1990b on social movements of protest and change, show a consistent defence of pluralism and civil society (nation) with good Indian empirical reference and unusual theoretical reference to all three terms (nation, state, society).

Savarkar 1923 is evidently the only book so far produced by the ideology of Hindu nationalism (cf Gandhi's *Hind swaraj*). It shows with apparent approval concerns of the state prevailing over those of civil society. Uberoi 1996 to the contrary evidences the martyrology of Shiah Islam, Sikhism and Gandhism in defence of the concern of salvation-in-society as being above the state as well as the authority of tradition as a principle of motion of history and civil society.

## References

Balandier, Georges. 1970. *Political anthropology*. London: Allen Lane, the Penguin Press.

Chandhoke, Neera. 1995. *State and civil society*. New Delhi: Sage.

de Tocqueville, Alexis. *1945. Democracy in America,* 2 vols. New York: Alfred Knopf.

Durkheim, Emile. 1957. *Professional ethics and civic morals.* London: Routledge and Kegal Paul.

Fortes, M. and E. E. Evans-Pritchard (eds). 1940. *African political systems*. London: Oxford University Press for International African Institute.

Frazer, James G. 1950. *The golden bough*, abridged ed. London/New York: Macmillan.

Gluckman, Max. 1965. *Politics, law and ritual in tribal society.* Oxford: Blackwell.

Hegel, G. W. F. 1967. *Hegel's philosophy of right*, ed. and transl. by T. M. Knox. London: Oxford University Press.

Jaffa, Harry V. 1968. 'Natural rights', *International encyclopaedia of the social sciences*, ed. David L. Sills, vol. 11, pp. 85-90. New York: Macmillan Co. and Free Press.

Kelley, Donald R. 1990. 'Altera natura: the idea of custom in historical perspective', in John Henry and Sarah Hutton (eds). *New perspectives on Renaissance thought*, pp. 83-100. London: Duckworth/Instituto Italiano per gli Studi di Filosofia.

Milner, J. and Ingram Cobbin (eds). n.d./1883. *Foxe's book of martyrs*. London: Morgan and Scott.

Oommen, T. K. 1990a. *State and society in India*. New Delhi: Sage.

____________. 1990b. *Protest and change*. New Delhi: Sage

Pandit, P. B. 1977. *Language in a plural society.* Delhi: Dev Raj Chanana Memorial Lectures/Delhi University Press.

Savarkar, V.D. 1923. *Hindutva.* Nagpur: V.V. Kelkar.

Shils, Edward. 1997. *The virtue of civility.* Indianapolis, Indiana: Liberty Fund.

Uberoi, J. P. S. 1996. *Religion, civil society and the state.* Delhi: Oxford University Press.

# 3

# State and Civil Society: Reframing the Question in the Indian Context

*Vikash N. Pandey*

*In our nightmares and consciences, the complex truths of the past are at risk of being sorted and pressed into the simplifying imperatives of the present. The act of 'looking' is partly 'pre-interpreted' through a range of intense personal and collective present meanings.... Other stories are less told and less well remembered because they jar in one way or another with current sensibilities or perceived truths. In this sense, we fail to use the past as a resource as fully as we could. Our memory is fractured.*

—A. Harrington

## Introduction

State and civil society are being widely debated in contemporary times. Yet, due to an uncritical employment of these concepts, the critique of the state and the celebration of civil society and culture (tradition in one sense and liberalism in the other) has acquired enormous influence in anti-modernist and resurgent market-friendly articulations. This paper attempts to (a) re-visit the backwaters of these concepts, and their place in different theoretical traditions; and (b) scrutinise the fallacious understanding of the relationship between state and society as mutually hostile, and its consequent polarising effects. It will be argued that such a dualism results in a retrogressive romanticisation of tradition/culture and civil society.

It is, perhaps, no accident that such political discourses are also co-terminus with the current eclipsing of an egalitarian thrust and the phenomenal resurgence of fundamentalism, and of ethnic religious and racial violence in all parts of the globe. Insurmountable human tragedies are taking place in the name of 'identity' salvation, and these are being counterposed to the violence of the modern state (making no distinction between government and state). On the one hand there is uncritical praise for the capitalist liberal state (posited as the only modern and democratic form possible or desirable) which forecloses any alternative formulation of democracy or an egalitarian polity. On the other we find a savage criticism of modernity counterposed by an equally non-reflexive praise of tradition/culture as opposed to the state. In such a view the 'modern' state is conceived as universalised and homogenising, acting against culture/ tradition and, thereby, the people. The pre-modern traditional polity is posited as the real democratic polity, thereby calling for privileging the culturally based social collectivities against the modern and anti-people, state-regulated ones as the only genuine future left before us. In this political discourse, the appeal for anti-modern social collectivities is, paradoxically, built on the liberal strategy of separating state from society. In short, a larger platform is covered by the dualism of culture/society vs. state, and tradition vs. modern. In opposition to their view this paper argues that state and/or society are intertwined concepts denoting a dynamic discourse, each affecting and getting affected by the other, and neither of them being socially frozen identities/entities.

In the first section of this paper the existing paradigms and what their formulations on the inter-linkages between state and civil society consist of are reviewed. The following section pays particular attention to the debate within India. In the Indian context, our main focus is on the culturalist critique of the modern Indian state and celebration of civil society/tradition. Therein, we offer a critique to expose the common fallacy culturalists share with the liberal-democratic framework. Overall, this paper intends to deal with the polemical intents of the neo-liberal celebration of globalisation and with the cultural cry of tradition against modern (that is, the weakening of the state against the proposed world as a free market or civil society), precisely in order to capitulate the relationship between the state and civil society, as attempted in the concluding section.

## State vs. Society

Leading modern societies claim to have a constitutional and democratic state, based on the rule of law which stems from the balance between the legislature and the executive. These bodies of governance are supposed to be accountable to the will of the people as expressed through electoral forms of political participation. As these governing institutions derive their power from the people, they are subject to the control of the people. This ensures, at least formally, that there is no monopoly of power in the hands of a single class or group and democratic rights are guaranteed to all members of society. Thus, under such an arrangement, the modern state is an expression of popular rule.

Based on this fundamental assumption about the 'formal' nature of the liberal-democratic state, it is argued that such a polity is essentially plural, cutting across social classes. Power is dispersed among groups, institutions and organisations. Inequalities do exist but being non-cumulative, they are negotiated and modified through democratic struggles and bargaining among various economic and socio-political interests. When we add issues such as language, gender, race, religion, ethnicity, and the like '... there is a dispersal of powerful individuals and groups throughout society and in so far as this heterogeneous system of checks and balances is subject to any unified control, it is a control established through the political system and accountable to the people through the ballot box' (Jessop 1991: 173).

Thus, such states serve to (a) mediate among competing interests, and (b) even acting, sometimes, against the interests of 'capital', maintain the public and national interests in opposition to sectional and international interests. These entities cannot afford to be partisan because it would result in an erosion of their legitimacy. This applies equally to all kinds of sectional interests such as regional, linguistic, sexual, racial, cultural. In this sense, if a state becomes partisan, it is because of the inadequacies in democratic accountability. Therefore, to maintain the neutral, balancing and mediating role of the state, it is necessary that democratic accountability in the political system is advanced. This democratic accountability lies in the expansion of 'civil society', a reduction in the role of the state (and collateral bureaucratic power). By mediating the role of the state under the supervision of civil society, democratic actualisation of plural groups can be furthered within the boundaries of a state.

It is argued that whenever the state expands and becomes strong (reducing or crushing civil society), its repressive and authoritarian tendencies become overwhelming. Gellner gives the example: 'Civil society (in the USSR) had been crushed and atomised by Bolshevik centralism, by the fusion of all hierarchy and organisation into a single nomenclature' (1991: 133). Gellner goes on to describe the restoration of capitalism, religious revivalism, ethnic conflicts and re-emergence of neo-fascism in Russia as 'a painful revival of civil society' (ibid). Though with a different vocabulary, some Indian scholars have found a similar process behind the contemporary assertion of plural groups and civil society in the shape of religious revivalism, ethnic and such other mobilisations against the Indian state. We shall talk about this in greater detail in the next section.

This whole edifice of a democratic polity is erected on the fundamental dualism of the state and civil society. This is based on two core assumptions: (a) that civil society, being essentially plural in character, is inherently democratic, non-repressive; and (b) that the state is essentially a repressive institution.

After separating the two a reconciliation is attempted by suggesting that to maintain the democratic nature of our polity, it is necessary that the state be minimal and put under the active control of civil society. Only then could the harmony between individual-civil/society-state be achieved..

Superficially ironical but fundamentally supplementary, the liberal construct as well as the culturalist critique of the state are premised on its supposed autonomy. The state is oppressive because it can weaken or negate the forces with divergent preferences/interests and thus reduce the plurality because of its universalising thrust. In other words, it is suggested that '… states and people may formulate and pursue goals that are not simply reflective of the demands or interests of social groups, classes or society' (Skocpol 1985: 20-21).

## Critique

Let us look at the achievements of the modern state with its democratic polity, which distinguishes it from the pre-modern and even classical liberal state. The purpose behind this stock-taking is three-fold: (1) the strength/claims will guide constructive criticism that there are inherent limitations to this approach. These limitations call for alternative conceptualisation of the state-society relationship for a better 'future'; (2) it will also guard against reductionist tendencies in the orthodox critique of the state and enable an alternative conceptualisation based on recent contributions of critical theories; and (3) it will also provide (by putting together a critique of the liberal foundations of the state-society dualism and from the lessons of the dissenting voices within Marxist thinking) a critique of neo-liberalism, a culturalist rejection of the modern state and a celebration of tradition and of 'nations' based on culture. (Sometimes, the name given to this institutionalisation is civilisation-nation/state.) In other words, it would help in exposing the liberal heritages within the culturalist construct of the polity based on state-society dualism.

First, the achievements of the liberal-democratic states:

1) At least in the later half of the 20th century, opportunities for political participation have got extended to larger sections of the population, and a tendency of rejecting 'formal' monopoly of power in the hands of dominant social groups, that is, capitalists, has been noted.
2) Within each liberal-democratic state, constitutional guarantees are available in terms of formal freedom and equality for all the citizens.

Put together, the legitimacy of the state accrues through 'welfare' intervention in mitigating substantial inequalities and extending popular participation in the electoral verdict. But, then, it raises doubts about the proposal for a 'minimal-state'. In fact, the greatest challenge faced by the leftist mobilisations in these states has been the modifications in the classical liberal agenda whereby the state played an active role in 're-distribution' rather than allowing free and brutal play of market.

Moreover, the question remains: does formal freedom and equality ensure substantial freedom and equality to every social group? Is democracy a notion restricted to formal equal opportunity to vote? If there is unequal distribution of resources (for example, education, capital and other means of production), there are necessarily unequal opportunities and bargaining capacities. For instance, how far do the elected assemblies/parliament reflect, in substantial terms, the concerns of unorganised labour or rural population of drought-prone regions? In recent decades, irrespective of political parties coming to power, facilitation of market forces has become the dominant governmental policy to be pursued in the Indian sub-continent. In this sense, capital has come to retain important control over the state, moving from a hesitant, indirect one during the 'welfare era' to an aggressive, almost unchallenged, direct one since the liberalisation drive.

Contrary to the claims of the liberals, resources and rights are not equally shared by each social group; moreover, their distribution also depends on the differential location of social groups and forces (both nationally and internationally). In this sense, plurality per se cannot ensure a democratic state or polity. It might simply be a contested process for regional, religious, ethnic, linguistic and other basis of electoral support and yet hide social discrimination and inequality by forwarding the illusion of expanding 'civil society' against the state. In this sense, a struggle against a particular state is not necessarily identical with the struggle for democracy, self-determination, an egalitarian society or in favour of a marginalised group. It might simply mean 'growing ideological antipathy to democracy' in the fundamentalist sense: celebration of traditional culture or facilitating the capitalist (multinational and domestic both) hegemony against the recurrent economic crisis faced by the state (Jessop 1991:18).

In short, a weak state does not mean a strong civil society. The implication is that the state is subject to social structural features and, therefore, state and civil society are not distinct and frozen entities. They are dynamically linked together in terms of a state-society couplet rather than being oppositional and mutually exclusive categories.

## Interrogating Civil Society

The cornerstone of the liberal and culturalist critique of the state is their advocacy of the expansion and privileging of civil society. Implied in this is the assumption about civil society as non-stratified and homogeneous (in specific cultural terms, civilisational unity as a natural sphere of human existence in contrast to the modernist fabrication of nation-state). In this section we will look into the historical emergence of the notion of civil society to point out (a) how the notion of civil society as a separate (and against the state) category itself is part of the liberal paradigm; and therefore (b) how the celebration of civil society by the culturalists shares the liberal programmatic of pushing the egalitarian reformulation of society into the background.

Historically, the notion of civil society re-surfaced during the 18th century.[1] The dualism of state and society and contemporaneously civil society, emerged for the first time, along with the decline of the feudal polity and the emergence of the middle classes. Thus, under Locke's *Social contract*, individuals surrendered all their powers and rights to the collectivity of 'civil society' and 'state' in return for the protection of their property. By the mid-19th century, 'civil society' implied formal (limited) legal equality, the protection of property and constitutionalism. The liberalism (articulated by Adam, Ferguson, Voltaire, Priestly and Bentham) posited civil society as a 'self-regulated society' against the state (Williams 1976). It '... laid the foundation ... to ex-nominate capitalist social organisation: economic man and minimal state; so that during the twentieth century it culminated into a critique of welfarism—as the road to serfdom-by Hayek and—"end of history" by Fukuyama' (Upadhyaya 1992: 91). So, '... wider the range of activities covered by the market ... fewer the issues on which government is necessary, the greater is the likelihood of getting agreement while maintaining free society ...' (Friedman 1963: 24).

In this invocation of the 'invisible hand' of the market, democracy also got equated with abstract legalism. However, a critique of this notion of 'civil society' and democracy was put forward simultaneously by Rousseau:

> the origin of society and law, which bound new fetters on the poor, and gave new powers to the rich; which irretrievably destroyed national liberty, eternally fixed the law of property and inequality, converted clever usurpations into unalterable right, and, for the advantages of a new ambitious individuals, subjected all mankind to perpetual labour, slavery and wretchedness... (Colletti 1978: 165).

The most severe criticism of this dualism of civil society vs. state, however, came from Marx:

> ... neither legal relations nor forms of state could be grasped, whether by themselves or on the basis of a so-called general development of the

> human mind, but on the contrary they have their origin in material conditions of existence, the totality of which Hegal, following the example of Englishmen and Frenchmen of the eighteenth century, embraces with the term 'civil society'; that the anatomy of this civil society has to be sought in political economy...(1975: n.a.).[2]

Civil society, thereby, cannot be seen as autonomous from the socio-economic and political processes and also from the state. By ignoring the dynamic intertwining of state and society, the liberals and culturalists both forget that state and society are interdependent and that they interpenetrate in a multitude of different ways (Block 1987).

## Celebrating Culture/Tradition in India

Having outlined the critique of the dualism of the state vs. civil society, we will now discuss the debate as imported in the Indian context and concurrently try to expose its underlying weaknesses of idealism and fundamentalism.

The required departure from the statist notion of 'India', as it is claimed, lies in the recognition that, (a) the secular modern-state of India universalises and homogenises in the name of unity. Privileging state over people, it denies the social space to plurality of traditions, religion, language, and the like. Thus, the agenda of the state is inherently modern, repressive; and (b) alternatively, India is a cultural notion imbibing multiplicity and is a civilisational unity rather than a modern state.

To set the tone for this critique of the Indian state, the emergence of capitalism (which is taken as another name for modernity) is seen as the collateral of the state. The capitalist process requires homogenisation for which it posits two simultaneous processes: (a) the centralisation of economic and political powers in the institution of the state; and (b) homogenisation and standardisation of culture to be formed as nation under the supervision of the state and thus the consolidation of the nation-state. In this sense it is a repeat of what had been the Western experience (Anderson 1983).

Against this interpretation, the contemporary Indian subcontinent dissents. With the resurgence of the nation-question all over the world and the crises at home (for example, in Punjab, Jammu and Kashmir, Uttarakhand, Jharkhand, Gorkhaland and the northeastern region) there is a renewed vigour with which the notion of the Indian state as a product of Western/modern statist repression of the diversity is being openly challenged. The move is based on one assumption, that India is a civilisational unity rather than a 'nation-state' (Kumar 1989: 39).

> [So] we need to remember that the essential identity of India is cultural, not political or economic. It is one civilisation that has withstood various vicissitudes and still endured, largely because of its basic identity being cultural. It never had a political centre except very recently (Kothari 1989: 81)

Pre-modern, non-nation-state civilisational forms of unity were based on the plural cultural ethos. The modern state tries to remove this plurality and togetherness inbuilt in Indian culture.[3] Nandy writes:

> It is from non-modern India, from the traditions and principles or religious tolerance encoded in everyday life associated with different faiths of India, that one will have to seek clues to the renewal of Indian political culture. The traditional ways of life have over the centuries developed internal principles of tolerance and these principles must play a part in contemporary politics... religious communities in traditional societies have known to live with each other (1988: 188).[4]

Taking one step further, it is argued that

> (1) the Hindu religion, in its traditional form, was a non-proselytising system against the various proselytising religions of the world namely Islam and Christianity. Therefore, it created federal Hindu cultural organisations and was democratic, tolerant and plural; and
>
> (2) this pure (ideal) Hinduism could, thereby, survive throughout the ages, through immutable ties of caste and ethnic identities of its members. Unlike Islam and Christianity, which seek total and absolute suppression of other beliefs to survive, federal Hindu cultural organisation as Brahmins, Shudras etc., does not impose universal community of Hindus. Age-old 'Indian' tradition was socially and culturally democratic (Kothari 1970: 253).

So the Sivakumars' claim that in pre-modern India there was a moral universe of local pluralism based on the organic solidarity of caste society:

> There are three important implications of dharmam as a central norm in the ideological universe: (1) moral obligations and entitlements associated with dharmam, constituted a powerful basis for redistribution of wealth; (2) in the process, the moral universe constituted a strong basis for the cohesiveness and solidarity of social

> groups; (3) the compulsive force of the norm of dharmam, acted as a strong counter to concentration of wealth and power (1996: 362-63).[5]

Thus, pre-modern was heterogeneous and yet harmonic. If there were conflicts, oppressions or wars they were sporadic, calamities or peripheral. The whole social fabric was universal in the sense that it tied the dispersed sites into the cosmic order of local pluralism (Indian culture). The inauguration of modern-Western universalisation-homogenisation negated this heterogeneous plural universe. The old moral order was erased and in its place was implanted the modern Indian state. This is the root of the cultural loss.

The modern state is repressive because by its nature it tries to create a single political entity out of this civilisational unity. Due to the suppression of pre-modern India, where various communities co-existed without an attempt to impose a uniform culture of a state, what we are witnessing today is, therefore, a 'clash of cultures' against a 'homogenising Indian state'. The invocation of those endangered traditions imprinted in religious and other cultural identities constitute the people's struggle for expansion of civil society against the hegemony of the state. So we must reduce the nation-state and extend civil society to regain cultural unity.

It is further argued that 'much of the fanaticism and violence associated with religion come today from a sense of defeat of the believers, from their feelings of impotence and from their free-floating anger and self-hatred while facing a world which is secular and desacralised' (Nandy 1988: 185). As tradition was a symbol of human dignity and authenticity, it is under attack 'because people are under attack' (ibid. 1984: 2081) through the state, essentially a modern-Western project.[6]

This argument, as it seems to me, celebrates caste, religion and ethnicity as the essential elements of democracy and the state is identified as the root of intolerance and communalism in modern India (ibid).

## Critique

Now, we will take up a critique of the culturalist critique of the modern state and its celebration of tradition-culture. It will be argued that there are problems in terms of (a) conceptual slippage, (b) substantial details, and, put together, (c) a similarity between the fundamentalist assumptions and liberalised prescriptions rooted in the basic fallacy of dualism.

The most disturbing aspect of the formulation of Hindu tradition as a 'harmonious and democratic whole' against the homogenising modern state is a complete negation of the social processes in India. Being totally blind to the social stratification and to ethnic/religious and communal strife along with repressions and violence in Indian history (Thapar 1987; Pandita 1995), the claims of democratic roots of Hindu culture vis-à-vis Islamic and Christian cultures are grossly a-historical and a-sociological. Precisely because of this, it is bound to fail in demonstrating the democratic content in the asymmetrical social relations. It completely ignores the anti-democratic and authoritarian potentials of such articulations (dismissing other cultures as proselytising systems), a common strategy of fundamentalisms of all variety.[7]

Then again, there is confusion between variety and pluralism. Simple variety without its political institutionalisation in terms of equal civic space, does not guarantee a body-politic of pluralism and democracy. As argues Kaviraj, Indian pluralism, in this sense is, 'simply a registration of variation. Indian animal or plant life also shows great pluralism. We do not however call it pluralist in the terms of democratic tolerance or even its preparation .... Several contiguous and mutually independent autocracies do not represent democratic culture' (1989: 5-6).

In specific details, diversity in the Hindu tradition/social order has been based on social hierarchy and discrimination. This stratification is premised on inegalitarian social relations (most nakedly evident in caste and gender ideologies and practices). In pre-modern times, social organisation was devoid of even formal equality, in addition to being based on substantial inequality. In India, the caste system meant unequal rights and therefore the so-called 'civilisational unity' of 'traditional India' was erected on discrimination and inequality between and within social groups. Even at the formal level, harmonious co-existence and democratic plurality in pre-modern India is a-historical romanticisation at best and a lie at worst. Conflating the democratisation process in the democratic state with modernist oppression and homogenisation is uncritical history and sociology and even (more importantly) dangerous. Simply because, '(t)raditional Indian culture (too) was deeply aristocratic, repressive and massively violent towards the oppressed' (ibid: 6). At the same time, mobilisation and struggle against such oppressive social relations have been, to a great extent, part of the democratic process in India. In short, it is fallacious to posit the polarity of tradition/democracy vs. modern/authoritarian, cultural plurality vs. modern statist homogenisation, and so forth.

Furthermore, to submerge all shades of pre-modern human existence and relations as 'traditional' itself is a homogenising practice. By giving a universal meaning to the term traditional for all kinds of pre-modern social relations it is '....difficult to understand which specific social practice is meant—pre-feudal, feudal, medieval, colonial, or any of the numerous discrete forms of feudal society? One underestimates the repressive and conservative creativity of the Indian tradition by giving in this misleading monolithic form'(Kaviraj 1989: 4). In fact, there is no single cultural mark that was common to all historical social processes in the Indian sub-continent. 'For good or ill, such cultural markers can only rest on "exclusivist" racial, tribal or religious claims' (Vanaik 1992: 5). In this sense, India cannot be a single cultural category.

Such articulations are only demands for other nation-state(s) against a state based on the particular homogenising 'national' identity markers. As such they do not necessarily reduce the space of the state. On the contrary, they facilitate non-secular (religious and other primordial forms of imaginary unities) 'exclusion' to evoke the divisions between different social blocs and increase the tensions between them (for example, Hindutva nationalism, Sikh nationalism, among others).

> To the extent such cultural exclusion serves to 'symbolically' unify the internally diverse communities (Hindu/Sikh/Muslims), the culturalist hope is on the similar terrain, that of fundamentalists: 'unity' to substantially diminish the questions of class, gender inequalities and a social mobilisation for egalitarian socio-political relations'. In effect, the culturalists and fundamentalists oppose such egalitarian processes in the name of enhancing a separate and distinctive tradition/culture. The anti-secularism (and celebration of such identities) by refusing to outlaw the 'politics of religious identity' as a strategic goals helps to extend and consolidate legitimacy (of communal politics) (ibid: 28).

Uncritical celebrations of tradition/culture ends up being anti-pluralism as it forgets in the process that (a) states are never a single cultural category; and (b) local cultures and their political practices themselves undergo change in a dynamic socio-economic and political context.

In fact, the critique of the state based on a cultural notion of 'India', itself betrays the over-indulgence with the state and the liberalist device of separating modern-tradition and state-society. This critique is possible only on the polarised entities of homogeneous tradition-modern and culture-state, which are posited against each other, one being privileged over the other. It fails to move beyond liberal dualism and acknowledge the dynamic discourse between the two.

Let us look into one concrete instance of such creation of false images. According to Nandy, Gandhi was a 'traditionalist because he was opposed to "state" for its secular roots (and not only because of its particular concrete manifestation as colonial state)' (Nandy 1987: 129; 1989: 1-3). The question is: if Gandhi was a traditionalist then why did he participate in the emergence of India as a modern state? Second, if Gandhi was a 'traditionalist', he would have joined Nandy in romanticising sati as symbolic of 'self-sacrifice' against modernity's tyranny (Nandi 1987). On the contrary, Gandhi wrote in *Young India* (1931) that the origin of sati is not in the spirit of sacrifice but in '*superstition,* ignorance and blind egotism of man'—'a statement of modernism par excellence' (Upadhyaya 1992: 26).

Sati is just one instance. Such discourse not only shares the prescriptions of liberalism but also the presumptions of fundamentalism. In concrete terms, such an agenda provides alternate languages by which social inequalities (hierarchies of wealth and power or class, caste and gender) get legitimised. Such a discourse constantly tries to evade the question of substantial inequality in civil society. Little attention is paid to the inegalitarian and oppressive structural elements and their live inter-linkages with (a) the unequal opportunities for different social strata and the resultant conflicts; and (b) the regional and sub-continental power pyramid sustaining and, in turn, sustained by the local power asymmetries. In other words, in pre-modern India, (a) all the communities/social groups did not have equal rights, and (b) the cultural fabric of the 'Indian civilisation' was woven around caste, class and gender discrimination. Overall, the pre-modern (tradition) was devoid of even formal equality, in addition to being based on substantial inequalities.

Paradoxically, this invented cultural nationalism is itself a form of cultural management and accusation ironically placed at the door of the modern state (Bhabha 1994: 208). Such boundary formations of cultural unities necessarily involve a process of homogenisation through abstraction of the socio-cultural spaces. These are, in fact, attempts to (a) carve 'national' cultures out of the fragmented civil society; and (b) establish a state where the particular versions of cultural unity and exclusiveness are superimposed over the inequality and internal contradictions within such socio-cultural existences.

Indian experiences are rich enough to argue that (1) such an invention of cultural unities does not mean an emancipation from socio-political and cultural oppression; and (2) by creating such unities all the members of such 'nationalities' do not acquire equal access to power. Bhabha's criticism of the closures and ethnocentrism inherent in such culturalist pedagogical neo-medievalism against the cultural 'loss' (ibid) applies, equally, to Hindutva nationalism and similar cultural-unity based articulations of Indian 'civilisation' and tradition.

> The manner in which differences in cultural systems are stressed, both by Sikh and Islamic fundamentalism, shows that, while opposing

> homogenisation into the dominant cultural systems of 'Hindu Indianness', they, in turn, wish to set up other homogenisations, homogenisations based on Sikh or Islamic religion-cultural systems. In this respect they are no different from the proponents of 'Hindu Indianness'. And it is because the objective is, during and after the liberation struggle, to set up new homogenisations that we may say that they are forms of bourgeois nationalism.... Inevitably then such bourgeois nations... will, as they gain state power, oppress their own minorities. ... the national question..., in general, does not end with overcoming one level of national oppression, that of the minorities still remains. Further, as seen in the episode of the Muslim Women's Bill, special forms of oppression might be allowed within the ...community. Anything may be allowed, other than an actual sharing of political and economic power ... (Nathan 1990: 21).

Such strategies are based on the rhetorical proclamation of concepts such as democracy, individual freedom, human rights and civil society, without locating their societal content and historical context. Thus the critique of the state are never applied to the concepts of traditional/cultural and liberal market-freedom. This one-sided debunking of the state in the name of self-determination and human rights actually clears the way for recent upsurge of capitalism by removing the equality discourse. Probably, this evasion is because of the distaste culturalists share with liberalism of the view that egalitarian social relations are inbuilt requisites for local self rule. One tends to suspect that it is simply a gesture of washing one's hands off the realities of social inequalities and allow contemporary oppressions to take over in the name of culture and civil society. Chatterjee writes:

> A considerable part of transnational activities today take place in the domain of non-state institutions under the sign of the modernisation of civil social formations. These are the activities of a transnational public sphere whose moral claims derive from the assumed existence of a domain of universal civil society. Many United Nations agencies, non-governmental organisations, peace-keeping missions, human rights groups, women's organisations, free speech activists, operate in this moral terrain. As such, they act as an *external* check on the sovereign powers of the nation-state and occupy the critical moral position of a global civil society.... This is the standpoint that produces the most aggressive charges... (against) the nation-state... many transnational activities and movements pursuing demands for social and cultural rights of individuals or groups seek to open up and institutionalise

> precisely such a sphere of global intervention, framed by a universalist notion of rights and grounded in a global civil society (1997:33).

In effect, this romanticisation of civil society and tradition/culture is essentially against equality and not against modernity (of capitalist/liberal variety) or non-democratic forms of a particular state. This makes the alternative politics, that is, the democratic social fabric based on equality subordinate to the market economy. For example, in post-USSR Europe, relations of domination and inequality are projected as a triumph of democracy, freedom and an expansion of civil society.

## Beyond Dualism

Marx had cautioned us against 'the chief defect of all hitherto existing materialism' for their tendency to project 'the external object, reality, the sensible world... in the form of an object'. Instead the world is projected by Marx 'as concrete human activity, as practice' and 'the interpretation of subjectivities is a practical-critical activity' (1975: 412-22).

Seen from this perspective, we have to conceptualise the state-society relationship as dynamically intertwined, mutually affecting and changing, as against being treated as mutually exclusive, separated into object-subject, material-cultural, tradition-modern, and so on. It calls our attention to at least two aspects of the state and its inter-linkages with the societal processes:

1. The state as a form or institutional ensemble.
2. The state as substance, that is, social relations.

Put together we must look into the concrete processes by which the state and society are affecting each other. Thus, a particular and specific configuration of social forces evokes a certain form of state and in turn gets affected. It implies that the social bases of the state are heterogeneous and there are contestations in the material manifestations of the state apparatus, policies and programmes. These contradictions and conflicts imply varying degree of support/approval/ rejection/dissent of various social groups to the state.[8]

This means that state is a social process, involving structural properties of social relations as emergent and not fixed. For a critical intervention in the process we need to grasp the complex dialectic between structures and agencies, social relations and the institutional ensembles. As a dynamic interaction of a form-determined social terrain and its material forces, subjects as well as the structural constraints and possibilities a particular state (at given pint of time and space) is 'structurally mediated "interactive" instance' (Jessop 1991: 103). Conceptualising the state this way implies that:

1. The state is an asymmetric structural ensemble with no pre-given form.
2. The interaction among an asymmetric institutional ensemble and groups means that the state is not fixed or static in time and space but is constantly reconstituted.
3. The state is not separate and autonomous from civil society. It is an emergent form and substance impacting the social relations. 'Sates never achieve complete separation from society and their precise boundaries are usually in doubt' (ibid: 342). The same applies to the civil society. Thus, both always involve contradictions and contestations among political actors, classes, gender, ethnic-religious-regional interests, and the like. Thereby, both are always in dynamic discourse between structure and agencies, cultural and material.

Thus, contrary to the claims of civil society being internally coherent, organisationally pure and operationally fixed 'systems', state and civil society are emergent, contradictory and hybrid. To understand the state as process ('in making') we must reject the 'metaphysics of presence'[9] which has been the basic fallacy of liberalist and culturalist conceptualisation. Instead, it is to be seen as an emergent correspondence among different discursive articulations, societal elements and structures. By name state-society is a couplet denoting structuration.[10]

To conclude, there seems to be a contemporary consensus amongst liberals and culturalists that state and democracy are inversely proportional. Therefore, democracy must increase as the state decreases. Social theories of liberalism have (mis)appropriated the term democracy to legitimise social inequalities under the banner of civil society. Of late, culturalists have joined the band-wagon of anti-statism (or trans-nationalism as the more respectable term for globalisation and multinational corporatism), arguing for the extension of civil society and tradition against state and modernity. In contradistinction, through a re-look at the complex relationship between structural process and political organisation, we have tried to argue that there is no necessary equation between decline of the state and rise of democracy. Second, democracy is linked with the question of social equality. We must continue to speak against the subjugating traces of the civil society along with the state. In the context of developing societies (and the Russian example of the decline of the 'socialist' world) there seems to be a stronger apprehension of an equation between inequalities, fundamentalism, and greater human subjugation, on the one hand, and the celebration of free market and civil society, on the other. A silence against oppressive features of civil society is, in many ways, participation in the violence inflicted in the name of cultural recovery:

> …the lack of response is a silence that perpetuates the violence …. The study of social suffering must contain a study of a society's silence toward it (or, say, the degree of its incapacity to acknowledge it), and that the study of that suffering and that silence must contain an awareness of its own dangers in mimicking the social silence that perpetuates the suffering (Cavell 1998: 94-95).

The problem, therefore, is not of liberating civil society from the state as such because both of them are not exclusive to each other. We must move beyond this dualism of state vs. society to grasp the dynamic process as both being intertwined together.

## Notes

I am thankful to P.N .Mukherjee, Chandan Sengupta and Neena Singh for their comments and suggestions on the earlier draft of this paper. However, the usual disclaimer applies.

1. I am skipping the antiquity and notion of civil society in thinkers like Aristotle as it differs substantially from the notion of civil society in use since the 18th century. For a detailed discussion on this see, Williams 1976; Chandhoke 1995; Upadhyaya 1992.
2. Gramsci, extending this reading to the cultural realm, rejected the artificial separation of civil society from state, and similarly individual from society (Gramsci 1971: 206-76).
3. Here Indian culturalism and anti-statism show the potential (but, nevertheless, hesitant) tendency to share the post-modernist celebration of disorder, seen as deeply located in civil society.
4. Against this over-sympathetic role ascribed to religion (and especially Hindu religion in the Indian context), I wish to only quote Dumm: 'To argue....that religion is not intrinsically conservative requires that one examines only the explicit pieties embraced by religions and not the ancillary role that religions play in support of reactive powers through the renunciation they impose upon believers and the incitements they provoke against those who live outside or on the margins of their communities, (Dumm 1996: 134).
5. The Sivakumars go on to claim that during the colonial era we were faced with the monotheist British state and the church of England vs. Pantheist Hinduism, where 'the former was exclusive in its outlook and hence propagated itself through proselytisation, while the latter was ever inclusive and propagated itself through constant addition to its corpus of mythology; and finally, the former had no social theory, the latter operated through the paradigm of Varna' (p. 370). A Brahminical arrogance about 'barbaric others'? Are not we just a few steps away from

fundamentalist claims? Otherwise, what is the compulsion to uncritically glorify the pre-colonial asymmetries in order to critique modernity? Don't we have an option?

6. Therefore, Sati is read as a defense of Indian women against the modern state (Nandy 1987, 1988). For a critique of Nandy, see Quadeer and Hasan (1987), Patel and Kumar (1988).
7. Ironically (and knowing Nandy and Kothari's politics, one can be sure that their anti-fundamentalist stand is quite vocal) with different routes and prescriptions, culturalism and the cultural nationalism (of the saffron variety at least) are one in celebrating religious identity based notions of India and the approval of Hinduism.
8. This is in contrast to the conceptualisation of state as being an essentially unitary institution, thereby fundamentally capitalist or modern in nature. This is also different from a plural concept of the liberal-democratic framework because it recognises the asymmetric terrain which does not allow equal relations in substantial terms.
9. Rejecting the search for universal properties of an 'entity', as being 'metaphysics of presence', Derrida (1980) explores the difference as constitutive of existence in general.
10. Structuration implies 'no proper or constitutive limits to the production of meaning in and around the multiple codes' (Norris and Benjamin 1989: 164)

## References


Anderson, Benedict. 1983. *Imagined communities: Reflections on the origin and spread of nationalism.* London: Verso.

Bhabha, H. 1994. 'Anxious nations, nervous states' in J. Copjee (ed.), *Supposing the subject.* London.

Block, F. 1987. *Revisiting state theory: Essays in politics and postindustrialism.* Philadelphia: Temple University Press.

Cavell, S. 1998. 'Comments on Veena Das's essay "Language and body: Transactions in the constructions of pain",' in A. Klanman, Veena Das and M. Lock (eds), *Social suffering.* Delhi: Oxford University Press.

Chandhoke, N. 1995. *State and civil society: Explorations in political theory.* New Delhi: Sage.

Chatterjee, Partha. 1997 'Beyond the nation? Or within ?', *Economic and Political Weekly,* January 4-11.

Colletti, Lucio. 1978. *From Rousseau to Lenin: Studies in ideology and society,* transl. from It. by John Merrington and Judith White. Oxford: Oxford University Press.

Derrida, Jacques. 1980. *Writing and difference,* transl. from Fr. by Alan Bassman. California: California University Press.

Dumm, T.L. 1996. *Michael Foucault and the politics of freedom.* New Delhi: Sage

Friedman, M. 1963. *Capitalism and freedom.* Chicago: University of Chicago Press.

Gellner, Ernest. 1991. 'Nationalism and politics in Eastern Europe', *New Left Review,* 189.

Gramsci, Antonio. 1971. *Selections from the prison notebooks,* transl. from It. by Quintin Hoare and Geoffrey N. Smith. London: International Publishing Company.

Harrington, A. 1998. 'Unmasking suffering's masks: Reflections on old and new memories of Nazi medicine', in A. Klanman, V. Das and M. Lock (eds). *Social suffering.*

Jessop, Bob. 1991. *State theory: Putting the capitalist state in its place.* Philadelphia: Philadelphia State University Press.

Kaviraj, S. 1989. 'Political culture in independent India: An antiromantic view', *Teaching Politics*, 7(1-2).

Kothari, R. 1970. *Politics in India.* New Delhi: Orient Longman

_________. 1989. 'Cultural context of communalism in India', *Economic and Political Weekly*, January 14: 81-85.

Kumar, R. 1989. 'India: "A nation-state" or a "civilisation-state",' *Occasional Papers, VIII.* New Delhi: Nehru Memorial Museum & Library.

Marx, K. 1975. 'The first thesis on Feurbach' in his *Early writings,* transl. by R. Livingstone and G. Benton. Harmondsworth: Penguin.

_______. 1970. 'Preface' and 'Introduction' of *Contribution to the critique of political economy.* Moscow: Progress Publishers.

Nandy, Ashis. 1987. *Traditions, tyranny and utopias.* Delhi: Oxford University Press.

___________. 1984. 'Culture, state and the rediscovery of Indian politics', *Economic and Political Weekly,* December 8: 2078-83.

___________. 1988. 'The politics of secularism and the recovery of religious tolerance', *Alternatives*, 13(2).

Nathan, D. 1990. 'From civilisation to nations', *Occasional Papers, XXI.* New Delhi: Nehru Memorial Museum & Library.

Norris, Christopher, and Andrew Benjamin. 1989. *What is deconstruction*? London: St. Martin

Pandita, Lalita. 1995. 'Patriarchy and paranoia: Imaginary infidelity in *Uttararmacarita* and *The winter's tale*', in P. C. Hogan and L. Pandita (eds), *Literary India: Comparative studies in aesthetic colonialism and culture*. Albany: State University of New York Press.

Patel, Sujata and K. Kumar. 1988. 'Defenders of sati', *Economic and Political Weekly,* January 23: 129-30.

Quadeer, Imrana and Zoya Hasan. 1987. 'Deadly politics of the state and its apologists', *Economic and Political Weekly,* November 14: 1946-49.

Sivakumar, S. S. and C. Sivakumar. 1996. 'The meaning of social order in the Tamil country', in P. Robb (ed.), *Meanings of agriculture: Essays in South Asian history and economics*, Delhi.

Skocpol, T. 1985. 'Bringing the state back in: Strategies of analysis in current research', in P. R. Evans, D. Rueschemeyer and T. Skocpol (eds), *Bringing the state back in.* Cambrige (UK): Cambridge University Press.

Thapar, R. 1987. *Cultural transactions and early India: Tradition and patronage*. Mumbai: Popular Prakashan.

Upadhyaya, P. C. 1992. 'The failure of socialism as the triumph of democracy? A critique of the post socialist consensus', *Occasional papers, LXIII.* New Delhi: Nehru Memorial Museum & Library.

Vanaik, Achin. 1992. 'Communalism and nationalism: Some tentative reflections', *Occasional Papers, LVI.* New Delhi: Nehru Memorial Museum & Library.

Williams, Raymond. 1976. *Keywords: A vocabulary of culture and society.* Oxford: Oxford University Press.

# 4

# Nation-State and Open Systems of Stratification: Making Room for the 'Politics of Commitment'

*Dipankar Gupta*

The age of nationalism was also the age when *ancien regimes* the world over began crumbling under the weight of their accumulated years. Old systems of stratification, which were closed and ascriptive in character, gave way to more open systems of social differentiation. Birth began to be replaced by achievement as a marker of social distinction. This impetus to break down closed stratificatory systems also dissolved localised juridical systems and solidarities. In many quarters it led to the fear that the basis of morality had been seriously undermined (Nisbet 1970: 16-23)). Urban slums, crime and a growing impatience with customs and manners of the Old World, made this apprehension very real.

## Nation-state and open stratification: Contradictory logics

It was not always noticed, given the social clamour that capitalism had introduced, that something new was replacing the old. An open system of stratification came with its own core values and ethical norms. These allowed a new kind of economic organisation to gradually consolidate itself. Neither absolutism, nor the feudal system it lived off, was in any deep sympathy with capitalist forces, or with the classes that appeared to promote them. As Karl Marx vividly recorded in the *Manifesto of the communist party,* old loyalties to preacher, teacher and feudal lord, were now being replaced by the sheer power of money. Money dissolved all these ties that had endured for centuries and replaced them instead with the ideology of freedom. Marx, however, saw this freedom as essentially double edged. It allowed workers to freely choose occupations or employers, but, by the same token, they could also be freely fired. Even so Marx could not, and did not, ignore the positive effects of capitalism, the great strides it had taken, and was taking, on the historical stage.

What has not been adequately theorised is why the impetus that dissolved old solidarities and parochial ties did not go far enough? Why did localised solidarities and affiliations give way to a territorial one based on emotions evoked by the nation-state? There is little doubt that the nation-state came into being to bring about another closure of sorts. Surely, this cannot be reconciled with the logic that overwhelmed *ancien regimes,* and closed stratificatory systems. Even the bitterest critic of capitalism will agree that capitalism recognises no national boundaries. This was the basis of Lenin's argument that capitalism was potentially 'imperialist' (Lenin 1969), while others, from Andre Gunder Frank (1971) to Samir Amin (1974), delve deep into this attribute to bolster their argument that capitalism is truly a world system.

It is difficult then to overlook the contradiction between capitalism not recognising boundaries, and the fact that capitalism and nationalism have been historic coevals all over the globe. Karl Marx too sensed this contradiction, but found a way out of it by claiming that the workers had no nation and that they constituted an international class. This obviously left behind the impression that the nation-state was typically a capitalist obsession. With the hindsight of history we can now be more categorical in our assessment that the nation-state was not just a capitalist cabal. A multitude of classes, from the bourgeoisie to the proletariat, from intellectuals to clerics and professionals, have in different combinations, been ardent advocates of nationalism, and of the nation-state. In the Greek struggle for independence (1821-30) the entire people, from the sheepherder to the bandit heroes, rose together. Besides the Greek paradigm case, historians have recorded a variety of instances when lesser landowners, or gentry, middle and lower middle classes, professional intellectuals, as well as the administrative strata, were fervent nationalist partisans (for example, Hobsbawm 1988a: 165-67). In Ireland, nationalism came in the wake of several rounds of agrarian revolt; in Hungary, Poland and Norway, the multi-class alliance that worked to overthrow foreign rule, almost naturally, turned to nationalism to shore up their gains. As Gramsci perceptively observed: 'In reality, the internal relations of any nation are the result of a combination which is "original" and (in a certain sense) unique' (1971: 240).

While it is indeed a good idea that the working class should be an international class, the sad truth is that as long as left wing activism did not cleave to nationalist sentiments, it remained a peripheral political option. China, Russia and Cuba were spurred by heavy doses of nationalism, even though in each instance token gestures were made to internationalism. On the other hand, socialists of pre-war England, or communists of pre-Independence India, were unable to effectively mobilise the proletariat in their respective countries, as they were both bound by Soviet Union style *internationalism*. Consequently, left champions like Sidney and Beatrice Webb, who found in nationalism everything that was distasteful, failed to inspire the workers on whose behalf they fought so valiantly and selflessly.

### The unfettered intellectual

The nation-state, as it came into being, was owned by all classes. It is true, however, that the educated classes, or intellectuals, probably played a relatively dominant role. In a sense Hans Kohn, the great scholar of nationalism, was right when he said that 'it was the poet, the philologist, and the historian who created nationalities' (quoted in Rich 1977: 46). This is why in the first stage of nationalism there is a general tendency to collect and recover folklore and historical anecdotes to build national pride. This itself is interesting. The literate classes, as Max Weber once pointed out, are the most pre-occupied with such nationalist urges. Indeed, why should this be the case? Intellectuals have traditionally been handmaidens of the ruling class (Gramsci 1971: 7), but were now seemingly striking out on their own. Objectively they represented a host of classes that were eager and restless to break away from the restraints of the old, natural, economy. The intellectuals could play a leadership role in this regard for even in tradition they represented an ideal that an average peasant looked up to. This was not an unrealisable ideal as it was not outside the realm of possibilities for a peasant to become a priest, lawyer, teacher, notary, or doctor (ibid: 14). This is probably why intellectuals could straddle the pre-capitalist and capitalist phases, and were thus best suited to be the ideològues of nationalism.

Structurally too the intellectuals were well placed for their new role as ideologues of nationalism. As intellectuals they were not as intimately tied to modes of economic production and dominance as most other classes were. Their relative freedom from the natural economy of feudalism provided them with a window to look outside the parish, the manor and the *zamindari*. Doubtless there were many who still clung to the Old World and lamented its loss, but many more were moving over. The new breed won because it had, to put it baldly, history on its side.

The espousal of nationalist cause was what separated the old from the new intellectuals. These new intellectuals often came from the ranks of the old and were not specifically ideologues of capitalism. In fact, many may well have been quite opposed to it. While they may not have been inspired by capitalism, they certainly saw the limits of pre-capitalist social relations very clearly. This judgement was possible because capitalism had already started eroding the bastions of the feudal order. As capitalism objectively requires greater space for its operation, a kind of twinning took place between nationalist ideology and economic rationality. It is not a coincidence really that intellectuals all over Europe in the 18th and 19th centuries, from Bishop Berkeley, to Immanuel Kant to Jean-Jacques Rousseau, were exhorting their country people to uphold the civic virtues of nationalism.

It was around these educated classes that a new morality was forming (Nisbet 1970:23; see also Gramsci 1971:334-5). The importance that the educated classes received at this stage was quite disproportionate to their numbers. In 1842 French state lycees had just 19,000 enrolments. In all of France only 70,000 children were in secondary schools. To take another example, around 1850, in all of Russia there were only 20,000 secondary pupils (Hobsbawm 1988a: 167). The influence that the educated people were able to exercise would have been impossible if capitalism had not given freedom (notwithstanding its double edge) a new expression, and a promise, that could be grasped at all levels of the social hierarchy. These intellectuals successfully elevated grand national sentiments over all the pre-existing local ties without which the nation-state would have been impossible to conceive.

The fact that intellectuals played such an important role is itself an indication that there was nothing logical about the boundaries that made up nation-states. These lineaments were not outcomes of structural logic or primordial pressure. When Italy was unified in 1860, it is said that just about two and a half per cent of the population spoke Italian. In 1860 Massimo d'Azeglio programmatically pronounced: 'We have made Italy; now we must make the Italians' (Hobsbawm 1988b: 110). Metternich too called Italy a 'mere geographical expression' (ibid). Neither did the fact that the Irish already spoke English, or that Norwegian was close to Danish, and that the Finns also spoke Swedish with equal fluency, take away from the stridency of their respective nationalisms. It was, therefore, not as if a primordial ethnic core was calling out to be recognised as a nation on which the state was later grafted. The conception of the 'nation' itself is an artifact, without anything natural about it. This then leads us to ask a supplementary to the first question: Why did intellectuals fight for establishing nation-states and not press instead for recognising the universalistic potential of open stratificatory systems?

## Two views on nation-state: Irreducible ethnos and capitalist engine

In order to be able to answer such questions with some efficacy it is necessary to quickly consider the prevalent views regarding the formation of nation-states. Broadly speaking there are two established positions on this subject. It is not as if they are always held in an exclusive way. Even so there is a general tendency to emphasize either one or the other.

According to one view, a nation-state is born out of the tremendous surge of passion that is located in the irreducible *ethnos* of a people. This position has several proponents and has many *avatars.* According to this school of thought, every nation-state has a primordial and pre-given cultural core that authentically realises itself in the form of a nation-state. This primordial core is sometimes expressed in terms of language, and on other occasions, in religious sectarianism, but most often, as a combination of the two.

There is a certain commonsensical allure to this view. It seems to match what people actually say about themselves and what motivates them to bond together as territorial compatriots. From blood soaked ethnic cleansers to soldiers in battle fatigue to humble farmers, this view is echoed often enough. Its lambent brilliance notwithstanding, the fact however remains that if this sentiment is such a strong stirring then how was it kept still for so many centuries only to be woken up some two hundred years ago. The 'sleeping beauty' character that this point of view seems to espouse makes it particularly fallible on analytical grounds (see Hall 1993:4). Its reliance on an irreducible, and incorruptible cultural essence and its inability to take on board the historical specifics of nation-state formation makes it vulnerable under sociological scrutiny.

The second view on nation-states has both structuralist and voluntaristic components. The common theme, however, is that the emergence of capitalism undermined local economies by its sheer organisational and structural supremacy. This forced parochial solidarities to yield and make way for nation-state sentiments to take their place. The structuralist version would go on to argue that this nation-state *denouement* is an ineluctable aspect of the growing power of capitalism. To this the voluntarists would add that national sentiment and territorial boundaries are essentially outcomes of compromises and machinations between leading capitalists in different parts of the world.

This position too has many advocates. It certainly scores over the earlier cultural argument in the sense that it takes into account the historical specifics of nation-states and locates their origin and their recency in the rise of capitalism. It can effectively answer the question: why are nation-states modern day phenomena?

The capitalist engine argument however finds it difficult to adequately respond to the question as to why nation-state boundaries need to be drawn at all. Why should there not be a universal capitalist world without nation-state distinctions? The proponents of the captialist engine argument, particularly the voluntarists among them, would *riposte* by saying that the leading capitalist factions find it in their interest to partition the world. In particular, the dependency theorists would argue that it is in the interest of capitalists in both the forward and backward sectors (the core metropolitan areas and the peripheral hinterlands, respectively), to come to an alliance. Such a tie in would keep the developing regions in perpetual dependence on the developed sectors of the world. In this alliance, capitalists in both areas do very well. It is only the workers in the peripheral outposts of capitalism that are the worst off. While this seems persuasive enough, it still does not explain what led to the initial demarcation of nation-states from which a series of dependencies could be worked out.

Even if geography is now economics, the structuralist and the voluntarist exponents of the capitalist engine argument must answer where the passions accompanying nation-state formations come from? Both in the developed and in the developing worlds the sentiment behind nation-state formations cannot be limited to capitalists. Nor can we satisfactorily explain the rise of nationalist feelings by taking recourse to notions of capitalist conspiracy. Proletarians, capitalists, farmers, and intellectuals all become nationalist partisans, though, as we noted earlier, intellectuals constitute the most vocal section. In the height of their collective zeal they are willing to kill, and on some occasions, even die, for the nation-state. One of the unfortunate aspects of a conspiracy theory is that it insults the intelligence of those who are supposed to be victims of machinations and plots hatched at more elevated social levels.

The structuralist endorsement of the capitalist engine argument ends up by requiring the voluntarist to shore up its flanks. What began by relying purely on the logic of structures had to accommodate the voluntarism of conspiracy in order to put up a semblance of defence against sociological scrutiny.

## Closed and open stratification: Power vs. authority

This then is the all-important and critical issue. Why did not the breakdown of closed systems of stratification and the emergence of open classes not charge down full steam ahead without countenancing any kind of territorial loyalty? Sure enough, in the localised loyalties of the past, the relationships were face to face, or at a remove that could still be summoned by familiarity of connection. These ties, as has often been averred in sociological literature, were multiplex and communitarian, at least up to a point. The modern bonds of nation-state solidarity are on the other hand largely imagined (but not imaginary). The problem then is why is it necessary to imagine such a community when localised closed systems of hierarchy were under attack by an open system inaugurated by capitalism? Where is it in capitalism, with its open class structure, that nation-states are made essential?

To answer such questions it is necessary to step back from the din of history and from the ideological noise that both the essential ethnos and the capitalist engine points of view make. We should instead look elsewhere and seek at least a partial solution to the conundrum from within the theories of social stratification. In this connection, it is not even necessary to burrow deep into the arcane segments of stratification theory, but merely to take a close look at some of its well known postulates and push them along a little further than is usually done.

Let us, as a first step, recall the distinction between open and closed systems of stratification. Along with this distinction let us also align the analytical differences between continuous hierarchies and discrete classes. In closed systems of stratification, any actually existing and operating hierarchy is primarily an expression of political power and not ideological acquiescence. It is quite another matter that domination is frequently couched in the language of patriarchy, caste or religion. While the dominated may have acquiesced to the broad principles of such ideologies, it was in their actual empirical embodiment that disputes arose. This is because these ideologies were invariably ascriptive in nature and foreclosed options for those who did not belong to the favoured community of the day.

Therefore, to be born a non-Rajput in a Rajput stronghold implied a host of disadvantages. To be born a Protestant in Catholic France entailed other kinds of severe disabilities. Such examples can be multiplied *ad infinitum* from medieval history the world over. Under these circumstances it is quite natural that those who have been kept out on ascriptive grounds should chafe at the indignities heaped on them. This is why when domination is based on purely ascriptive grounds, there are no agreed reasons as to why the dominated should ideologically accept their domination. They might still believe that ascription is important but they would dispute their subjugation on that account. The subordinate peoples may still believe in caste and religion but dispute their position in the current structure of domination. Therefore, even though the stated ideology of the medieval ruling classes was put out in the name of patriarchy, religion or caste, it was actually brutal instruments of physical coercion that kept the others down.

In feudal estates, for example, various strata interacted on the basis of ground rules that were guaranteed by sheer political power. It is for this reason there was no great intellectual challenge to discuss the actual sources of legitimacy in a feudal state. Power became authority without any major transformation. In contrast, the theories of the capitalist state are much more problematically positioned. This is because in capitalist societies the transition from power to authority is mediated by popular acquiescence. This demarcates power from authority at both analytical and empirical planes. A moment's reflection will reveal that in closed systems of stratification the problem of distinguishing power from authority was not quite germane. If such distinctions were made, they were premised on the successful use of physical force and not moral pressure. This is why from Weber to Marx to Parsons, it is the establishment, modalities, and exercise of authority in capitalist/democratic societies that are the most challenging

In pre-modern India there have been many instances of peace between communities and strata that lasted for centuries. In no case, however, was this relative tranquility easily bought. Peace followed war only if the vanquished agreed to live by the terms set in place by the victors. After 150 years of strife the Turks finally subjugated Bengal. From then on peace ensued but on terms set by the Turkish court. In a Hindu kingdom beef eating or cow slaughter would hardly be entertained, and likewise in a Muslim principality the *mazhar* of a mosque should never be dwarfed by a *shivalaya* (Pandey 1990:134).

### The principle of repulsion and identity formation

As power largely decided the nature of hierarchy, identities and deeply held loyalties were of the kind that were mutually exclusive when not actually hostile to one another. If caste is an extreme form of 'closed' system of stratification, to slightly paraphrase Weber, then Celestine Bougle's argument that *jatis* are mutually repulsive expresses this category hostility best (Bougle 1991:64-73). As strata in a closed system of stratification mutually repel, or are hostile to, one another, any hierarchy that is expressed in a workable form must necessarily subordinate these tensions through the medium of power.

The eventual hierarchies arrived at are nearly always internally fragile. This is why they need to be externally imposed. The principle of repulsion and the character of mutual exclusivity remain through all this. It is not as if closed systems of stratification cannot experience mobility. History is replete with instances when they did. The crucial fact is that while closed stratificatory systems experienced mobility, they never did allow for it. Which is why every time a hierarchy had to be established in a manifest and workable form, it needed to be reinforced by physical power and by naked instruments of coercion. Closed systems relied on coercion and not acquiescence and this is what separates them from open systems of stratification.

The fact that strata in closed systems of stratification are mutually repulsed by one another tells us why such systems are characterised by discrete classes. These discrete classes are brought in line by power to give the semblance of a continuous hierarchy. As I have tried to demonstrate in the past, caste is an ideal example of how discrete units are forced into submission along a hierarchical grid, giving the superficial impression that a continuous gradation is at work both empirically and logically. Logically, there are great problems in establishing such a slope as the units are not just mutually repelled, but are also incommensurate with one another. Any empirical imposition of a hierarchy is then a matter of externalities and not of internal cohesion.

### Open stratificatory systems and the politics of responsibility

In contrast to closed systems of stratification, the open system is characterised by a continuous hierarchy. In a continuous hierarchy the different strata are not mutually repelled by one another, but actually cohere together because they are arranged on a scale that measures more or less of a certain variable. The cohesion in such a continuous hierarchy arises from the fact that it is organised around a single variable, or a cluster of variables (for example, of the SES index type), which is shared in common down the different strata but in varying quantities. A continuous hierarchy is then characterised by two features. The first is that it is this variation of a *common* variable that makes for a continuous hierarchy. The second feature is that there is a general admission of *consensus* that the hierarchy indeed is correct. This admission does not mean that one is always happy with the position one occupies in the hierarchy, but this is not because the hierarchy is considered to be idiosyncratically constructed. Short people, or poor people, may resent the position they occupy in the hierarchy of height or wealth, respectively, but they accept the validity of the scale itself. A short person cannot claim to be tall, nor a poor person rich without sounding absurd. In a closed system of stratification (for example, caste) the hierarchy of purity is hotly disputed. Different castes have divergent hierarchies that are not commensurate with one another. This is what fuels caste wars. Distinctions based on race again are incommensurable and cannot be arranged in a hierarchy. Likewise, deprivations imposed on minority religions and language groups are premised again on incommensurabilities. In all these cases the principle of repulsion is constantly at work.

On the other hand, the hierarchy of class, or of authority, are manifestations of open systems of stratification. Such hierarchies obey the two features of open systems of stratification mentioned above. In modern classes there is a logical and systemic tie that binds the foreman in a factory to the worker and to the executives. Hierarchies of this sort allow for mobility and do not just experience it. This is because the strata in a continuous hierarchy share a variable in common, and are therefore not governed by the principle of repulsion. Hierarchy in such cases is not idiosyncratically, or incommensurably, realised. This is why a worker could aspire to be a foreman, a foreman a manager, and so on. In the case of discrete classes, a Scandinavian would not want to be English, a Marathi would be unwilling to be a Bengali, a Kshatriya would balk at the idea of being a Brahman.

In cases of caste mobility too, Izhavas do not become Nambudris when they rise in social esteem, they just occupy positions of privilege that were the preserve of certain other castes in the past. Unlike discrete classes, in a continuous hierarchy there is overall acquiescence that the common variable is indeed legitimately distributed across different levels, or tiers. The workers, foremen and managers all belong to the same power hierarchy. There may be disagreements over how a certain personnel performs the allotted role, but the position itself is not disputed. This is why it is logically and empirically possible for those in a continuous hierarchy to move both up and down.

An important consequence flows from this. In these open systems of stratification it is not quite as easy to build identities at any one level, as each level is labile and prone to changes. It is not as if those who occupy a certain slot in the continuous hierarchy are aesthetically or primordially attached to that position alone, as is the case with discrete classes. The open character of a continuous hierarchy does not allow for such strong feelings of sentimental attachment. The principle of repulsion, after all, does not quite operate here. This is ultimately the reason that sustains what Weber had called the politics of responsibility (Weber 1946). For politics of commitment to emerge, there must be strong identities. In open systems of stratification, strong identities are discouraged, simply because the situation is inherently mobile. In closed stratificatory societies, on the other hand there is greater scope for identity politics as movement from one stratum to another is not allowed, and this is also because the strata mutually repulse one another.

In the politics of responsibility, the focus of attention is on the exigencies of experience and not so much on commitment to a pre-given ideological or value position. One immediately realises that the terrain of open systems is not suited for commitment politics. For this kind of politics to sustain itself, barriers and distinctions have to be erected which are of the kind that do not allow transposability and mobility from one to the other. Capitalism, which broke down localised loyalties and juridical authority, thus seems ideally equipped to establish open systems of stratification. Marx too acknowledged capitalism's historical contribution on this score.

### Capitalism in search of commitment

The emergence of capitalism was not buoyed by popular drives to be worker, foreman or manager, as much as by the possibility of freeing oneself from the fetters of localised and closed pre-capitalist constraints (see Fanon 1967:119) There were no clear identities then that the partisans of capitalism could cling on to in their efforts to supercede pre-capitalist forms of social order and production. The forces resisting the forward march of capitalism, on the other hand, had the advantage of pulling out all the identities that closed systems of stratification and the principle of repulsion allowed. Identities based on sect, caste, estate, and feudal loyalties were pressed into service to contest, and sometimes successfully block, the demand for freedom and individual rights that capitalism generated.

As the protagonists of the open system were bereft of the earlier exclusivist identities that the closed systems readily made available, they cast about in search of a new one (Rich 1977: 44-5). It was not as if feudalism obligingly withdrew. In the long struggle ahead capitalism needed the politics of commitment to sustain it in its epochal battle against feudalism and absolutism. Economic rationality was not good enough when the battle lines were drawn on the streets. To generate this commitment, neither locality, nor caste, nor feudal estate could be summoned, as none of these allows the opening of space necessary for capitalism to gain ground. Capitalism, after all, cannot function in localised spaces as feudalism can (see O'Connor 1970:103).

Keeping in mind this distinction between open and closed systems of stratification (and along with it the distinction between discrete classes and continuous hierarchies), let us enquire why is it that capitalism which brought in open systems of stratification, was forced to erect discrete classes at the level of nation-state? Where was the need for politics of responsibility to yield ground and allow politics of commitment to flourish as it did in the many passionate mobilisations on behalf of nation-states? As Ernest Renan once said, all nation-states are built on a grief (Renan 1990). So the identity of belonging to a nation-state exists because there are other nation-states to which one does not belong, and which may, on occasions, be the source of that grief (for e.g., India and Pakistan, America and Iraq, England and France)

Thus far we have argued from within the precincts of stratification theory. It is about time that we brought in the exigencies of nation-state formation to be able to somewhat answer the question why capitalism had to erect national boundaries when its internal logic is that of universalism?

Capitalism does not emerge noiselessly from the wombs of feudalism. Two differing economic forms must battle it out for there is so much at stake on both sides. It is this pressure to overwhelm pre-capitalist systems that drives capitalism to seek, for purely objective reasons, a politics of commitment. As capitalism sponsors a continuous hierarchy, it is unable to internally fuel a politics of commitment. As we mentioned earlier, a politics of commitment emerges when identities are informed on the principle of repulsion. This is why the forces of capitalism must necessarily takes recourse to creating a supra-local allegiance based on territorial attachment to the nation-state. This gives its continuous hierarchies more space to realise themselves, and at the same time fashions an exclusivist identity based on the principle of repulsion. From this identity then, a politics of commitment can be more realistically commandeered. From now on members of a nation-state are on guard against those who belong to other territories and other nation-states. The principle of repulsion has thus worked itself in without over constraining the logic of capitalism.

### Arbitrary territory, exclusivist identity

What the territorial lineaments will be is difficult to forecast in advance. Much depends on contingent historical conditions that set the terrain for the battle between pre-capitalist and capitalist impulses. Sometimes it can be the format left behind by colonialism, on other occasions it can be empires, or it can be contiguity, or even natural geographical factors. Quite often, the exigencies and demands of the struggle for the establishment of capitalism contingently set up territories. Several nation-states came out of the erstwhile Hapsburg Empire. Sometimes language, at other times religion, gave these nationalisms their emotional appeal. Even when it was ostensibly language, as we discussed earlier, the bond had to be made: it was not already there. Partisanship to the German nation did not prevent the Mecklenbergers from speaking a dialect that was closer to Dutch than it was to German (Hobsbawm 1988b: 108).

As nation-state loyalty, however arrived at, was now the only basis for a kind of exclusivist membership, territory became sacralised for the first time. When empires existed it is likely that the emperors and the ruling classes had a certain attachment towards a political domain. This was certainly untrue of the subordinate classes. It is said when Napoleon's army marched into Russia the peasants welcomed him hoping for a kinder dispensation from that which they enjoyed under the Czar. But when Hitler's army marched into Russia every Russian became a patriot and recited Pushkin to keep their spirits alive. The contributions of the Russian soldiers cannot be understood in any other way than in terms of loyalty to the nation-state and its territories.

As the territorial boundaries of nation-states are not logically marked but are contingently created, they are bound to change over time. If nation-states change, or if their territories undergo modifications, there is no reason to believe that the earlier boundaries were inauthentic and only the latter ones are true expressions of nation-state sentiments. Now that the erstwhile nation-states of Yugoslavia and USSR have disintegrated and given way to the formation of other nation-states, this does not mean that the earlier nation-states were based on a lie. If that had been the case Russian soldiers would not have fought as valiantly as they did to send back Hitler and deliver the death blow to Nazism and firm up the Soviet state. Nation-states are ultimately constructions, and in many cases (even in such instances as Italy and France), very self-consciously so. But it is from these constructions alone that an exclusivist identity based on territory can be derived. This is what helped capitalism to sustain its protracted struggle against feudalism which drew its ideological energies from localised and closed systems of stratification.

## Conclusion: Citizenship, stratification and the nation-state

The concept of citizenship is therefore critical for nation-states to survive. It is through citizenship that nation-states aspire to undermine previous solidarities with mutually exclusive categories that breed on the principle of repulsion. At any rate, citizenship, consistently advocated and adhered to, takes away the efficacy of these earlier ties and confines them to the private sphere. In fact, contrary to Niklas Luhman's view, I think society emerges as a living reality only with the breakdown of medieval institutions. In earlier times one's identity was linked parochially to phenomena like caste, clan and neighbourhood. The whole was indeed less than the sum total of its parts (Luhmann 1982:238, 257). Nobody really cared what happened outside the range of one's immediate and proximate experiences. This explains why it was possible to retain the old village economy in India, more or less unperturbed by different waves of invasion, over hundreds of years.

The distinction between open and closed systems of stratification, and the structural pressures on capitalism to inaugurate a fresh exclusivist identity, help further to understand why citizenship is always at odds with prior forms of memberships. Excessive attachment to caste, clan, religion and language is now considered 'divisive' in character. In earlier years a person was recommended highly for subscribing to such values. Yet today, because of the ascendance of nation-state sentiments, earlier exclusivist identities are disparaged. It is not as if the nation-state itself does not propound separation and exclusion, but it cannot tolerate others doing the same. This is because through partisanship to the nation-state a supra-local community is created, and this is why other more localised loyalties have necessarily to be disparaged and undermined. As we said earlier the nation-state brought forth a larger supra-local community identity that powered capitalism with the politics of commitment. Without this kind of ideological charge capitalism would have found it difficult to assume the position of dominance it enjoys today.

The linkage between politics of commitment with exclusivist identities nursed on mutual repulsion, and the politics of responsibility based on open stratification systems, which are premised on continuous hierarchies, helps us to analytically strengthen both studies on stratification and of those on social movements. It also helps us to appreciate why certain kinds of solidarities are historically favoured at certain junctures, while others are not.

The arrival of 'new social movements' in contemporary society is further illustration of the fact that the politics of commitment is losing out on their efficacy and appeal. New social movements are not about displacing entrenched classes, or the hated 'others', as much as seeking further accomodation within a system that is resilient and open to mobility from within. It is in the sphere of nation-state loyalties that the politics of commitment is most strident today. What has embourgeoisified the trade union movement was not so much labour aristocracy but the ability of capitalism to realistically present an open system of stratification with an appreciable degree of social mobility. This does not mean that classes and class exploitation does not exist. It only means that being a member of a certain class need not always be determined by accident of birth.

## References

Amin, Samir. 1974. *Accumulation on a world scale.* 2 vols . New York: Monthly Review Press.

Bougle, C. 1991. 'The essence and reality of the caste system', in Dipankar Gupta (ed.), *Social stratification*, pp 64-73. Delhi: Oxford University Press.

Fanon, Frantz 1967. *The wretched of the earth.* Harmondsworth: Penguin

Frank, A. G. 1971. *Capitalism and underdevelopment in Latin America*. Harmondsworth: Penguin

Gramsci, A. 1971. *Selections from prison notebooks*. New York: International Publishers.

Hall, John A.1993. 'Nationalism: classified and explained', *Daedalus,* 122:-28.

Hobsbawm, E. J. 1988a. *The age of revolution, 1789-1848.* London: Cardinal

____________. 1988b. *The age of capital, 1848-1875.* London: Cardinal

____________. 1990. *Nations and nationalism since 1780.* Cambridge: Cambridge University Press.

Lenin, V. I. 1969. *Imperialism, The highest stage of capitalism.* Moscow: Progress Publishers.

Luhman, Niklas. 1982. *The differentiation of society.* New York: Columbia University Press.

Nisbet, Robert. 1970. *The sociological tradition.* London: Heinemann.

O' Connor, James. 1970. 'The meaning of economic imperialism', in Robert R. Rhodes, ed., *Imperialism and underdevelopment: A reader.* New York: Monthly Review Press.

Pandey, Gyanendra. 1990. *The construction of communalism in colonial north India.* Delhi: Oxford University Press.

Renan, Ernest. 1990. 'What is a nation', in Homi Bhaba (ed.), *Nation and narration.* London: Routledge.

Rich, Norman. 1977. *The age of nationalism and reform, 1850-1890.* New York: W. W. Norton.

Weber, Max. 1946. 'Class, status and party', reprinted in Dipankar Gupta (ed.). 1991. *Social stratification,* pp. 455-70. New Delhi: Oxford University Press.

# 5

# Language, Region and National Identity

*M. N. Karna*

My intention in this paper is to explore the nature and role of some key forces, which have shaped and fashioned the patterns of state and nation in the developing world. To illustrate my thesis I have primarily drawn on examples from India with which I am more familiar. But most of the arguments may also apply *mutatis mutandis* to other South Asian countries. I have attempted to address this subject within the broader disciplinary perspective of sociology but with an historical approach to the topic. However, in no way do I seek to focus on all the essential aspects considered crucial for constituting the nation. Given the objective of the present exercise, I consider closely only issues of language and region in the context of a national question.

## I

Nation and nationalism have become an integral part of the people's psyche today. However, our understanding of nation and nationalism is still amorphous and blurred because of the confusion created by the interchangeable use of the terms nation, state and territory. In fact, these three major dimensions–the nation as a collective identity, the state as an expression of political sovereignty, and territory as a geographical area—have to be properly delineated to grasp the coincidence between nation and state.

The historiography of nationalism unequivocally suggests the ancient origins of a nation state. The past traditions of a nation have been articulated in terms of history, culture, language, folklore, territory or religion to demonstrate its antiquity and continuity. In these historical interpretations the nation subsumed the state. Hegel's famous definition, 'nations may have had a long history before they finally reach their destination, that of forming themselves into states' (cited by Gellner 1983:48) became the basis for all subsequent analyses. A similar formulation appeared in the writings of Ernest Gellner (ibid: 55): 'It is nationalism which engenders nations, and not the other way round.' These points were particularly highlighted taking into account the developments in Europe during the mid-19th and early 20th centuries.

Elie Kedourie (1960: 1) stated as early as 1960 that 'Nationalism is a doctrine invented in Europe at the beginning of the nineteenth century.' However, having realised the socio-political consequences of aggressive European nationalism some revision took place in the very conceptualisation of nationalism. The disastrous wars and their international fallout forced the analysts to see nationalism not as a positive and inevitable fact but as a 'negative ideological creation'.

Another perspective on nationalism emerged through the writings of East European historians, who treated struggles for national independence as fights against imperial autocracy. Nationalism was understood as an embodiment of the forces of progress and betterment. Contemporaneously, in French historical analysis a distinction was made between national movement and nationalism. While national movement was considered to be the legitimate expression of popular sentiment, nationalism was defined as a narrower ideology. Such a distinction was however not noticed in English language historiography, where national movements and nationalism are part of the same formation. Thus, nationalism is perceived as an ideology of unusual force, an instrument of political manipulation.

Although the central theoretical position of these discussions has been somewhat different, all of them accept the historicity of national sentiment and identity. The growth and development of national identity as a potent political force determined by specificities of contexts and conditions are regulated and guided by the social processes. It is through the social process that the ideology of nationalism was spread, the composition of its bases determined and the functioning of its cultural symbols handled.

Geneaologically speaking, the national question did not form the core of early Marxist writings. While Marx and Engels talked in general about the national struggles of the Irish and the Poles and commented on the national demands of the other East European Slav nationalities, it was for other major Marxist theorists like Kautsky, Luxemberg and Lenin to dwell upon the national question and its political importance. Lenin treated nationalism as a real social issue and endorsed the principle of national self-determination. But nothing specific can possibly be derived from his voluminous writings on the sources of national discontent (see, specifically, Lenin 1964a, 1964b, 1964c). However, the most enduring Soviet-Marxist treatment of the national question was provided by Stalin in 1913, which pointed to the numerous social contexts in which national conflicts might be defined. 'The urban petty bourgeoisie of an oppressed nation could be set against the bourgeoisie of a dominant nation (as in the case of the Czech-German conflict), rural bourgeoisie might be set against landlords (as in the Ukrainian-Polish conflict in Galicia), or an entire "national" bourgeoisie might be in conflict with a ruling nobility as in the case of the Poles, Lithuanians and Ukrainians in Russia' (Stalin 1953).

Contemporary Marxist writings on the theme have heavily relied upon the classical Marxist-Leninist approach, particularly Lenin's major theoretical work on imperialism but some amount of freshness is noticeable in their articulation and coherence. The paradigms developed in these studies are essentially evolutionist and in the context of the Marxist stages of social and economic development, they have identified successive stages in the modern nations in their bourgeois and socialist forms. Most have focused on the early stages of national evolution but without highlighting the patterns and mechanics of formation of nations. The development of nationalism in Central Europe in relation to its evolutionary stages is especially analysed in the work of the Pole, Chlebowczyk (1980) and the Yugoslav, Zwitter. The Czech historian Miloslav Hroch (1985) has been more influential in the comparative study of national movements. By taking cases of smaller nationalities of Europe in his major work, Hroch examines the sequence of events as national movements develop and analyses the social background of nationalist activists. He illustrates his model with reference to the Czech, Lithuanian, Estonian, Finnish, Norwegian, Flemish and Slovak national movements.

More recently, the relationship between European powers and their present or former colonies has been interpreted in terms of core-periphery theory. By drawing attention to the conflicting interests of different groups within the periphery and their relations with the metropolitan centre, Johan Galtung (1971) shows the tension between the two in terms of an imbalance due to a differential location of economic, political and cultural power. The internal colonialism perspective thus suggests that centre and periphery need not be separated by a great distance but they might be located within the area of the same state. Hechter's (1975) investigation into the process of nationality formation in the United Kingdom is a substantive work here in terms of its influence on the study of nationalism. It has been argued that like many other states, the UK is characterised by a powerful, culturally distinct core which exercises monopolistic control over commerce, credit and political life. The people in peripheral areas are just left with the option of joining the core. Under such circumstances, a peripheral nationalist movement emerges, particularly when the extent of economic inequality between core and periphery increases and communications between the two are intensified. Hechter (1985) thus defines nationalism as a popular protest against oppression and elaborates his model with additional ideas of the cultural division of labour and rational choice theory.

In recent non-Marxist approaches to nationalism more methodological rigour is found because the conceptual schemes adopted by them reflect more analytical power as they have been developed within the framework of general theories of society. Another development here shows the critical role of the relationship between nationalism and ethnicity. Smith recognises that there is no direct link between ethnies and modern nations. He defines ethnies 'as named human populations with shared ancestry myths, histories and cultures, having an association with a specific territory and sense of solidarity' (1986:32). Modern nations possess in addition to the characteristics of ethnies identified above, legal, political and economic unity. However, in a more recent work Smith (1991) has analysed many transformations of modernity, which are required to turn an ethnie into a nation. The objective reality of a past ethnie does matter for modern nations. In the absence of the 'myth-symbol complexes' which generate and express ethnic identity, Smith suggests modern nationalism would be rootless and arbitrary. Another influential work in this field is of Michael Banton (1983) who has devised a useful rational model of ethnic group formation and consolidation.

Some theorists, on the other hand, focus their attention primarily on a political perspective and relate growth of nationalism to economic and social development. Deutsch's theory of social communications asserts that the existence of a socially mobilised population within a distinctive ethnic group is a precondition for the development of nationalism among its members (Deutsch 1961, 1966). The balance in a state system is disturbed if social mobilisation grows faster than assimilation to the dominant culture. The section of population which is socially mobilised but not assimilated into the dominant culture is most likely to turn its back on the dominant culture and on the political system which supports it. Ultimately, the mobilised section of the population will start developing its own culture and will also move towards a political domain marking the beginning of a nationalist movement in the unassimilated peripheral community. If the rate of assimilation is equal to or greater than the pace of mobilisation, the process of nationality formation does not threaten the integrity of the state; but if the rate of assimilation is slower than that of mobilisation, an alternative nationality is likely to develop. Deutsch has taken up cases of Finland, Bohemia, India and Scotland to illustrate his model.

The political perspective finds a central place in the work of Paul Brass. He presents a distinctive theory concerning the origins of ethnic identity and modern nationalism (1974, 1976, 1980, 1991). Using a more explicit political framework and focussing on the elites rather than on the masses, Brass bases his formulation on two main arguments: one, that ethnicity and nationalism are not 'givens' but are social and political constructions, and, two that ethnicity and nationalism are modern phenomena 'inseparably connected' with the working of the modern centralising state. The nature and specificities of interactions between the leadership of centralising states and elites from non-dominant ethnic groups located in the peripheries of those states have been examined to develop the theory of elite competition. He has drawn examples mainly from India, Eastern Europe and the erstwhile Soviet Union to illuminate the various patterns of ethnic mobilisation and nation formation.

Anderson's analysis of the origin and growth of nationalism has been the most influential in the last few years in generating new theoretical ideas on nationalism. He shows that nations were not the determinate products of given sociological conditions such as language or race or religion; they had been 'imagined' into existence everywhere in the world (Anderson 1983). He has described some of the major institutional forms through which this 'imagined community' came to acquire concrete shape. The critical role of institutions of what he calls 'print capitalism' have especially been taken up to illustrate the arguments. Moreover, he demonstrates that the historical experiences of nationalism in Western Europe, the Americas and in Russia had provided models to all subsequent nationalisms in Asia and Africa, out of which nationalist elites selected the ones they liked.

The above appraisal of the selective approaches analysing nation, nationalism and national identity can conclude with a summary of some of the essential issues discussed above:

1. Nationalism is an ideological phenomenon, a matter of ideas and concepts, adhered to by certain groups and communities. The fundamental issue to be addressed here is not that of the real nation or national identity which lies behind the concept of nationalism employed in political practice, but that of the formation, articulation and propagation of the concepts themselves.
2. Nationalist ideologies are formulated in order to gain and retain hegemony. They are not 'givens' but are constructed and expressed in political terms. Accordingly, national movements have been studied as manifestations of political power in which social, economic and cultural aspects are considered as explanatory factors.
3. Some theorists consider nation as a natural unit that has always existed albeit for long in a passive and dormant state. Nationalism

for this reason is a reflection of primordial identities like the family, inherently superior to other loyalties.

4. National identity is an abstract concept that subsumes the collective expression of a subjective individual sense of belonging to a socio-political unit: the nation state. It is a cultural construct, not a fixed objective reality but an ongoing and changeable process, dependent on and deriving from social relations and hence not exclusive of other identities.
5. Nationalism in its identification of a people with the territorial nation state is a historically modern phenomenon. It may be seen as a response to the consequences of modernisation. Modernisation disrupts social life, causes role differentiation, creates new and different modes of communication flows and transforms the political system. Thus, at the origins of nationalism is modernisation, which consists of the processes of social mobilisation, cultural standardisation and growing political participation.
6. A series of elements are identified, constructed and placed together to constitute the nation. Some such decisive elements recognised so far are common territory, common origin, common historical experiences, common language, common religion and morals, and common customs. These objective characteristics cannot possibly be juxtaposed but can only be understood in terms of complementarity or interdependence.

These issues have undoubtedly made the narratives of nation and nationalism more comprehensible as they concentrate on the processes of construction of ideologies of nationalism, the conditions which facilitated their spread and the social mechanisms through which they operated. However, equally important is their failure to illuminate why national sentiment, or the pride that an individual takes in belonging to a nation has become such a pervasive reality despite his disappointment with or hostility to the state apparatus of the nation.

## II

One of the major elements in nationality formation is linguistic allegiance. The interface between linguistic identity and national consciousness is obvious because ordinarily one cannot locate a historic nation which is not associated with a linguistic marker. In this sense, language is the demiurge of nationalism and it acts also as a vehicle of expansion.

It is believed that each nation is a linguistic entity. The situation in Europe coincided with this presumption as native speakers of French, German and Italian were a Frenchman, German or Italian. It was emphasised that 'Mankind instinctively takes language as the badge of nationality' (Freeman 1879). But such a principle applied only to the reality existing in monolingual nations which covered substantial areas of Europe. However, even in this region, there were apparent exceptions like the Swiss and Belgian nations. Not only that but English, Spanish, Portuguese, French and German languages all crossed national boundaries. The common pattern was thus the reality of linguistic diversity.

The merits of linguistic uniformity for the development of national identity have been succinctly expressed by Rupert Emerson in the following statement:

> Leaving aside the fascinating if unanswerable query as to the extent of which each particular language both mirrors and fashions unique patterns of thought and thus reflects and molds a distinctive national soul it is evident that language is the primary instrument of social communication (1970: 133).

The speakers of the same language develop a common bond and share a 'common store of social memories'. Language establishes a link with the 'glorious past'. No society likes to snap this link as it is taken to be great and grand. It is particularly so with the people who do not feel so great about their present. It is because of this that 'the mother tongue became almost sacred, the mysterious vehicle of all national endeavours' (Jaszi 1929: 262, also cited by Fishman 1973). It is further emphasised that:

> in its mother tongue every people honours itself; in the treasury of its speech is contained the charter of its cultural history. For the 'peoples without history, history and language were two sides of the same coin. The vernacular was not merely the highroad to history,' it was itself the voice of years that are gone' (ibid).

Joshua Fishman expressed this view most succinctly:

> ...the essence of a nationality is its spirit, its individuality, its soul. This soul is not only reflected and protected by the mother tongue but, in a sense, *the mother tongue is itself an aspect of the soul*, a part of

the soul, if not the soul made manifest (1973: 153, emphasis in original).

However, the idea that language signifies nationality and nationality signifies language is modern. Language does not automatically become the basis for making political distinctions. When language acquires institutional importance in some major domains of nationality—law, polity and economy—it may assume political significance. Thus, the link between language and nationality cannot be taken as natural or God-given, based exclusively on people's faith and belief. Sapir amply clarifies this point by stating that 'a particular language tends to become the fitting expression of a self-conscious nationality' but 'such a group will construct for itself… a race to which is to be attributed the mystic power of creating a language and a culture as twin expressions of its psychic peculiarities' (1942: 660). Actually 'the link is man-made but ascribed to supernatural forces in order to hallow it' (ibid).

The entire relationship between language and nationality has become more complex and demanding with the coming of modern nationalism. What was initially taken as a natural link has now turned into an espoused cause. With the increasing importance of the mass media, the standardisation of language became a necessity because ideas of the people were now expressed through newspapers, periodicals and pamphlets. Similarly, the expansion of the modern organised courts made the choice of language a matter of more popular concern. The extension of market relations and the development of mass education further boosted the interest in the use of specific languages. Thus, language gains relevance not only as a repository of national culture and reminiscences, as a storehouse of myths but also as a matter of political, economic, legal and educational interest.

But here a fundamental question arises. How significant is language as a component of nationality? How does it fare when placed in association with other decisive components such as territory, origin, religion, historical experiences, customs and morals? Analysing this question Fishman says: 'The ideological pinnacle of language nationalism is not reached until language is clearly pictured as more crucial than the other symbols and expressions of nationality' (1973:163).

The primacy of the nationality-language tie-up in pre-nationalist days was essentially in terms of its greater collective significance but in subsequent phases it turned out to be just a symbol with which only the elite and intellectuals were concerned. In other words, language became merely a representation or an emblem in the nationalist phase which was put to use by nationalist activists to accomplish their goals. For this reason, the supremacy of language from the perspective of nationalist ideology can be attributed only by comparing it with other collective symbols.

Some commentators argue that language is more important than territory for defining nation. For, language provides the most immediate link among people and helps to establish well-defined boundaries. In fact, the boundaries between languages are clearer and lasting. It was this issue that prompted Davies to state 'A people without a language of its own is only half a nation. A nation should guard its language more than its territories–'tis a surer barrier, a more important frontier than fortress or river' (1945:71). Almost a similar stand is taken when it is asserted that language is more abiding than the institutions of government. The linguistic identity of a nation may remain intact even if its state boundaries are lost. A state may be geographically or politically divided but its language does not break its promise. A nation remains intact if it maintains its distinctive linguistic traditions.

Likewise when language is placed face-to-face with religion in the context of nationality, the primacy of the former is distinctly discernible. The historical experiences of 19th century Europe, the cradle of modern nationalism, apparently suggest that the rise of nationalism coincided with a decline in the hold of religion. The advent of modernism weakened the grip of religion. Of course, the scenario substantially changed in the subsequent phases, particularly in the ex-colonial countries where it was inconceivable that nations could emerge without being profoundly influenced by religious issues. However, even in this period 'only an arbitrary line of coincidence links religion and nation'. Several instances of contemporary nationalisms show that the 'unity of language is more durable for survival and permanence than the unity of religion'. In language one has a secular symbol whereas religion is often an embarrassment for the modern man. The issues of linkages between language and nation and the primacy of the former in terms of other elements of nationality formation have been discussed so far to provide the background for analysing the problem in the context of the South Asian region which I shall do now. But before that, it remains to be noted that the idea of a single national language is a product of European historical experience. It does not essentially hold good for a large number of nation-states in other parts of the world, Asia included, where the reality is linguistic diversity rather than linguistic uniformity.

## III

People's attachment and love for their own language is not new but the mobilisation of linguistic loyalty for political purposes is a recent phenomenon. The invention and growth of printing technology, the spread of education, particularly among the lower strata of society, and the increasing participation of the people in mass politics obviously facilitated the use of language for the politics of nationalism. While the question of a national language assumed a central place very early in different European regions, the idea of linguistic nationalism gained in salience in multilingual states of Asia and Africa in the wake of the Second World War. Most of these countries were either in the phase of attaining success in their anti-colonial struggles or had already achieved freedom from colonial rule. Language was a critical issue in the national struggles of these new states as it acted as a symbol of identity and distinction which in turn provided access to their own cultural tradition. However, these newly liberated nations were multilingual in a majority of cases. But one common feature ascertainable in these developing nationalisms was the role of languages introduced by the colonial masters on the one hand and conscious standardisation of the major vernacular languages on the other. Under such circumstances, several patterns of language diversity have emerged in these nation states.

First, a variety of closely related languages co-exist, one of which may acquire the position of a major link language (Das Gupta 1970). The situation in Indonesia corresponds to this pattern. Second, there may be a variety of unrelated languages but none of them can claim a long literary tradition. One witnesses this situation in many parts of tropical Africa. Another pattern may be where several languages, all with some degree of literary tradition co-exist but no one can claim a distinct dominance over others. Such a situation is found in India, Pakistan, Srilanka, Malaysia and so on. While in the first pattern there is ordinarily no possibility of intense antagonism on the language issue, in the other two situations political rivalry on this issue is bound to be generated in the absence of dominance by a single language. The concurrent claims of several languages for national status may even lead to boisterous fights endangering the very existence of the nation. Language is thus not only a primary element in nationality formation but remains a significant issue even in the process of nation building.

India is a nation sharply divided along linguistic lines. A large number of linguistic regions have begun to compete with each other to impair the sense of national identity. Stalin's remark in 1925 that while India was spoken of as a single whole there could be little doubt that 'in the event of a revolutionary upheaval in India hitherto unknown nationalities, each with its own language and its own distinctive culture, will emerge on the scene' has proved prophetic.

The demand for a reorganisation of provinces on a linguistic basis has a linkage with the struggle for Indian independence. The Indian National

Congress had ever since 1921 started supporting 'the idea of the creation in British India of administrative units based on linguistic homogeneity'. As early as 1928 the Nehru Report talked about the desirability of creating linguistic provinces and this principle was subsequently included in the election manifesto of the Congress. Immediately after Independence on 27 November 1947 Prime Minister Nehru, on behalf of the Government of India accepted in the Constituent Assembly the principle underlying the demand for linguistic provinces. It was against this background that two commissions—one, the Linguistic Provinces Commission appointed by the Constituent Assembly in 1948, and the other, States Reorganisation Commission in 1955—were appointed to go into all relevant matters concerning the formation of linguistic states.

The idea of linguistic states rested primarily on the premise that these linguistic groups are sub-nations and as such they are contracting parties to the Constitution from which the Federation and the Centre derive their existence and power (Indian Institute of Public Administration 1968b: 443). However, this question raised not only an intense debate but attracted sharp reactions from various corners of the country. It brought out two sharply conflicting views with regard to the formation of these linguistic states. The cases for and against the formation of the linguistic states were advanced. Several violent agitations and protests were launched to gain recognition for one's respective language. Its serious political consequences were also highlighted. The Linguistic Provinces Commission wrote:

> An autonomous linguistic province ... means an autonomous linguistic state and an autonomous state means ... that its territories are inviolate. And if in a linguistic province the majority language group comes to regard the territory of the entire province as exclusively its own, the time cannot be far distant when it will come to regard the minority living in that province and people living outside it as not their own. And once that stage is reached, it will only be a question of time for that sub-nation to consider itself a full nation (IIPA 1968a: 474).

The nature of dangers involved in new separatisms based on politically consolidated linguistic communities was further highlighted by the members of the commission in these words :

> This inquiry in some ways has been an eye-opener to us. The work of sixty years of the Indian National Congress was standing before us face to face with centuries-old India of narrow loyalties, petty

> jealousies, and ignorant prejudice engaged in a mortal conflict, and we were simply horrified to see how thin was the ice upon which we were skating. Some of the ablest men in the country came before us and confidently and emphatically stated that language in this country stood for and represented the culture, tradition, race, history, individuality and finally, a sub-nation, that the government of a linguistic group could not be safely left in the hands of a multi-lingual group; and that each linguistic group must have a territory of its own and that its territory was inviolate and could not be shared by any other linguistic group (ibid: 479-80).

The subsequent developments reinforced further the primacy of language as a national question. The language issue did not subside even after the reorganisation of states on the basis of linguistic regions. The consensus on official language arrived at within the Constituent Assembly and the adoption of the Official Languages Act in 1965 could not conclude this debate. Several new issues were added to the vexed problem inherited from the past.

As Indian nationalism has been deeply wedded to the question of regional languages, India's independence and the formation of linguistic states released certain social forces which culminated in the growing assertion of the unrecognised local contact languages for recognition of their rights. This further fostered a consciousness and an assertion of linguistic regionalism, the roots of which were already there in India's history and culture. Ray's contention that 'India's history and culture have always oscillated between an ideal of pan-Indianness and that of regional self-assertion' (1968: 6) appropriately captures the socio-political situation prevailing in the country today. Indian consciousness is co-existing, despite the multilingual situation, with another corporate consciousness at the regional linguistic level.

Given the complexity of multilingualism, it was not very easy to deal with several emerging issues involved in the language question in post-independence India. Some of the unresolved subjects included questions of national language, official language(s) of the union and the states, link language between the state and the union and among the states, not to speak of the question of language of education, the medium of instruction and the languages to be taught at the school level.

While the reorganisation of states 'sought a balance between the advantages flowing from federal units based on linguistically homogeneous peoples and the particularism and discrimination likely to be fostered by such units', bestowing national status on all the major regional languages through their inclusion in Schedule Eight of the

Constitution achieved some measure of amity on the language front. Of course, several other languages spoken by large sections of the people in certain regions, used as media of instruction at the secondary level and recognised by the Sahitya Akademi for purposes of national awards, have still not gained the honour and prestige of being designated as national languages. The recent inclusion of Konkani, Manipuri and Nepali in the Eighth Schedule has further stepped up the demand for the inclusion of Dogri, Maithili and Rajasthani languages, which are already recognised by the Sahitya Academi.

Nonetheless, the most intense debate has been on the issue of the official language of the union and the states. This problem has broadly been solved at the level of the states, but it is only partially resolved at the national level. Initially, as is well known, it had aroused one of the keenest controversies in the Constituent Assembly and produced so much heat and debate that it was felt necessary to keep it out of direct discussion in the assembly. The central debate was confined to the issue of English versus Hindi. Colonial rule had established the hegemony of English by adopting it for official correspondence and as the medium of instruction in higher education, which also provided a medium of communication for the Indian intelligentsia throughout the country. It was thus widely accepted that English served as a force for national unity and for developing national consciousness as well as for administrative convenience.

The linguistic divide had another dimension as well. The major regional languages used in different regions of the country are classified into two broad categories–the Sanskrit-based languages, important among them being Hindi, Bengali, Gujarati and Marathi, and the Dravidian languages, that is, Tamil, Telugu, Kannada and Malayalam. Although Sanskrit had influenced and contributed towards the development of most of the Indian languages, nonetheless each of these languages has its distinct character with its own script and grammar but in the absence of a pan-Indian unity, a common language could never become the goal.

Given these circumstances, Hindi, being the major language in several states, emerged as a strong contender for acquiring the status of official language. Besides, an enormous section of speakers of Hindi/Hindustani received substantial patronage by the leaders of the freedom struggle including Gandhi and Nehru. It was contended that English could under no circumstances be the national language of India and it had to be replaced by Hindustani. Gandhi wrote 'Our love of the English language in preference to our own mother-tongue has caused a deep chasm between the educated and the politically-minded classes and the masses.' The state of affairs in the Hindi belt was also perplexing and confused. The language issue in northern India had taken a communal turn from the early decades of the 19th century in the shape of the Hindi-Urdu controversy. In the Moghul period, Persian was the court language but with the fall of the empire, Persian was replaced by Urdu. Thus, in spite of several essential common features in Hindi and Urdu, both these languages began to signify something different from each other, particularly from the second half of the 19th century. The separatist tendency in language got a further boost when Hindi and Urdu were identified with the two major religious groups , the Hindu and the Muslim, which actually had no base in the prevailing reality.

Reverting to the wrangling over the official language it may be pointed out that the sharp differences of opinion which were expressed at the time of the framing of India's Constitution revealed the extent of violent sentiments this issue had engendered. The protagonists of Hindi led by Seth Govind Das demanded that the Constitution should specifically provide for Hindi in the Devanagiri script as the official language of the country. Feelings on this issue were so strong that Govind Das once made an impatient remark:

> I want to tell my brethren from Madras that if after 25 years of efforts on the part of Mahatma Gandhi they have not been able to understand Hindustani, the blame lies at their door. It is beyond our patience to bear that because some of our brethren from Madras do not understand Hindustani, English should reign supreme in a Constituent Assembly which is said to be a sovereign body and which has assembled to frame a constitution for a free India (IIPA 1968b: 783-84).

The opinion of non-Hindi speaking areas was that while they were not antagonistic to Hindi, they would resent what appeared to them to constitute the imposition of one language over the whole country and over vast numbers of people who were not acquainted with the language. The most vigorous exponent of this view was T. T. Krishnamachari who termed it as 'language imperialism' and forcefully argued that the Hindi issue, pressed too far, might result in a secessionist movement. Without demur he said:

> I would convey a warning on behalf of the people of the South for the reason that there are already elements in South India who want separation and it is up to us to tax the maximum strength we have to keep those elements down, and my honourable friends in the U.P. do not help us in any way by flogging their idea of 'Hindi imperialism'

> to the maximum extent possible. It is up to my friends in the U.P. to have a whole India, it is up to them to have a 'Hindi India'. The choice is theirs and they can incorporate it in this Constitution; and if we are left out, well, we will only curse our luck and hope for better times to come (IIPA 1968b: 788-89).

However, subsequent development suggest that a consensus was arrived at on the issue of recognising Hindi in Devanagiri script as the official language of the union and English as the associate language until all states agree to the exclusive adoption of Hindi. Likewise, the problem of link-language for intra-state and between state and union now does not pose a serious threat to unity because a workable system has already been evolved for this purpose. Similarly, with regard to the language of education there is almost universal agreement on the use of the mother tongue as the medium of instruction at the primary level and the Three-Language Formula at the secondary level. Some distortions have no doubt taken place in the actual implementation of the Three-Language Formula but they have not caused any bitter dispute among the various states. All told, it may be asserted that despite the far-reaching implications of the language issue, India has been able to balance the conflicting forces unleased by the political mobilisations for language.

Nonetheless, separatism based on politically consolidated linguistic communities will not wither away because culture-based regionalism centring on language communities represents values more easily intelligible to the average Indian than Indian nationalism. That is so because when a vast majority of people will achieve literacy and education in their local languages, the consequence may well be the rise of a sense of local provincial identity which may not necessarily coincide with national identity.

## IV

Apart from language, region is another important variable relevant to the idea of nation. A region is a geographical unit characterised by a particular biological cycle and an ecological equilibrium. A natural region acquires its boundaries and area by the expanse of a valley or a watershed. Life in the valley is made possible by the ever-replenished flow of water, which activates land fertility and the complex functions of the ecological cycle (Glikson 1955). Man built his society and culture in river valleys which served as their natural foundation. Ever renewed fertility of soil, water and easy communication among communities settled along the river were guaranteed by such a landscape. This fundamental basis of civilisation remains important up to this day. The network of socio-economic relations had expanded over those natural geographical regions. Nonetheless, the content and form of the socio-economic organism was determined by the quantity, quality and location of the region's natural resources and the size of the population living in it. Thus, two broad facets of region were identified–the physical and the social; the first has existed since the beginning of time, the second has acquired its shape through thousands of years of human history. The socio-economic region fulfilled the natural tendency of man to settle in groups and to form local nuclei of settlements, which in their turn strongly enhanced social and regional coherence and centralised regional life around focal points of settlement (ibid: 50).

A region is located between a community and a nation-state. Although the geographical distinctiveness is a significant determinant of a region, its entity does not always possess formal physical boundaries. The latter may be identified in cultural, linguistic, economic and administrative terms. However, these specific domains may coincide in some cases and may not in some others. For example, cultural and linguistic confines may transcend the political and administrative boundaries. The Hindi region in India provides a ready reference in this regard. Thus regions may lack formal boundaries identifiable in physical terms. That is why some analysts consider 'region as a mental construction' (Hartshrone 1939: 253), 'a reservoir of energy' whose 'origin lies in the nature but whose development depends on man' (ibid.).

Closely related to the concept of region is the idea of regionalism. The latter has been conveniently used to explicate the tendency of various regions of a country to assign primacy to the region as a value in comparison to the country as a whole. This tendency may be concretely expressed in terms of language, culture, economy or polity. Accordingly, regionalism represents the regional idea in action as an ideology or as a movement. But more often it is used in the political sense to describe the nature of mobilisation of people of a certain region to ventilate their grievances. Paul Brass, for instance, defines regionalism in the Indian context as:

> ... patterns of politics in the states that are best explained primarily in terms of conflicts and issue that arise within the states rather than in the national political arena and that deviate in easily discernible ways, such as in political party formations and voting patterns, from national trends (1991: 161).

However, this term, of late, has acquired notoriety in India and is used in a pejorative sense. It is perceived negatively and taken as a danger to the territorial integrity of the country. But to my understanding, regionalism or regional movement is not always a challenge to the survival of a nation-state. History shows us that states have not only existed but also progressed faster with numerous regional identities. The people of different ethno-linguistic groups located in various regions have lived together harmoniously in a nation-state and strengthened each other with mutual advantage. Thus, regionalism *per se* is neither a risk factor nor a hazard to the integrity of states. However, it needs to be emphasized that regionalism may grow into a formidable challenge to the nation-state if the latter fails to accommodate the legitimate aspirations of various regions. In a situation of multi-regional national identities there are several regions which are not only relatively small in size but possess distinct cultural, linguistic particularisms. Conversely, there may exist a sizeable majority, which is politically and socially dominant. Under such a structural condition, it is possible that even justifiable rights of smaller identities are neglected and ignored. Their demands and genuine grievances are overlooked more often under the pressure of the dominant majority. As such, smaller communities remain under constant threat of deprivation and discrimination. There is a constant fear for the loss of culture, language, tradition and even religion among the smaller groups. The notion of 'mainstream' is expounded by the dominant group to pressurise the smaller identities to assimilate with the larger whole. Historical evidences and justifications are invented to show linkages among various regions and ethnic groups on the one hand and the dominant groups on the other.

An impression has gained ground of late that there exists in India a dominant national group identified as a Hindu-Hindi community apart from a number of other smaller linguistic, cultural and religious groups. The dominant national group comprising the Hindi-speaking states of north and central India is acknowledged as the largest single block of states with Hindu-Hindi as a major concern. From the point of view of political, economic and administrative interests the Hindu-Hindi region does not essentially present a homogeneous block, but as long as language and religion continue to be the essence of national politics, the linguistic and religious affinities of such a large block of states tend to give an impression that the Hindu-Hindi area constitutes the 'mainstream' and represents the heartland of India. Whether such a notion of dominant national identity coincides with ground level reality requires further examination but frequent charges of 'northern domination' and 'Hindi imperialism' from the southern language groups and the mutual distrust arising out of the unevenness of development in various regions of the country definitely supports this contention. It is frequently observed that all regional demands and grievances are considered 'anti-national' by the so-called mainstream India. In most cases these grievances give rise to a number of questions about the socio-economic origins of regionalism. As mentioned earlier, it is possible to find an answer in the peripheral position of different regions in the background of various grievances.

Regional demands articulated in India may broadly be considered under three headings: institutional, economic and cultural. Institutional demands have been primarily raised in the context of reorganisation of states, provision for the devolution of power to these states, constitutional safeguards for different 'special' regions (Sixth Schedule of the Constitution), the greater degree of administrative, political and financial autonomy to the units, and so forth. No doubt, these institutional provisions seem to have been made initially to accommodate regional demands but in actual practice the nation-state has used them as instruments to assimilate the regional political elites into the Indian state. It is pertinent to point out here that the degree of autonomy for each region has been defined by individual regional statutes. For example, we have Article 370 for Jammu and Kashmir, 371A for Nagaland, the Fifth Schedule for tribal regions of central India, and the Sixth Schedule for certain hill regions of north-eastern India. There is no single constitutional arrangement applicable uniformly to every unit. In most of the cases new provisions were made under heavy regional pressures created by the organised regional political parties and groups. In effect, all institutional demands such as further reorganisation of states, more autonomy, secessionist threats have been met by the central government under similar pressure. For example, once the linguistic reorganisation of states passed through the first phase, the subsequent compulsion led to the bifurcation of Bombay into Maharashtra and Gujarat, of Punjab into Punjab and Haryana. Likewise, the creation of Nagaland as a separate state and bestowal of full statehood to Manipur, Tripura, Arunachal Pradesh and Mizoram are some other instances in point.

Economic demands have arisen out of a context of uneven development, or better still regional disparities in development, more particularly under-development of peripheral regions. Even a passing reference to the situation obtaining in the north-eastern region of the country will adequately illustrate this point. While both central and regional planning agencies have recognised the specificities of the north-eastern situation, they have failed to adopt a suitable alternative developmental strategy that could develop the region without disturbing its ecological balance and the people's psychology. The primary objective of the developmental policy is to utilise the natural resources of the region, with scant regard for its impact on the socio-economic life of the indigenous people. Such a strategy has led to destabilisation of the socio-economic life of the locals. Moreover, the developmental programmes entail emphasis on the growth of linkages with national and global markets, commercialisation of indigenous designs and skills, competitive use of land and forests and far-reaching changes in the pattern of land ownership and property relations. This, in turn, involves establishment of linkages between unequal formations, one highly developed and competitive and the other still at the stage of slash-and-burn cultivation. The former expropriates maximum benefits, the latter increases its dependence on market forces. The fact of the matter is that the planning strategy envisaged for the northeastern region is premised upon an ethos and value *gestalt* entirely unconnected with the socio-economic reality of the area. Consequently, there is a rather minimal impact of development measures, leading to growing disparities among various regions (Karna 1990). Such imbalances in socio-economic development inevitably result in political fragmentation. The emerging regional elites and middle classes tend to utilise the inherent conflict potential for a larger share of power. Regional political parties and groups emerge to articulate and mobilise large sections of the population on issues pertaining to common economic interests in their regions (ibid. 1998).

The cultural dimension of regional demands is equally significant and centres around issues of linguistic and cultural identity. The question of language has already been discussed in some detail. It remains to be noted, however, that language and its associated features are the symbols most easily available to ethno-nationalist organisations for constructing an ethnic identity. In addition to language, the shared socio-cultural experiences in terms of a whole series of traditions, art forms, behavioural patterns and images are articulated to promote regional awareness.

In fact, these three major issues–institutional, economic and cultural–form part of regional demands in India today in most cases. But the nature of articulation of the demands is not uniform in all such regions. It varies, depending on the specificities of the social structure and the historical conditions, and so also the character of regional movements. In some cases it may take the shape of constitutional or democratic struggles, in some others it may assume a direct secessionist form. There is also the likelihood of the assertion of regional identity taking a communal turn in certain areas, leading to conflicts between 'tribals-non-tribals', or 'insiders-outsiders'. As long as regional-cultural identities insist on their right to preserve and develop their language, tradition and ways of life, the problem remains manageable but when they assert their economic and political rights the system faces stresses and strains. The latter often aggravates conflicts (Oommen 1986).

## V

I have argued in this paper that a proper understanding of nation and nationality in India is possible if one adopts an alternative model of state-nation relations. The issue of state-nation relationship is different in Asian and African countries as compared to the nation-states of Western Europe. The model suitable for the latter cannot therefore be transplanted on a country like India.

When an ethnic group uses its cultural identity to seek economic and political rights, the process of nationality-formation comes into existence. The articulation of political and economic demands assumes a critical role in this context. They may range from merely a demand for regional economic development to increasing control over local resources or full economic and political autonomy. The group may even claim a separate homeland within the country or a separate country with full sovereignty. This is how a group aspires to have some kind of recognition as a national group. Such ethnic groups become nationalities when they succeed in gaining recognition not merely due to the sharpness of their demands but also because of their distinct culture, common heritage and political unity within a more or less well defined geographical area. In this process a nationality becomes a nation when it possesses an additional power to compel its members and back up group aspirations. Eventually, a nation becomes a state when it has successfully acquired sovereignty and attained all these aspirations.

Against this background, I am in agreement with the characterisation of India as a multi-national state. India's nationalities vary in size and are at varying stages of development. This contention is objectively based on the fact that pan-Indianness co-exists with the regional national consciousness. Nonetheless, the most crucial and substantive issue here is whether India's several nationalities together form or tend to form the Indian nation-in-the-making. The fact of the matter is that such an assumption gives rise to serious difficulties because the regional identities in the country have adjusted to the reality of an Indian state but are yet to harmonise with the idea of the Indian nation.

## References

Anderson, Benedict. 1983. *Imagined communities: Reflections on the origin and spread of nationalism*. London: Verso.

Banton, M. 1983. *Racial and ethnic competition*. Cambridge: Cambridge University Press.

Brass, Paul R. 1974. *Language, religion and politics in north India*. Cambridge: Cambridge University Press.

____________. 1976. 'Ethnicity and nationality formation', *Ethnicity*, 3(3): 225-241.

____________. 1980. 'Ethnic groups and nationalities', in P.F. Sugar (ed.), *Ethnic diversity and conflict in Eastern Europe*, pp. 1-68. Santa Barbara, Oxford: ABC-Clio.

____________. 1991. *Ethnicity and nationalism: Theory and comparison*. New Delhi: Sage Publications.

Chlebowczyk, J. 1980. *On small and young nations in Europe. Nation-forming processes in ethnic borderlands in East Central Europe*. Wrodsclaw, Warsaw: Zaklad Narodowy Imiemia Ossdinskich Wydawnictwo Polskiej akademii Nauk.

Das Gupta, Jyotirinda. 1970. *Language conflict and national development*. Bombay: Oxford University Press.

Davies, T. 1945. *Essays and poems with a centenary memoir*. Dublin.

Deutsch, K. W. 1961. 'Social mobilisation and political development', *American Political Science Review*, 55(3-4): 493-514.

____________. 1966. *Nationalism and social communication: An enquiry into the foundations of nationality*, 2nd edn. Cambridge, MA: MIT Press (first edn., 1953).

Emerson, Rupert. 1970. *From empire to nation*. Calcutta: Scientific Book Agency (Indian reprint).

Fishman, Joshua. 1973. *Language and nationalism*. Rowley, Mass: Newbury House Also included in Stuart Woolf (ed.), *Nationalism in Europe, 1815 to the present: A reader*, London: Routledge.

Freeman, Edward A. 1879. 'Race and language', *Historical essays*, 3rd Series, London: Macmillan and Company.

Galtung, J. 1971. 'A structural theory of imperialism', *Journal of Peace Research*, 8(2): 81-117.

Gellner, E. 1983. *Nation and nationalism*. Oxford: Basil Blackwell.

Glikson, Artur. 1955. *Regional planning and development*. Laiden: L.A.W. Sijthaff's Uitgeversmaatschappij N.V.

Hartshrone, R. 1939. *The nature of geography: A critical survey of current thoughts in the light of the past*. Pennsylvania: Association of the Lancaster.

Hechter, M. 1975. *Internal colonialism: The Celtic fringe in British national development, 1536-1966*. London: Routledge & Kegan Paul.

____________. 1985. 'Internal colonialism revisited', in E. A. Tiryakian and R. Rogowski (eds). *New nationalisms of the developed West: Toward explanation*. pp.17-26. Boston/London/Sydney: Allen & Unwin.

Hroch, M. 1985. *Social preconditions of national revival in Europe: A comparative analysis of the social composition of patriotic groups among the smaller European nations*. Ben Fowkes, Cambridge: Cambridge University Press.

Indian Institute of Public Administration (IIPA). 1968a. *The framing of India's Constitution: Select documents*. Vol. IV. New Delhi: IIPA.

____________. 1968b. *The framing of India's Constitution: A study*. New Delhi: IIPA.

Jaszi, O. 1929. *The dissolution of the Habsburg monarchy*, Chicago.

Karna, M.N. 1990. 'Aspects of tribal development in North Eastern India', in Ashish Bose et al, *Tribal demography and development in North-East India*. Delhi: B.R. Publishing Corporation.

____________ 1998. 'Socio-economic aspects of ethnic identity in North-Eastern India', in Gurudas Das and R.K. Purkayastha (eds), *Liberalisation and India's North-East,* pp. 223-35. New Delhi: Commonwealth Publications.

Kedourie, E. 1960. *Nationalism*. London: Hutchinson.

Lenin, V.I. 1964a. 'Critical remarks on the national question' (originally published 1913), in *Collected works*. Vol. 20, pp.17-51. Moscow: Foreign Languages Publishing House.

____________. 1964b. 'Imperialism, the highest stage of capitalism: A popular outline (originally published in 1917), in *Collected works*. Vol. 22, pp. 185-304.

____________. 1964c. 'The discussion on self-determination summed-up' (originally published in 1916), in *Collected works*. Vol. 22, pp. 320-60.

Oommen, T. K. 1986. 'Insiders and outsiders in India: Primordial collectivism and cultural pluralism in nation building', *International Sociology*, I(1): 53-74.

Ray, Niharranjan. 1968. 'Introductory address', in *Language and society in India: Proceedings of a seminar*. Shimla: Indian Institute of Advanced Study.

Sapir, E. 1942. 'Language and national antagonism' in A. Locke and B. J. Stern (eds), *When people meet*. New York.

Smith, A. D. 1983. *State and nation in the Third World*. Brighton, Sussex: Wheatsheaf Books.

__________ . 1991. *National identity*. London.

__________. 1986. *The ethnic origins of nations*. Oxford: Basil Blackwell.

Stalin, J. V. 1953. 'Marxism and the national question' (originally published 1913) in *Collected works*, Vol. 2, pp. 300-381. Moscow: Foreign Languages Publishing House.

# 6

# Tribe, Region and Nation in the Context of the Indian State

*Jaganath Pathy*

## I

Not too long ago, the idea of tribe, region and nation conveyed a single complex whole and thus, each could only be comprehended if studied along with the others. Each term simultaneously incorporated social, geographical and political dimensions. Hence, even analytically, these were hardly distinguishable. This merely meant that a given socio-cultural collectivity, or closely related socio-ethnic categories occupied an ecological territory and had a kind of political structure to manage the system as well as interactions with outsiders, or the 'others'. But like all concepts and terms, they too had to adjust to newer political and ideological realities and meet emerging professional exigencies. Small wonder the meaning of terms currently used are often incomprehensible.

The reasons for conceptual revisions could be many, but some significant ones may be worth reiterating. Previously unquestionable terms have now been decentered, largely due to the newly emerging political identities. For instance, a tribe or tribal social formations once referred to a stage destined to move towards the ubiquitous mainstream by means of education, modernisation, and so on. Today, they happen to be subjects of history with their own political space and cognitive specificity, promising to change whatever had existed for long. Similarly, both the concept of region—rooted in the concept of distance and de-essentialised due to the development of technology of transport and communication—and the concept of nation, which envisions a political organisation unique to itself and subscribed by a given culture, have never materialised. Instead, supranational and multi-national entities have grown in formidable strength. In brief, political compulsions force us to rethink and if need be, change the classical categories. Besides, the dimension of time has, in the final analysis, reduced the holistic multidimensional premise to analytically separable and operative wholes with distinct spaces of their own. Both political economy and the sociological profession tend to desire these separations for reasons of praxis and epistemology. The internal differentiation, heterogeneity, fissures and fusions in each of these categories appear merely to camouflage the urgent political and professional needs. Most researchers, however, may be reluctant to buy the argument of external motive forces influencing conceptual dynamics. But perhaps a majority of scholars may agree that these terms have still some instrumental and operative value.

Even this is very positive. For it ultimately means that the need for intense revision is very much called for and there can be no certainty about an essentialist position in relation to these codified categories. And these terms pose severe conceptual, theoretical and empirical difficulties in coming to terms with the contemporary situation. There is an inbuilt obfuscation of specificities—way of life, and political discourse from ethnographic concerns to manipulative politics or struggles for emancipation. As long as nothing is built into the given state structure—colonialism, capitalism and neo-colonialism—it is difficult to modify the used (or abused) terms in some detail and vitality. In the following pages we strive to question the validity of these general terms, and then situate them in the Indian context.

When Confucius was asked what was the first thing he would do if he became the emperor of China, his immediate reply was that the most important thing is the rectification of the words. How true it was then, and how equally true now. The term tribe is shrouded in ambiguity and often totally erroneous; the semantics are thus crucial and logically relevant.

Despite its wide currency in social science literature, the term tribe and allied terms like native, aborgines, first nations, indigenous, and the like, have never been defined with any scientific rigour and precision and existing definitions continue to characterise certain categories of pre-literate cultures, covering a wide range of forms, of social organisations and levels of techno-economic development. It appears that what is missing in the process of conceptualisation is the acknowledgement of history and of a complex political economy.

Needless to emphasise that the term and the community of people so designated belong to a particular era and to a social complex. Disciplines simply followed the dictates. We may say that the term originated with the rise of European colonialism and with racist ideology. It is worth acknowledging that several of the tribes were once considered nations, peoples and kingdoms by the same colonisers who wanted to establish commercial and diplomatic relations with them. It was colonial subjugation that transformed nations, countries, kingdoms and peoples into the so-called tribes. Prior to colonial annexation, the term had no equivalent in Africa, Asia, Australia or America. It is not merely accidental that only in the heydays of colonialism were most of the peoples named as tribes. The term tribe thus reflects the vocabulary of the colonial powers which, overladen by the 'Whiteman's burden', described it in several disparaging and contemptuous terms. Of course, even after achieving independence, the post-colonial states were not able to wholly expose the completely political nature of the term. Thus the limited definition continues to be used in order to manage the unequal national/international system.

Not only has tribe been identified as a type of non-state society organised on the basis of multifunctional kinship network but also as a stage in economic development and history (Godelier 1977). That necessarily means moving along the path traversed by the European colonial powers as the ultimate and true path. Religion, especially the Christian religion, was to come handy in this. Meanwhile, there is little historical record to convey how many peoples and their cultures were decimated or destroyed through the acceptance of this simple logic.

Similarly, region is not merely a concept of space. It is a political phenomenon, determined by the existing power matrix. It is not simply an ecological niche, where a community of people manages to survive with its own culture and social organisation. The region is not necessarily the cradle of the homeland, of the given community/sister communities. With the formation of the nation-state, the region came to signify only a province/administrative block in the eyes of the state in terms of certain demographic and linguistic/cultural traits. Nowhere does the term incorporate a region's other traits, like its unique history, culture and social formation. It is simply a politico-administrative unit, whose continued survival is dictated by the power matrix within which it is located.

In short, the region is referred to not simply as an ecological niche, as seen by the powers that be–near to the centre or far–but also represents a probable near-homogeneity of the people living there with some degree of autonomy under the centralised nation-state system. Post-colonial exigencies and a lack of consideration of history and culture determine the term region, thereby implying that such spaces are unchangeable or immune to change.

The current notions of regions are thus problematic insofar as they have been homogenised and trivialised within the Eurocentric matrix and lately by the dominant classes and communities seeking to domesticate the diversity of peoples, cultures, languages and terrains. Reality is constructed and framed by colonial and global encounters–a terrain of discourses and practices organised around the construction of fictitive regions and imagined communities. True, there is a constant process of being reworked within a developing political contestation.

Consequently, a region, based on the inherent geographical/territorial inertia, can hardly ignore for long the rising political and cultural connotations. Obviously then, the meaning of region tends to change, and should change for the better or worse, since there is no clearly defined space with order and rationality in the centralised and concentrated political system. The talk of decentralisation as a more efficient form of democratic organisation demands a newer mode of localisation.

Curiously, following the colonial wars and annexations, administrators and subsequent scholarship have largely downplayed the important similarities and connections between different regions, like northeast India, the Chittagong hill tracts of Bangladesh, Melanesia-Micronesia, Polynesia in the Pacific, and so on. The regions thus demarcated never seriously bothered about the history, culture and politics of the given peoples, let alone the similarities and connections outside these boundaries. Needless to stress that this has distorted the scientific analysis of contemporary regions of the globe (Tonn and Feldman 1995).

Finally, after the crisis of the European feudal system and the near breakdown of absolutist forms of power, the political structure of the current nation-states had grown over the last couple of centuries under the supposed defence of individual human rights and democratic practices. This structure stood for firm progress, rationality, modernity and civilisation. Subsequently the system of nation states became the sole basis of the legitimate international political order.

Recently however, there has been a growing awareness of the limitations of the given political structure. The sovereignty of states tends to prevent solutions to problems with global dimensions, like the ecological crisis, human poverty and peaceful solution to conflicts. Internally, and in the name of national security and cultural integration, several collectivities are directly or indirectly forced to follow the 'mainstream' values and institutions of the dominant class and community, although traditionally they have their own systems of values and institutions (Moore 1987). But more often than not, the established states often deny them the political, economic and cultural autonomy they deserve.

In a sense, the nation-state has become an antiquated political structure, which hardly responds to the need for an independent world authority, at least outside its borders. Most states, having been constituted artificially, contain a varied make-up of peoples, races, languages and cultures, among whom there have been wars, oppressions and structures of dominance of one people by another; rationality and peace thus appear unthinkable. If all peoples and cultures have their right to exist, to govern themselves, and to take part in solving problems common to humanity, the resulting political map would be much more different and complex than the political map of the states currently honoured.

The concept of nation, with its limited and fragile history, carries with it massive problems of juxtaposing the earlier nations, kingdoms and empires with the contemporary nation-states. The former were essentially political institutions based on cultural configurations and on cultural exchanges. The latter however divided the world into some two hundred political units, each supposedly carrying a near-homogeneous cultural, social, linguistic and customary whole; and if they did not, maybe by persuasion, welfare, cooptation or coercion they could be brought over to that homogeneity. Consequently over a couple of centuries, millions have and are still being assaulted due to this process of building a culturally homogeneous entity. Endemically, peace, prosperity and tranquility are questioned. Earlier, nations were mostly *sui generis* but now they are forced into creation for political ends.

Recapturing the problematic of the nation-state, it is worth reiterating that often colonial expediency alone, without any concern for history, tradition, culture, language, economy and geography had determined national boundaries. The post-colonial states are thus composed of a multiplicity of heterogeneous cultural and linguistic groups within, whereas there is a considerable cultural contiguity across national frontiers. This speaks volumes for the arbitrariness of modern state boundaries. Nevertheless, the post-colonial leadership has uncritically adopted and legitimised the imperatives of the nation-state and emphasized this by invoking inviolability and security of territory. This empirical predicament is frequently used as an excuse to repress and persecute the marginalised ethnics and others. The emphasis on a standardised and unified cultural mould emasculates democratic institutions and the federal character of the state.

Given the unequal global political economy, lack of rights to self-determination of peoples and cultures, centralisation and globalisation, the so-called nation-state needs to re-evaluate the absurdity of state boundaries. Rightly Raymond Williams (1983) argued that the nation-state is a project by and for the bourgeoisie in the interest of capital accumulation, but it is rather only one part of a complex story. The nation is an 'imagined community' (Anderson 1983) organised via the legal apparatus of citizenship and the specific geo-politics. Despite the fact that most of the current nation-states have ratified the International Covenant on Civil and Political Rights which holds that all peoples shall have the right to self-determination and by virtue of that right, shall freely determine their political status and cultural development, no state is prepared to honour the provision. Small wonder the nation-states are contested areas opposed to popular hegemonic myths and recurrent conflicts, both regional and global. So much for the terms; let us now turn to the Indian context.

## II

We have said that India contains the largest number of tribes in the world and that almost half of the tribal researchers are located in this country. But sad it is that we are nowhere near a conceptual definition of tribe, acceptable to the scientific community. In brief, the term tribe has never been defined with any scientific precision. Of course, some superficial and empirical characteristics are attributed to the term, namely: (1) homogeneity; (2) isolation and non-assimilation; (3) territorial integrity; (4) consciousness of unique identity; (5) animism (now defunct), but religion all-pervasive; (6) absence of exploiting classes and organised state structure; (7) multi-functionality of kinship relations; (8) segmentary nature of the socio-economic unit; (9) frequent cooperation for common goals; and many other ambiguous empirical external attributes which have been presumed to have remained unchanged for over a century since the time of Morgan, although these social formations have changed radically.

Some serious critiques demonstrate that the term tribe is at a theoretical dead-end and ideologically manipulative. The question of homogeneity and the idea of equality among the tribes have been increasingly found to be of little significance. Even in lineage-based societies there are economic and political inequalities in terms of control of marriage, exchange of allied goods and the redistribution process. In the Indian context, where the equivalent of the term was non-existent before colonial domination, several studies have shown the differential control of assets and the marked diversity among the tribes. Likewise, the geographical isolation of tribes ignores the historical process of interaction with the non-tribes (Kosambi 1965: 49). In short, the assumption that a-historic and static tribal societies have survived as a cultural lag is misleading.

Of course, for Indian researchers it is by now almost a taboo to define the term. Any attempt from whatever criterion would inevitably exclude a large number of officially recognised scheduled tribes from being designated as tribes. Hence, tribes simply refer to those communities included in the list of scheduled tribes. Whereas this juridical terminology and categorisation has been uncritically accepted in Indian social research, the term is nowhere defined in the Indian Constitution. Only Article 342(i) provides that the President of India with due consultation with the governors of the states may designate the 'tribe and tribal communities or parts of groups within tribes or tribal communities' to be the scheduled tribes for each state. Obviously then, there is no clear sociological basis of identifying a community as tribe.

Accordingly in 1950, the President of India promulgated a list of the scheduled tribes of India, apparently by making some additions to the 1935 list of backward tribes. No uniform test for distinguishing the scheduled tribes has ever been formulated, even in the amendments of 1956 and 1976. Since 1960 there has been no serious attempt by any legal or sociological expert to identify any community as tribe.

Of course, most concepts are prone to change, and carry largely instrumental and operative values; the notion of tribe cannot be otherwise. Whereas the term largely remains in conceptual confusion, the designated scheduled tribes broadly share certain common features. These peoples in general are historically evolved entities and are biologically self-perpetuating, marked by certain common cultural features, and are subordinated in several ways to the dominant society; its institutions and values. They had been for long engaged in struggles to preserve and promote their distinguishable features as well as territorial survival resources.

Leaving aside the conceptual problematique, let us turn to certain aspects of their culture and demography. According to the 1991 Census, India's tribal population was about 68 million, that is, about 8 per cent of the country's population. The number is large; much more than the population of many a country around the world. As some tribes were temporarily accommodated in the other backward classes category, they numbered only 19 million persons distributed among 212 communities in the 1951 Census. Their strength had increased to 38 and 52 millions in 1971 and 1981 respectively, constituting about 7.0 and 7.8 per cent respectively of the total population of the country. Currently there are between 258 to 540 scheduled tribe communities, depending on whether synonyms and sub-tribes are treated separately or not. Thus these numbers should be treated as indicative rather than conclusive. Incidentally the strength of these communities varied widely, from 31 persons of Jarwa to over 7 million Gonds. The numerically small tribal communities, comprising less than a thousand persons, include the Andamanese, Onge, Shampen, Toda, among others, whereas the Bhil,

Santal, Oraon, Munda, Mina, Khond, Saora, and the like had more than a million persons each.

Likewise, although the tribals are spread in all regions–East, West, North, South, and in the altitudes–they do convey little on history, ecology, political economy, and on socio-cultural complexities. Additionally the nation-state can hardly recognise regional autonomy, internal self-determination, multi-culturalism and even federalism. Despite the oft-repeated slogans of unity in diversity, the practice in the last fifty years has revealed that in order to build a manufactured homogeneous syndrome on a basically heterogeneous landscape with diverse political, economic and socio-cultural dimensions, the diversities have rarely been honoured. Given the aspirations of 'regionalities' and sub-nationalities, it is high time to think in terms of a civilisational/communitarian state where every people receive an honourable place in the generalised system without any discrimination of whatever kind. This will finally mean resolution of internal conflicts and building humanistic, democratic and federal structures with devolution of power from the union to the regional and cultural entities down on to further socio-cultural complexes.

The tribals are found in almost all the states and union territories. In terms of geographical distribution, about 55 per cent of the tribals live in central India, 28 per cent in western India, 12 per cent in northeast India and 4 per cent in south India, and one per cent elsewhere. With minor exceptions there seems to be a contiguous belt of tribal habitat from the Thane district of Maharashtra to the Tengnoupal district of Manipur (Roy Burman 1994: 6). At the *taluka* (revenue block) level, barring a few gaps, there is a contiguous belt of tribal peoples. Cartographic distribution of scheduled tribes even at district level gives an idea of a fair degree of contiguity (Raza and Ahmed 1990: 60). A few of the scheduled tribes within the borders of Arunachal, Nagaland, Manipur, and Mizoram have their counterparts across the border in China, Bhutan, Burma and Bangladesh as well as in Thailand, Laos and Cambodia. Besides, it is important to note that the scheduled tribes are mostly located at the meeting points of the linguistic and political regions of the country and on the international borders. This is not surprising as the national territory and the formation of the states rarely bothered about common history, culture and political economy.

Anyway, currently it appears there are two major concentrations: (i) the central mountainous tracts stretching from sea to sea on an east-west axis and bound by the river Godavari to the south and spanned by the Vindhya and Satpura ranges, covering the states of Andhra Pradesh, Bihar, Gujarat, Madhya Pradesh, Maharashtra, Orissa, Rajasthan, West

Bengal and others with about 83 per cent of tribal population; and, (ii) the mountainous tracts of northeast India, separated by the Brahmputra Valley, covering a part of Assam, Manipur, Meghalaya, Nagaland, Sikkim, Tripura, Arunachal and Mizoram states with a strength of over 12 per cent of the tribal population. The rest (5 per cent) are distributed over the peninsular south, among the Oceanic groups and in the northwest Himalayas.

In the 1960s, and maybe even now, one-third of the tribals lived in the districts where they were in a majority. In fact over 60 per cent lived in the districts where they comprised 30 per cent or more of the population. It is thus not very difficult to demarcate the regional or sub-regional autonomy of the tribes in most parts of tribal India. Small wonder several of the tribal regions like Jharkhand, Bodoland, Gurkhaland, Bhilistan, and the like, are struggling for political and cultural autonomy.

Moreover, a common feature shared by the tribal habitats is that of remoteness and the marginal quality of their resources. Earlier exploitation of such poor regions was found both difficult and uneconomic but in the recent decades of technological advancement and the unrivalled economic and political strength of world capitalism, we witness a creation of favourable conditions for invasion and extraction of natural resources from the ecologically fragile regions inhabited by the tribal peoples. Accordingly, the mammoth development projects like dams, mines, agro-businesses, security aspects, and so on, have become distressingly routine and an ever-increasing phenomenon threatening the integrity of the tribes. In the name of development, public interest, national security, millions of tribals have lost their traditional territorial resources. After all, the tribals, constituting only 8 per cent of the population, occupy nearly 20 per cent of the geographical area which contains over 70 per cent of the minerals, the bulk of forests and water resources. The powerlessness of the inhabitants provide easy access for the MNCs and their agents. The new corporate forces will soon lead to the loss of food entitlements and to the cultural degeneration of the tribal peoples. Suffice it to note that tribal regions have become arenas of the global 'free' market economy.

Of the two major tribal regions of India, the central tribal belt has been prone to capital-global and national-penetrations. True, even earlier, this region had attracted non-tribal immigrants historically, especially since the colonial days. Now as the region has become the nerve-centre of national development, mines, dams, massive factories including army enterprises have sprung up to a great extent. In the past different cultures were used to adjusting among themselves through mutually beneficial complexes and civilisations. But the recent happenings reveal unilateral imposition of alien forces, almost totally ignoring indigenous knowledge, practice, values and institutions. The resultant loss of survival resources and cultural complexes has led to a number of massive struggles of the tribal peoples. In the last century, in order to defend the land, territory, forest and culture they had launched a large number of movements. Indeed in the 19th century the tribals were credited with a much larger number of struggles than the rest of India. Of course, their movements were more often than not crushed through colonial might, with the support of the non-tribal populace of the country, while the anti-imperialist thrust was not articulated very well. Suffice it to note that almost all settled tribal peasants, given some numerical strength, fought against the British and their subordinates. Often they took to violence and arms to protect themselves, when sadly the non-tribals, especially the Western educated elite were critical of such struggles in the name of progress, rationality and civilisation.

In the post colonial decades, despite two dozen protective and promotive provisions for tribals in the Constitution, Nehru's *Panchsheel* doctrine and extensive legislations protecting tribal lands from alienation, their lands and forest resources have been taken away not only by the non-tribal rich manipulators but also the very state in the name of public interest and under the Land Acquisition Act (1894, as amended in 1984). Representatives of the dominant communities and classes, both local and alien, have managed to usurp not only the survival resources of the tribals but also the socio-cultural and political milieus. Hence despite constitutional and legal safeguards, the lives of the overwhelming masses of the tribals have worsened. Small wonder their political movements continue as fiercely as before. The agrarian question remains crucial in this region; and none has so far got political autonomy in the form of a state.

Unlike the central Indian tribal belt, the scenario in the northeast tribal belt is very distinct. This region, with about 119 tribal communities, is largely occupied by the so-called Mongoloid groups having cultural and historical affiliations with the neighbouring countries, like Bangladesh, Mynmar, China and Bhutan. This region hardly permitted immigration from the north Indian plains and Bengal (except Tripura, Assam and Manipur) even in colonial days. Now, inspite of the Inner Line Regulations and the provisions of the Sixth Schedule of the Indian Constitution, the tribals in some regions have become a minority, and their land and other resources have been alienated. Nonetheless, compared to the central tribal belt, the tribals in this region control their survival resources (82 per cent are cultivators here while only 52 per cent are likewise in central India and 36 per cent in the peninsular south). They are in fact a majority in Arunachal Pradesh, Nagaland, Mizoram and Meghalaya. There the non-tribal population—mostly traders and businessmen—continues to remain almost urban, and thus does not very seriously contemplate alienating tribal lands. Small wonder that the tribal struggles of northeast India have little to do with land alienation or expropriation of survival resources by the state. The movements there are for political autonomy, including secession and independent state-formation. The official formation of mini-states has not yet curtailed the urge for freedom with dignity. It is almost daily news to find militant insurgency in some or the other part of this tribal region.

During the last decade, whereas the general population grew at 2.1 per cent per annum, the tribal population grew at 2.6 per cent per annum and it was the highest in the northeast with 4.6 per cent per annum. This information is very confusing to the extent that it neither considers the inclusion of new communities in the schedule tribe's list nor does it consider international migration in the northeastern region. The very low growth rates (1.5 per cent) among the tribes in the peninsular south and in the Oceanic groups is also not explained very convincingly. Among other reasons, external forces and intelligence agencies too are said to be causing this. How can any convincing analysis treat the tribal peoples of the region as easily prone to manipulation by others? The explanation ought to be more complex. Individual and collective human rights with dignity have been the long-standing urges of humanity. Two different matrices cannot be accommodated together without ever challenging the concepts, theories, and ideologies of the dominant and the subjugated.

## III

The formation of the nation-state led to the denial of diversity of cultures and value systems of the peoples, and the creation of a single standardised pattern. The modernisation syndrome disregarded the heterogeneity of communities and thereby not only threatened their ecological base but also their cultural viability as groups. In brief, the diversity that should have been preserved and valued has been reduced to a near historical memory under world capitalism. The post-colonial nations have emulated not only Western culture and values but have also forced others, especially the marginalised, to be convinced of their intrinsic inferiority. Nonetheless, ironically enough, the theory that every sovereign state is a national society or ought to be a national society has been legitimised in post-colonial societies. That all these states contain different cultural-linguistic groups within their boundaries and that they have a tendency to maintain their distinctiveness is something that has been derecognised. Indeed the 'nation-state remains the exception and not the rule' (Despres 1984: 19). Of course, during the freedom struggle, the aspiration for nation-state formation was considered the prime embodiment of the anti-imperialistic programme and crucial for freedom and equality but this aspiration has remained largely unfulfilled. It may be remembered that often colonial expediency alone without any concern for history, tradition, culture, language, economy and geography, among others, had determined state boundaries. Not only do we find a multiplicity of heterogeneous cultural and linguistic groups within, but there is also considerable cultural contiguity across national frontiers. What separates these contiguous cultural areas is the modern state system. Nonetheless, the post-colonial leadership has uncritically adopted and legitimised the imperatives of a nation-state and emphasised inviolability and security of territory. This empirical predicament is often used as an excuse to repress and persecute the marginalised communities, especially the tribals of the border regions. Their value structures are rejected as obscurantist, whereas those of the dominant communities are imposed upon them, by cajoling and coercing as per the need. The assimilationist policy of nation building has contributed towards the endangering of the collective rights of several tribal communities.

The notion of India as a multi-national federal republic is strongly contradicted by the ruling classes themselves. The overriding concern for nation building and monolithic nationalism has transformed itself into an intolerance of plurality. The off-repeated 'unity in diversity' should have at least retained the diversities to create the essence of shared history and positive values. Instead, there are increasing attacks on other religious groups, converted tribals and others, reflecting a perilous centralising trend of Indian reality. There are forces which enjoy powerful official support and which have been aggressively equating Hindu chauvinistic ideology with Indian nationalism.

In the 'interest' of the nation-state, the tribals have been deprived of much of their land and land-based resources, their livelihood has been ruptured and their language, religion and culture severely impaired and stigmatised. The theories of internal colonialism and the Fourth World are being increasingly articulated to comprehend the tribal peoples' relation with the modern state. It is not only global capitalism and its epistemology but also the national cultural policy of assimilation that has devastated tribal cultures, languages and their collectivities. They are made to think that they are inferior in matters of their own lifestyle, customs and folklore. Myths have been nurtured that tribal social formations are archaic hangovers, remnants of a bygone era, unchanging entities paralysed by custom and thus their ways of life should be raised to the advanced cultural life enjoyed by the 'national society'. In order to maintain national integration, their identities must be replaced by loyalty to the 'national mainstream' or at least made compatible with national interests.

The threatened socio-cultural tribal collectivities face a formidable challenge from the dominant religion, culture and language. And sadly, they receive little protection from the state system, which has recently abandoned its role as an impartial arbiter for the citizens and instead become, often, a party to aggression. Only one of the Austro-Asiatic or Sino-Tibetan linguistic groups, namely, Manipuri, has been recognised by the Indian state. A few northeastern tribes have been granted statehood after a prolonged and protracted struggle but many are still struggling for some administrative and political autonomy. These are perfectly legitimate movements with aspirations that remain within the framework of the Indian Constitution.

Faced with continuous pauperisation and endangering of linguistic and cultural identity, several of the tribal peoples across the country have independently launched struggles of various types directed towards recuperating their traditional rights over their resources and in order to maintain and develop their legitimate cultural, social, linguistic and political rights, as well as to demand a cessation of abuse and discrimination. This is not parochialisation of social consciousness but the outcome of long years of neglect, discrimination and misunderstanding. Their movements are, however, brutally repressed in the name of secession or diabolical international conspiracy. Yet many of their movements do survive and are recurrent. The strategies of divide and rule, distribution of patronage, cooptation, mediation structures, intimidation, illegal and arbitrary detention, mass population removals, concentration camps, torture and fake encounters have yielded small dividends.

The resolution of the crisis demands a simultaneous struggle against economic and cultural domination. The principle of internal self-determination should be the guide in setting up the standards for control over their own economic, social and cultural development. This is neither autarchy nor anthropological romanticism. Rather, it provides for the removal of certain traditional customs and practices, after proper evaluation; but the overall choice of adjusting with the larger society should be left to the tribes themselves. Internal self-determination does not mean secession but redefining the composite multi-cultural fabric of society and the nature of nation building. The right to enjoy as much control as possible over their own economic organisation and socio-cultural development would be an effort at conflict-resolution in multi-national societies on the one hand and could form a front against cultural imperialism. Being an integral part of decolonisation and democratisation, it assumes that both tribal and class identity are socially integrating principles of development. Stavenhagen calls this strategy ethno-development/self-development, wherein the ethnic group 'retains control over it's own land, resources, social organisation and culture and is free to negotiate with the state the kind of relationship it wishes to have' (1987: 74-78). Considering the enormous problems created by the technocratic models of development, globalisation and nation-state, this appears promising, although the details need to be worked out.

As a postscript, it needs to be said that though the tribal peoples of India, like their brethren elsewhere, have been traumatised by deculturation, cooption and negative identity, they have largely managed to preserve their positive identity, and their values of kinship, institutional reciprocity, shared history, territorial occupancy and are discovering their own philosophical and cultural uniqueness and potentialities. They are increasingly forming inter-tribal unity and consciousness, undermining the internal structuration and divisions, and may thus legitimately allow for greater autonomy within the so-called nation-state system. The principle then ought to be internal self-determination, including legal recognition of all tribal organisations, respect of customary rights on survival resources and their own practices and which do not clash with the accepted standards of human rights. Simultaneously, all development strategies must be fired by informed consent, self-sufficiency, social justice and ecological equilibrium.

It is high time we acknowledge that the traditional tribal cultures and knowledge systems have much to offer to this imperilled planet; and hence, internal self-determination and ethno or self-development cannot be separated from the collective rights of peoples in diverse regions as well as different countries with cultural contiguity. This could be the beginning of the process of emancipation of the tribal peoples and thus of others also. The detailed contours however need to be worked out in individual regions, cultural complexes and states. Meanwhile, maybe the Sixth Schedule of the Indian Constitution in its original form and even the provisions of the Panchayats (Extension to the Scheduled Areas) Act, 1996, could form the preliminary basis for working out the principle of internal self-determination and ethno-development.

## References

Anderson, Benedict. 1983. *Imagined communities: Reflections on the origin and spread of nationalism*. London: Verso.

Despres, L.A. 1984. 'Ethnicity: What data and theory portend for plural societies', in David Maybury-Lewis (ed.). *The prospects for plural societies.* Washington: American Anthropological Society.

Godelier, Maurice. 1977. *Perspectives in Marxist anthropology*. Cambridge: Cambridge University Press.

Kosambi, D.D. 1965. *The culture and civilisation of ancient India in historical outline*. London: Routledge and Kegan Paul.

Moore, S.F. 1987. 'Cultural pluralism and national cohesion', *Sociological Bulletin*, 36(2): 35-59.

Raza, Moonis and A. Ahmed. 1990. *An atlas of tribal India.* New Delhi: Concept Publication Co.

Roy Burman, B.K. 1994. *Tribes in perspective.* New Delhi: Mittal Publications.

Stavenhagen, Rodolfo. 1987. 'Ethnocide or ethnodevelopment', *Development: Seeds of change*, 1: 74-78.

Tonn, B.E. and David Feldman. 1995. 'Non spatial government', *Futures*, 27(1).

Williams, Raymond. 1983. *Towards 2000.* London: Chatto and Windus.

# 7

# Gender in the Making of the Indian Nation-State

*Maitrayee Chaudhuri*

## Introduction

I attempt here a very broad mapping of the manner in which women have been addressed in both the making of the Indian nation and in the running of the Indian state. As I understand it, there are three major ways that the national movement first and the Indian state later imagined the role of women. These are: (a) women as agents and recipients of development; (b) women's political participation in the nation as equal citizens of a state that does not discriminate on grounds of gender; (c) women as emblems of 'national culture'. These three facets of women's location within 'nationalism' and 'nation building' reflect three aspects of the 'national movement 'which were 'germane to the making of the Indian nation'. *One*, it was based on 'a well-developed critique of colonialism in its economic aspects and on an economic programme leading to independent economic development' (Chandra1999: 17). Economic self- reliance, sovereignty, growth with equity were part of the very identity of Indian nationalism. *Two*, the movement was committed to political democracy and civil liberties which were seen as building blocs of nation-making (Chandra: ibid). Political participation of women both in the national movement and then in the running of the independent state were therefore important. *Three*, Indian nationalism was also a cultural critique of colonialism and an assertion of 'national culture'. In this assertion the image of 'Indian womanhood' was significant

As one committed to the view that history is a determining influence in shaping the parameters within which we imagine and practice, I return to the past many times in the course of this paper, including the section on conceptual clarifications. The past is however very generally invoked, both within academic and popular writings, when narrating the story of the status of Indian women. Indeed the need for a historical past is an inextricable part of modern nationalist consciousness. The nation, itself a modernist enterprise however has to summon a legacy stretching to an ancient, time-immemorial past. The story of the Indian woman can therefore only begin with a customary reference to her high status in the

Vedic period. The contentiousness of such a project has been increasingly questioned (Chakravarti:1989) and I for my part am happier to locate myself in the colonial past as the starting point of India's journey to modernity, to state, nation and the woman citizen.

My reasons for doing so are not very complex. India entered modernity and capitalism through colonialism. Nationalism and the modern states, which are posited as nation states, are essentially modern. Likewise the women's question has to be understood as part of the modern democratic project. But liberal democracy's relationship with the question of rights of women was never simple. Thus while equal rights necessarily meant rights of all, men and women, it was not unusual to define citizenship as exclusive of both women and the dispossessed. On the other hand, modernity, with the corollary processes of capitalism and the refashioning of households and families meant that women were recast as creatures of domesticity and to be a housewife came to represent once more both a full time and natural vocation. It was also part of the 19th century package of ideas that claimed that the status of a nation ought to be gauged by the status of women. Indians were thus berated for their inability to attain heights as a nation because of the pitiable condition of their womenkind. Indian social reformers responded to this challenge and we had a major recasting of women in modern India. In this recasting we had a construction of middle class domesticity, much in the line of Victorian England, that defined the normative Indian woman as gentle, refined and skilled in running a 'home'. We also had a simultaneous assertion of the virtues of an ancient Hindu past and culture. With the intensification of the national movement however new ideas of socialism, of equality and development also gained ground. The actual entry of women into political action altered the parameters of imagining women's role in the nation. And at the same time the issue of cultural pride for a colonised society continued to be of great importance. It is only correct therefore to locate the making of both the nation and the women's question in this complex crucible of the colonial encounter. For therein lay the seed of much of the discord that marked contending ideas of women as democratic citizens and women as markers of culture, or women as dependent housewives and women as independent workers.

### State, Nation and Women

Perhaps a few conceptual remarks about the modern *state*, about nationalism and women may not be out of order here. I attempt below to etch (with a very broad brush): i) the ambiguous relationship between the liberal state and women; ii) the specificity of women's role in the nation; and iii) the historical legacy of colonialism.

### Women and the liberal state

The state is not a unified entity. It is a multi-dimensional phenomenon, the nature of which varies across time and space. Here our concern is with the *modern liberal state* with its legally circumscribed structure of power with supreme jurisdiction over a territory. Such a view may find echoes in ancient texts but clearly could not prevail while political rights, obligations and duties were closely tied to property rights and religious tradition. Similarly, the idea that human beings as 'individuals' or as 'a people' could be active citizens of this order–citizens of their state–and not merely dutiful subjects of a monarch or emperor could only develop in modern conditions.

I proceed with Held's definition of liberalism as an effort to delineate 'a private sphere independent of the state and thus to redefine the state itself, i.e., the freeing of civil society–personal, family and business life–from political interference and the simultaneous delimitation of the state's authority' (Held 1984:3). Liberalism was about a world of 'free and equal' individuals with natural rights. Politics came to be understood as the defence of the rights of these individuals. And the mechanisms for regulating these individuals' pursuit of their interests were to be the constitutional state, private property, the competitive market economy–and for us here the most important–the distinctively patriarchal family.

While liberalism celebrated the rights of individuals to 'life, liberty and property', it was the male property-owning individual who was the focus of attention. The liberal state by definition had an uneasy relationship with women 'individuals'. While the West granted universal franchise only after bitter battles, in India where a more critical understanding of liberalism was part of a nationalist discourse the tension persisted. I have shown elsewhere that eventually even in the 1938 Plan Document where 'near communists' were members, the rights 'to hold, acquire, inherit and dispose of property' won over the view voicing the rights of working class women as 'instruments of labour' (Chaudhuri 1996: 227-29). More significantly however, the rights of bourgeois women as independent individuals was itself challenged on the basis of customary practices. We witness this in the incredible opposition to the Hindu Code Bill after independence, where it was opposed tooth and nail on the grounds that the very fabric of the Hindu society would collapse (ibid. 1993: 182-92). We witness this in the debates over the first Plan Document expressed in the view that the 'State should follow a policy to assure women the same rights as men' but without 'prejudice to Muslim personal law' (ibid. 1996). And we see this in the conflicts between the Church and women's rights (Roy 1991).

The problem is not just attitudinal but one bolstered both by structures[1] and theoretical legacy. Theoretically, within liberalism women were not easily accepted as citizens. Rousseau excluded all women from 'the people', that is, the citizenry, as well as the poor. For citizenship is made conditional upon a small property qualification and/ or upon the absence of dependency on others (Held 1984:23). Wollstonecraft (1975) thus wrote:

> But to render her really virtuous and useful, (woman) must not, if she discharge her civil duties, want individually the protection of civil laws; she must not depend upon her husband's bounty for her subsistence during his life, or support after his death; for how can a being be generous who has nothing of its own/ or virtuous who is not free ...?

Structurally the family and the community mediates between the 'individual woman' and the state. An inevitable gap therefore exists between the liberal state's commitment to gender equality on the one hand and to a patriarchal family, male property rights and free market on the other.

**Nation, nationalism and women**

Scholars have repeatedly warned us of the dangers of conflating state and nation (Oommen 1997:13). Modern states however continue to posit themselves as 'nation states' irrespective of the fact that there could be more than one 'nation' encompassed in them or that there would be members of the same 'nation' under the rubric of another state. The desire for cultural recognition and identity–hallmarks of modern nationalism–has a tendency to get mixed up with the right to have a state to practice one's cultural distinctiveness and also be equal in a world of 'nation states'. This conflation of terms is precisely the manner in which the curious entity, the 'nation state' operates. Anderson (1983) had emphasised the misplaced nature of studying nationalism in political theory when we ought to really address it as a package with family, kinship and marriage. But herein lies the tension between the coupling of the modern, bureaucratic, rationalised state and the passion of a nationalism that can both kill and get killed in the glory of the nation.[2] One can rightly speak, as Anderson does, of 'political love', a love that retains the fraternal dimensions of medieval caritas but incorporates as well a maternalised loyalty symbolised domestically; *the nation is home and home is mother* (Anderson 1983, emphasis mine).

Hence it is not surprising that Rousseau who, we saw a little earlier, had no place for women as citizens, eulogises the Spartan mothers. Rousseau repeats Plutarch's 'Sayings of Spartan Mothers' reproducing tales, anecdotes and epigrams of the Spartan woman as a mother who reared her sons to be sacrificed on the altar of civic necessity (Elshtain 1991:546-47). The Spartans, models for later civic republicans and early modern state builders, honoured but two identities with inscriptions on tombstones–men who had died in war and women who had succumbed in childbirth: both embodying the sacrificial moment of civic identity (ibid: 549-50).

This theme of *women and sacrifice for the nation* is woven into the body of Indian nationalist thought. For the militant nationalists, India herself became the mother, at whose altar men and women were sacrificed. More often they were called upon to play a very special role as mothers and daughters of the nation. Gandhi's views resonate with this idea. Gandhi states that 'woman…(is)… mother to the Nation…' (1917).

> The economic and the moral salvation of India thus rests mainly with you. The future of India lies on your knees, for *you will nurture the future generation*… The destiny of India is far safer in your hands of a government that has so exploited India's resources that she has lost faith in herself (ibid. 1921, emphasis mine)

Drawing from different historical experiences, Yuval-Davis and Anthias (1989) sum up the ways in which women have tended to participate in ethnic and national processes and in relation to state practices. These are: (a) as biological reproducers of members of ethnic collectivities; (b) as reproducers of the boundaries of the ethnic/national groups; (c) as participating centrally in the ideological reproduction of the collectivity and as transmitters of its culture; (d) as signifiers of ethnic/national differences–as a focus and symbol in ideological discourses used in the construction, reproduction and transformation of ethnic/national categories; (e) as participants in national, economic, political and military struggles.

In practice these would tend to blur into each other. The above propositions do hold true for India. But I would like to contend that the specificity of an anti-imperialist nationalism also brought questions of political participation and development centre-stage to the women's question. At the same time I would argue that the inherent contradictions of a liberal state–wedded to equality on the one hand and patriarchal private property on the other, to individual rights of women on the one hand and to rights of 'cultural and 'religious' practices on the other– inevitability led to a bind that this paper looks into. To repeat, I seek to analyse these within the three axes on which I see the women's question defined in the Indian context. They are: i) women as agents and recipients of development; ii) women as politically equal citizens; and iii) women as cultural emblems of the nation.

**Legacies of the colonial encounter**

Generations have studied the 19th century reform movements as simple straightforward measures to do away with sundry social evils like sati and child marriage. The last fifteen years have witnessed a plethora of literature in this field belying any such notion and foregrounding both the complexity and ambiguity of the processes. Central to this problematising of social reform was exploring the far-reaching implications of the fact that the early initiatives on the women's question had been taken largely by men; that the reformers belonged mostly to the upper castes; and that the specific problems addressed and the mode of addressing were very often restricted by region and caste location. A more dramatic instance of how these researches have made us rethink issues is the case of the Widow Remarriage Act which legally allowed upper caste widows to remarry, but simultaneously through codification of laws obliterated the rights lower caste widows had traditionally availed of under their customary laws (Chaudhuri 1993: 31-38). This move towards increased homogenisation and *construction of a monolithic image and practice of Indian womanhood* persists to this day.

The other process initiated was the reinterpretation of 'Indian culture' and the special role within it for 'Indian women'. In this cultural regeneration are embedded complex ideas of what constitutes culture. Cultural practices often chosen as embematic of community identity pertain to women's mobility, control of sexuality, for example, child marriage, purdah, sati, the social death of widows. But if *women are icons of Indian culture*, the contentious question in a plural society like India is which of its women and which of its cultures ought to become the 'national' icon. And one of the most vexing issues of modern India has been fought over the *rights of community identity versus rights of women and rights of the state*.

While the concerns of the 19th century reform movement left their mark on the women's question it is important to emphasise that with the intensification of the national movement and the spread of *internationalist ideas of socialism and democracy,* the women's question could not be contained within the restrictive parameters of one or other reformer. Women within women's organisations like the All-India

Women's Conference and women within the national movement insisted on greater political and economic participation. The legacy of women revolutionaries, trade union activists, underground nationalists is as much part of the historical legacy that the independent Indian state inherited. Unfortunately however the persistent tendency of much of modern theory to dehistoricise the private sphere, celebrating male entry into the public sphere and condemning women to remain in the 'timeless universe' of domesticity and doomed to repeat the cycles of life' (Benhabib 1987: 86) seems to have had the final say after India's independence.

## Women as Agents and Recipients of Development

Economic critiques of colonialism were a key component of Indian nationalism. With independence the state's commitment to the nation was expressed in the pledge to development. Much before India actually attained independence serious thought was given to the question of development. The Indian National Congress constituted the National Planning Committee (NPC) in 1938 to chalk out blueprints for independent India's development. One of the 29 sub- committees formed was on 'Women's Role in Planned Economy' (WRPE). The formation of the NPC clearly expressed the intention of the Congress to adopt planning as the most effective means for the comprehensive economic development of the new nation. The WRPE is truly remarkable for both the details it has on the status of women of that time as well its breadth of interest and concern (Chaudhuri 1996:211-235). I quote at length its stated objective particularly to contrast it with the amazing fact that women and development disappeared from the first 'five' Five-Year Plans in an era where planning was the major issue.

> This Sub-Committee will deal with the place of women in the planned economy of India, including consideration of her social, economic and legal status, her right to hold property, carry on any trade, profession or occupation and remove all obstacles or handicaps in the way of an equal status and opportunity for women. In particular it will confine itself to: a) the family life and organisation, and women's employment in the house and the changes therein in recent years; b) marriage and succession and the laws governing these; c) the condition of industrial employment of women and the protection of working women in mines, factories, plantations, workshops and cottage industries as well as domestic employment and retail trade; d) social customs and institutions

which preclude women from taking her full share in India's planned economy; e) the types and methods of appropriate education to play her due role in household work, in the professions and social and national services; and f) any other questions connected therewith.

The WRPE, I have argued elsewhere (ibid), clearly shows the imprint of the ideas of liberalism and socialism. The socialist argument that the emancipation of women becomes possible only when women are enabled to take part in production on a large scale, and when domestic duties require their attention only to a minor degree, comes across sharply in the document. What also comes through and far more effectively is the liberal thrust on 'the free and full development of woman's personality' so that the individual can 'contribute to national progress'. The WRPE's state-centric vision moves far ahead of its time by acknowledging the 'home work' done within the house as well as by arguing for recognition of women's labour as a 'separate unit of production' and not as 'a corporate part of the family work'. The intent of the state to ensure property rights for women and enable her to carry on trade and other occupations equally reflects an understanding of women as independent economic individuals. As I glean through independent Indian state's formulations, the reader will be struck by the disappearance, not marginalisation of these issues

What has baffled scholars is the complete turnabout in the manner women were understood in the development paradigm once India attained independence and once planning really began. Indeed women virtually disappeared from the idiom of development, even work, and entered wholly the world of welfare. The Central Social Welfare Board was established by the government in 1953 with a nation-wide programme of grants-in-aid for promoting welfare and development services for women and children. The Planning Commission's Plans and Prospects for Social Welfare in India, 1951-61, spells out social welfare services as intending to cater to the special needs of persons and groups who by reason of some handicap–social, economic, physical or mental–are unable to avail of, or are traditionally denied, the amenities and services provided by the community. Thus women were considered to be handicapped by social customs and values and social welfare services were thought of to rehabilitate them. This is a far cry from the systematic analysis of marriage and family, rights to property and rights at work which marked India's first plan document–the WRPE.

The break with the past seems absolute. A new, fresh beginning takes place with distinct ideological moorings. The analysis shifted from addressing questions of systemic powerlessness to behavioral issues to be addressed by training. The origin of the women's programme has to be now studied within the context of the overall rural development programme, known as the Community Development Programme (CDP). The CDP was formulated soon after independence in 1952 with the help of American aid. The objectives of CDP were essentially two-fold: material and psychological betterment of villages. Material improvement was to be brought about through government aid (financial and technical) for agricultural development. The government also planned to provide the villagers welfare services such as educational, recreational and health facilities wherever possible. The psychological aspect concerned the creation of community consciousness among villagers so that they became aware of their own needs and responsibilities. But this programme with its main focus on agriculture, had nothing to offer to those who were not large agriculturists.

Women were integrated into this programme almost as an afterthought, when it was realised that the lack of participation of women in the programme was responsible to a considerable extent for the programme not making the desirable impact. Later when they introduced the women component in the rural development programme it was designed after the Home Science Extension programme. In this programme women were taught some practical skills aimed at making them better housewives and using their time more fruitfully. Mahila Mandals in the rural areas were visualised as the catalysts for such development. Accordingly, in the belief that better home-making skills would improve the living standards, the government devised the Mahila Mandal scheme in 1954 to integrate women into the CDP. Needless to say this programme did not merit any success because of its sheer irrelevance to the needs of the rural masses.

After the CDPs receded into the background, the focus of policy regarding women throughout the period of the Second to the Fifth Plans (1955-86) was welfare. (Government of India 1995: 24-30) Health and family planning concerns about women found explicit expression. In the Third Plan period we have the Applied Nutrition Programme (ANP) with the objectives of imparting nutrition education to mothers through demonstration feeding, production programme and training of women functionaries. Similar measures persisted until the time when the Sixth Five-Year Plan (1980-85) was being drafted, and a group of national women's organisations demanded that the strategies recommended by these working groups needed incorporation in the Five-Year Plan. The Planning Commission responded by including for the first time a chapter on Women and Development in the plan document. Simultaneously, the commission initiated a discussion on science and technology in development and the Ministry of Social Welfare appointed a Working Group for this purpose. Reviewing the outcome of these policy debates in its Report to the United Nations in 1985, the government of India noted that the major result was:

> A shift in recognition–from viewing women as targets of welfare policies in the social sector to their emergence as critical groups for development...This shift represents reassertion of the principle of women's equality of rights–to participate effectively in the process of development, ensuring thereby movement in the direction of the Constitutional goals. It is also a reassertion of an ideology enunciated by the Father of the nation that the future of India cannot be built without the willing and conscious participation of one half of its population–women...(GOI 1985: 6).

What is of significance here is that the tone is not of a new beginning but a return to the constitutional goals and commitments of the 'Father of the nation'. But even here the first plan document goes unmentioned. In 1995 the government brought out yet another document 'Towards Empowering Women' in response to the felt need of many 'in the context of the Fourth World Conference on Women at Beijing'. The document has little except a listing of women-specific and women-related initiatives towards 'empowering women'. It has little to say on poverty and exploitation but has pages of tables indicating projects sanctioned and the number of women benefited.

At one level the concept of empowerment could be read as in continuity with earlier discourses of economic rights and political participation. On closer scrutiny this is the buzz word of international aid agencies who have over the last decade appropriated 'the past years of research, activism and government action in India' (John 1996: 3074). As John has sought to show that 'as the "agency discourses" have been saying for some time now, the informal sector is at the heart of the market economy and represents its prime model. In their view, although "restrictive" third wold state regulations are responsible for the growth of the informal sector in the first place, it is nonetheless here that high productivity is possible with low capital costs' (ibid). This is of defining importance at a time when the Indian state is in a process of liberalising the economy, initiating and implementing structural adjustments and speaking of empowering the poor. What is also to be noted is that production is no longer definitive for national identity. I have argued elsewhere that consumption perhaps is (Chaudhuri 1999).

It is not as though the Indian state is oblivious of the implications of liberalisation. The Country Report 1995 has an entire section on the macro-economic policies and their impact on women (GOI 1995: 54-57). While fearing that the new economic policies may lead to an increase in employment, with 'women bearing a disproportionate share of the brunt', it ends with the remark that the 'feminisation of "work" that may be a consequence of the policies may, therefore, throw up both challenges and opportunities' (ibid.54-55). The aid agency discourses and increasingly the state discourse however shifts away from macro-economic policies to micro-interventions for 'empowering' of women.

There are two points that I wish to underscore. *One* is the gap between the state's intent to address women as workers and contributors to national production and the unfailing lapse into a more powerful discourse of women as passive recipients of welfare and of women as dependent members in male-headed households. *Two* is the fact that with liberalisation, and the exit of the socialist bloc, we have entered a new world where aid donors like the World Bank committed to entry of global capital also appropriate the findings of the women's movement and women's studies to argue that poor women are 'more efficient economic actors' with 'greater managerial and entrepreneurial skills than men'. Therefore what they need is credit and social services, not 'the conditions of employment that obtain in the formal sector, which would stifle productivity' (John 1996: 3074). Though recent government reports seek to connect the new discourse of empowerment—political or economic, to the legacy of nationalism, it is important to demonstrate that the two are not linked.

## Women as Politically Equal Citizens

That nationalist leaders desired women's political participation[3] and that women participated in the national movement are accepted facts.[4] Less accepted is any consensus as what exactly did political participation mean for the women and for the nationalist leaders. One view would argue that 'even the most cursory examination of women's organised activism from the beginning of the twentieth century explodes the myth still being pursued by many, that women's role in the national movement(s) against imperialism was male-dictated and male-manipulated (Kasturi and Mazumdar 1994:16). The other, as Mies points out, is:

> To draw women into the political struggle is a tactical necessity of any anti-colonial or national liberation struggle. But it depends on the strategic goals of such a movement whether the patriarchal family is

> protected as the basic social unit or not. The fact that the women themselves accepted their limited tactical function within the independence movement made them excellent instruments in the struggle. But they did not work out a strategy for their own liberation struggle for their own interests. By subordinating these goals to the national cause they conformed to the traditional *pativrata* or *sati* ideal of the self-sacrificing woman (1980: 121).

Other scholars like Gail Minault and Geraldine Forbes argue that the concept of the extended family in Indian culture[5] could extend virtually indefinitely and be used to justify women's concerns beyond the kin group. The metaphor of the extended family certainly assisted middle class women's performance of some public roles through their associations (Minault 1982: 220-21).

While at one time an uncritical lauding of women's political participation in the national movement was common, more recent views have veered around the belief that women's political participation 'gave the illusion of change while women were kept within the structural confines of family and society' (Jayawardena 1986:107). Partha Chatterjee has further blurred boundaries between the 19th century Bengal reform movement and the political activism of women at an all India level in the 20th century to pronounce what he calls the nationalist resolution of the women's question. The argument is that by separating the colonial, material, public world from the indigenous, spiritual, private world the nationalists defined what the parameters of women's change ought to be.

I would contend that active political participation often challenges the boundaries of intended models. And I would not see the question of political participation of women only from the confines of a set of reform ideas. Indian women also had a history of militant participation in political struggles–in working class strikes, in peasant rebellions, in anti-imperialist and democratic movements for a long time. It was simply not ideas (important as they were) which led to the Congress adopting the Fundamental Rights Resolution in 1931.[6]

As in the case of development, women's political rights were not seriously addressed in independent India's state discourse where women were primarily understood as recipients of welfare as wives, mothers and daughters. The state documents themselves accept that 'while women have often been in the forefront in mass movements, their presence has not been felt strongly in structured decision-making and institutions' (GOI 1995: 67). The reason they argue is that 'working in a predominantly patriarchal structure with no gender sensitivity has made it difficult to bring about real and sustained changes for women' (ibid). No further explanation is given about what gender sensitisation may mean but we are left with the feeling that state policy debates have left the kind of interrogation of structures, evident in the first plan document in favour of a discourse on attitudinal changes.

The failure of the state not surprisingly led to a resurgence of the women's movement in the seventies along with wide-ranging left and democratic movements. The state was confronted with the questions that the women's movements were raising, to name but a few: land rights; the gender-blinded nature of development; political representation; laws pertaining to divorce, custody, guardianship or sexual harassment at work; about alcohol, dowry and rape. The women's movement in turn interrogated their own relationship to the state. While on the one hand women, particularly poor women faced the violent edge of the state, it is the state from which the women's movement sought ameliorative intervention.

A decade after the upsurge of democratic and radical movements, the state, it is important to recall opted for economic liberalisation in the late eighties with the concomitant presence and pressures of international aid agencies in the country. Today we are in times where two parallel processes are underway. On the one hand international financial organisations, the Indian state and Western states herald India's entry into the global market, encourage withdrawal of the state from 'welfare' activities. On the other the same set of actors promote economic and political empowerment of the grassroots women. Economically this implies, as we saw in the last section, valorisation of the poor women's efficiency and a championing of the informal sector as the heart of the market economy. Politically , I would go along with the view that transnational capital supports the idea of 'low intensity democracy' or 'polyarchy' with the idea of legitmising internal orders which favour foreign investment and provide stable social and political conditions for its operation (Chimni 1999: 342).

The Indian government has projected the new economic policies as representing a consensus, above 'politics'. Along with the stress on production a commitment to what is called 'empowerment' of the people is reiterated. We can look at the 73rd and 74th constitution amendment acts of 1993 ensuring one-third of total seats for women in all elected offices of local bodies in rural and urban areas in this light. The 1995 Country Report thus states, 'Women have thus been brought to the centre-stage in the nation's efforts to strengthen democratic institutions' (GOI 1995). State documents suggest that at last we are going back to the constitutional pledges of political rights irrespective of caste, creed and gender. I am sceptical of the intent and would go along with Mohanty's argument that 'empowerment, civil society and democratisation form the new package of liberalisation discourse which on their face value respond to the long-standing demands of struggling groups' (Mohanty 1995). At the same time it would be spurious to dismiss the significance of these measures. That these are not empty gestures is evident by the fact that the promise to legislate 33 per cent reservation for women in Parliament has been repeatedly scuttled.

Recent years have seen abortive efforts to introduce what has come to be known as the Reservation Bill for women. That women are not adequately represented in the Parliament is widely accepted In the 12th Lok Sabha, out of 547 members of the Lok Sabha only 32 were women. It has been observed that as long as the promise of 33 per cent reservation 'remained in the realm of pious hope and pontification', there was 'uniform goodwill towards women and their cause' (Natarajan 1996). In parliamentary circles, the main opposition to the bill came from those who demanded sub-reservation for the OBC women within the 33 per cent quota. Critics[7] have wondered what 'these champions of the OBC had been doing these 50 years long...?' (ibid). The other views opposing it were that: one, 'women were not yet ready for political office' and they have to be 'sensitised and educated' and two, that 'reservation for women will lead to the perpetuation of dynastic politics'. In a political clime where a large number of male members in both the Parliament and legislatures are 'charged in cases ranging from murder and dacoity to rape and economic offences' (ibid) and where nepotism is widespread, both criticisms sound hollow. That the bill was unsuccessfully sought to be introduced after 1996 only shows a very concerted attempt to oppose it.

There is a strong tendency to project a view that political space for women in India in the past was granted to women without resistance. Debates on women's suffrage in colonial Bengal, which I draw upon only as one illustrative evidence, suggest otherwise. Opposition to a woman's right to vote were made on various grounds. One, that since 'she is quite unfit for defence and administration of a country, franchise cannot be her birthright' (Southard 1995:100). Two, that it would lead to 'discontent with domestic duties and neglect of husband and children, "even during illness", that "politics and other brainworks"' (sic) would make women 'unable to breastfeed her children' (ibid:101). It was the active intervention and struggle of women's organisations that got women their right to vote. Today too political participation of women is a contested terrain between a hesitant state, double-faced political parties, international aid agencies and growing womens' movements.

## Women as Cultural Emblems

This paper is premised on the assumption that notwithstanding the liberal 'nation state's' pledge for women's political and economic participation in the nation, women continue to be seen primarily as biological reproducers of members of nations and as cultural reproducers of national/ethnic boundaries. If *'the nation is home and home is mother'* women cannot but be signifiers of ethnic/national differences. They participate centrally in the ideological reproduction of the collectivity and as transmitters of its culture. It is in a discourse on 'national culture' that women therefore are most often and most 'naturally' referred to. Most 'naturally' for the middle class who dominated the 'national' debate, women's economic participation was cognitively invisible and political participation was alien. Women's role in the 'home' was natural. And we know the etiology of common sense is central to hegemony.

It is well documented that both the 'home' and the 'Indian woman' which were being eulogised as eternal were specific to a particular historical moment and marked a definite break from the past. Indeed the 19th century reformers and nationalists alike wanted to liberate the upper caste women from her world of superstition and ignorance. An audience of educated men was thus asked whether they did not feel in their daily lives that their mothers and wives were 'great impediments' in the way of their own intellectual and moral improvement (Chaudhuri 1993: 470). Reformers thus wanted to devise a system of education for females that would 'enable the wife to serve as a solace to her husband in his bright and dark moments ... to superintend the early instruction of her child, and the lady of the house to provide those sweet social comfort, idealised in the English word–Home' (ibid). This 'home' is therefore new but 'homes' like 'nations' appear as natural entities with a history that extends to a past that is 'time immemorial'. This process also happily coincides with what I have referred to earlier as the persistent tendency of much of modern theory to dehistoricise the private sphere,... condemning women to remain in the 'timeless universe' of domesticity...(Benhabib 1987: 86).

Thus while the economic and political spheres are 'alien' spaces women have to enter, the 'home' is the 'natural' realm where women already exist. Western feminists have claimed that in the Western world women have been seen as nature and men as culture. In India we know women are represented as cultural emblems. But what I want to argue further is that this 'culture' is at once 'nature' in the sense that like the 'family', the 'home' and 'women', 'culture' here evokes a past beyond history. It is primordial and thus inspires a passion that 'development' and 'political participation' can only be envious of.

Culture and nation are thus seen as natural. On the other hand culture in the modern nation state can really be understood as a 'garden' culture, not wild and therefore not natural. While wild culture like wild nature can grow unattended and still look beautiful, artificial gardens can be left unattended only to be destroyed. Likewise modern 'national culture(s)' are thought out entities which are administered under the specialised services of the state. Debates on cultural policies within Indian nationalism and nation building was important. Defining what constitutes 'national culture' however was a contentious project from the very start. Both the trends towards a hegemonic, homogenous Hindu upper caste notion of culture as well as a well articulated idea of a 'composite culture' with the far-sighted slogan of 'unity and diversity' fought itself through the trajectory of Indian nationalism and the doings of the Indian state. For women it implied once too often a conflict between women's rights as equal citizens and a community's rights to cultural practices which hinged upon gender discriminatory practices be it sati, *purdah*, child marriage or denial of inheritance rights or polygamy.

Even in the national and women's movement in the colonial period fissures had clearly cropped up between the promise of political and economic equality of women and equality for cultural practices that more often than not were discriminatory to women. Amrit Kaur and Hansa Mehta had objected to the guarantee of religious propaganda and practice. They felt that the term 'propagation' and 'practice' might invalidate future legislation prohibiting child marriage, polygamy, unequal inheritance laws and untouchability as these customs could be construed part of religious worship. Kaur suggested that freedom of religion be limited to religious worship (Chaudhuri 1993:185).

I have been arguing that culture is perceived as 'natural' but is a very artificial construct in the modern state. Groups who have power seek to shape the content of 'national' culture' In a culturally diverse society like India, in a clime where women came to represent 'culture', community leaders actively defined what constituted authentic cultural practices of a community. It has been argued that the women's question itself became a site for defining what tradition is. Women's political activism sought to question this as we saw in Amrit Kaur's attempts. But that the opposition to this was strong is evident from the fact that her views did not have the final say. Today we thus have a Constitution with Article 15 which deals with the Right to Equality. But the Constitution also contains articles dealing with other categories of rights, like the Right to Freedom of Religion, as embodied in Articles 25-28. And the question can be asked:

'Can a State which proclaims opposition to discrimination based on sex... permit religious personal laws, which affect the life of women in a basic manner?' (Desai: 1994).

Almost sixty years later the fears of India's early feminists have come true. Worse still, today the state's secular credentials are so weak that there is almost all-round consensus that the Uniform Code Bill is best kept away. The demand for a uniform civil code has been appropriated by the Bharatiya Janata Party. It is important to recall today therefore that the stiffest opposition to the Hindu Code Bill came from the then Hindu Mahasabha. One of its leading members, Chatterjee, had argued that the act would encourage the conversion of Hindus to Islam And Amrit Kaur lamented that ' "religion" in danger is a very potent caveat which scares even seemingly intelligent persons...' (Chaudhuri 1993:190).

Questions of culture, community identity and scriptural sanctions have been very much part of the manner in which the women's question emerged in India. One of the first issues where this comes up is the sati dispute. While the Brahmo Samaj marshalled enormous Shastric evidence to show that sati is not mandatory, the Dharma Sabha pleaded with the British to disallow those who know nothing of their customs and religion to deter them from speaking. Raja Rammohun argued that Manu enjoined a widow to live a life of denial and austerity while the Dharma Sabha petitioned 'that in a question so delicate as the interpretation of our sacred books, and the authority of our religious usages none but Pundits and Brahmins and teachers of holy lives, and known learning ought to be consulted–not men who have neither faith nor care for the memory of their ancestors or their religion' (Chaudhuri 1993: 17-21). The Age of Consent Bill that raged through India at the end of the 19th century asserted the natural and nationalist right of a community to decide when and how to reform, rejecting the right of an alien and unresponsive state to legislate on the private matters of Indians (ibid: 68-74).

While the establishment of an independent state in a way alters the terms of discourse, the problem of differing identification of communities to the state persists. The majority community 'naturally' identifies with the 'nation state' while degrees of discomfort persist with the other communities. That India attained independence with the partitioning of the country and unprecedented killings on 'communal' grounds have marked the discourse of state and communities till date. So far as women are concerned the questions persists: Who decides who speaks legitimately for a 'community'? Who decides what constitutes the 'culture' of a community?

The Shah Bano case dramatically brought all these questions to the fore. On 23 April 1985 the Supreme Court of India passed a judgement granting maintenance to a divorced Muslim woman Shahbano. The court awarded Shahbano maintenance of Rs.179.20 per month from her husband and dismissed the husband's appeal against the award of maintenance. The judgment of the Supreme Court sparked of a nation-wide controversy. The principal argument put forward by conservative Muslim opinion was that the Muslim Personal Law was based on the Shariat, which is divine and immutable. Though sections from the Muslim community defended the judgment the state was more willing to listen to the voice of conservative spokespersons of the community. Shahbano herself was pressurised to such an extent that in an open letter she denounced the Supreme Court judgment:

> …which is apparently in my favour; but since this judgement which is contrary to the Quran and the hadith and is an open interference in Muslim personal law, I, Shahbano, being a Muslim, reject it and dissociate myself from every judgement which is contrary to the Islamic shariat. I am aware of the agony and distress which this judgement has subjected the Muslims of India today (*Radiance* 1985).

The state passed the Muslim Women's Bill and the Hindu communal forces saw this move as an appeasement of the state to the minorities. Significantly, the fact that it was the Muslim women who were at the losing end passed them by. The question that arose is who exactly was the bill seeking to protect–community leaders, divorced husbands or women? (Pathak and Rajan 1986)

It is important to emphasise that the tendency for the conservative leadership of a community to affirm gender discriminatory practices as authentic culture is not confined to the minority community. Soon after the Indian state passed the Muslim Women's Bill an eighteen-year old widow, Roop Kanwar, was burnt alive on her husband's pyre in full view of about 3,000 spectators, 'accompanied by the full panoply of Rajput valour' (Bhasin and Menon 1988:12). Despite the Rajasthan High Court's directives to the state government to prevent the celebration of 'Chunari festival' in honour of Roop Kanwar, it was celebrated. About two lakh people assembled at the Chunri Mahotsava and paid obeisance to the *sati-sthal* (site of the self-immolation). Many leading politicians participated. The women of the Rani Sewa Sangha, a voluntary social movement to preserve India's 'ancient traditions' dressed as brides and marched through the streets of Chandni Chowk, Delhi, to commemorate 'the historic act of self-immolation'. Sati was projected as the highest ideal of female spirituality and renunciation, the highest achievement of *naridharma* and *pativrata*. And it was imbued with the aura of sacrifice associated with Rajput history (Sangari 1998: 26). The sentiments expressed at the sati case were perceived to be in keeping with the 'natural cultural' and 'national' sentiments of the people. The state perceived no threat unlike in the Shah Bano case, widely projected as an instance of a community's disloyalty to the state and nation. Quite clearly women to be cultural emblems of the nation have to conform to a particular culture.

## Conclusion

The kind of synoptic view that this paper has sought to present necessarily falls short of a nuanced understanding. The basic argument that it has sought to put forward is that the Indian state has perceived women primarily at three levels: women as agents and recipients of development, as citizens, and finally as cultural emblems. While India's specific colonial history and national movement have shaped these issues in a particular manner, this paper also believes that some of the basic anomalies which we perceive between what the state says and what it does flow from the very logic of a liberal state. In other words the liberal state is formally committed to the economic, political and cultural rights of individuals. But so far as women 'individuals' are concerned, the state tends to relate to them through the 'family' and 'community as evidenced in all the three cases of development, political participation and culture. This process gets further aggravated in India with its complex legacy of colonial history and embittered community relationships.

This paper has also sought to identify the major shifts in policies of the Indian state and has attempted to understand the implications of the state's liberalisation policies on the women's question–be it development or political participation. The question that may arise is where does 'culture' come in? But as has been argued all along, culture is not something that is added on. It is intrinsic to the imaginings of nations and doings of states. Empirically we know that along with liberalisation we have had heightened ethnic, communal tensions where the issue of women as emblems of culture has meant negation of women's political and economic rights. Theoretically this paper rests on the assumption that the 'nation-state' couples in itself a commitment to a rule-bound order premised on the equality of all individuals (women are equal citizens and economic actors), 'natural' and supreme love for the nation and its culture, where nation is the home (and mother), and on the freedom of the market which is increasingly disinclined to allow for a state to protect the weak and the marginal.

## Notes

1. For details on how inheritance, marriage rules and command over property determine the status of women in South Asia see Agarwal (1994).
2. The recent war at Kargil repeatedly brought images of bereaved women who had lost their sons or husbands in the battlefield.
3. '… unless women of India work side by side with men, there is no salvation for India, salvation in more senses than one. I mean political salvation in the greater sense, and I mean the economic salvation and spiritual salvation also' (Gandhi 1925).
4. 'It was a stirring spectacle, that of tens of thousands of women, who for centuries were chained to the narrow domestic life and whom an authoritarian social system had assigned the position of helots at home, stepping out into the streets and marching with their fellow-patriots in illegal political demonstrations' (A.R. Desai 1994: 346).
5. As I write and elections to the Lok Sabha heat up, we have BJP pitting Sushma Swaraj as the 'desi beti' against Sonia Gandhi, the 'videshi bahu' who asserts her claim to the nation through her marriage, children and widowhood.
6. Significantly, the Lahore Congress of Asian Women for Equality, the Geneva International Conference on Women's Equality and the Congress of the Chinese Communist Party adopted a resolution on gender equality in the same year.
7. That the Lok Sabha in 1996 had some 169 OBC men (in the unreserved category) and no women finds no mention in the whole debate (*Sunday*, 1-7 June 1997).

## References

Agarwal, Bina. 1994. 'Gender and command over property: A critical gap in economic analysis and policy in South Asia', *World Development*, 22 (10): 1455-78.

Anderson, Benedict. 1983. *Imagined communities*. London: Verso.

Benhabib, Seyla; 1987. 'The generalised and the concrete other', in Seyla Benhabib and Drucilla Cornell (eds). *Feminism as critique*, pp. 1-15. Oxford/Mineapolis: Blackwell and University of Minnesota Press.

Bhasin, Kamla and Ritu Menon. 1988. 'The problem' *Seminar*, 342, February: 12-13

Chakravarti, U. 1989. 'Whatever happened to the Vedic dasi?' in Kumkum Sangari and Suresh Vaid (eds). *Recasting women: Essays in colonial history*, pp. 27-87. New Delhi: Kali for Women.

Chandra, Bipan. 1999. 'The making of the Indian nation', in Anand Kumar (ed.). *Nation building in India: Culture, power and society*, pp.9-22. New Delhi: Radiant.

Chaudhuri, Maitrayee. 1993. *Indian women's movement: Reform and revival*. New Delhi: Radiant.

_________. 1996. 'Citizens, workers and emblems of culture: An analysis of the first plan document on women', in Patricia Uberoi (ed.). *Social reform, sexuality and the state*, pp. 211-35. New Delhi: Sage Publications.

_________. 1999. 'Models of development and images of women', in Anand Kumar (ed.). *Nation building in India*, pp. 124-38. New Delhi: Radiant.

Chimni, B. S. 1999. 'Marxism and international law: A contemporary analysis', *Economic and Political Weekly*, 34 (6), 6 February: 337-49.

Desai, A. R. 1994. 'Gender role in the Constituton' in Lotika Sarkar and B. Sivaramayya (eds). *Women and the law: Contemporary problems,* pp. 41-49. New Delhi: Vikas.

Elshtain, Jean Bethke. 1991. 'Sovereignty, identity, sacrifice', *Social research,* 58(3): 545-64.

Gandhi, M.K. 1917. Speech at second Gujarat educational conference, Broach, 20 October 1917, in *Collected works of Mohandas Karamchand Gandhi* (CWMG), 14: 31-36.

__________. 1921. 'To the women of India', *Young India*, CWMG, 20, 11 August: 495-97.

___________. I925. 'Gandhi's speech at Women's Christian College, Madras, 24 March', in CWMG, 26: 395-98).

Government of India (GOI). 1985. 'Women in India,' Country paper. New Delhi: Ministry of Social Welfare.

___________. 1995. *Country report. Fourth world conference on women, Beijing*. New Delhi: Department of Women and Child Development, Ministry of Human Resource Development.

Held, David. (ed.). 1984. *States and societies*. Oxford: Basil Blackwell and The Open University.

Jayawardene, Kumari. 1986. *Feminism and nationalism in the Third World.* Colombo: Sanjiva.

John, Mary. 1996. 'Gender and development in India, 1970s-1990s: Some reflections on the constitutive role of contexts', *Economic and Political Weekly,* 23 November: 3071-77.

Kasturi, Leela and Vina Mazumdar. 1994. 'Women and Indian nationalism', Occasional paper No. 20. Delhi: Centre for Women's Development Studies.

Mohanty, Manoranjan. 1995. 'On the concept of empowerment', *Economic and Political Weekly*, 17 June: 1434-36.

Mies, Maria. 1980. *Indian women and patriarchy.* New Delhi: Vikas.

Minault, Gail. 1982. 'Purdah politics: The role of Muslim women in Indian nationalism 1911-1924' in Hanna Papaneck and Gail Minault (eds). *Separate worlds*. pp. 245-61. Delhi: Chanakya.

Natarajan, Jayanthi. 1996. 'A political hypocrisy', *The Hindu*, December.

Oommen, T.K. (ed.). 1997. *Citizenship and national identity. From colonialism to globalism.* New Delhi: Sage Publications.

Pathak, Zakia and Rajeshwari Sunder Rajan. 1989. 'Shahbano', *Signs,* 14 (3) 558-52.

*Radiance,* 24-30 November 1985. 'Open letter to Muslims', (translated and reprinted from the original in *Inquilab* of 13 November 1985).

Roy, Mary. 1991. 'Women and law: Striking down a succession act'. Paper presented at the 5th National Conference of the Indian Association for Women's Studies at Jadavpur University, 9-12 February.

Sangari, Kumkum. 1988. 'Perpetuating the myth', *Seminar,* 342, (February): 24-30

Southard, Barbara. 1995. *The women's movement and colonial politics in Bengal 1921-1936*. Delhi: Manohar.

Wollstonecraft, Mary. 1975. *From vindication of the rights of women* (first published in 1792). Harmondsworth: Penguin.

Yuval-Davis, Nira, and Floya Anthias. 1989. *Woman-nation-state,* Basingstoke: Macmillan.

# 8

# Visions of Nationhood and Religiosity among Early Freedom Fighters in India

*Proshanta Nandi*

## Introduction

Some fifty years ago an ancient civilisation broke away from the yoke of colonialism to become a newly independent sovereign democracy called India. That august occasion heralded the beginning of one of the most remarkable chapters in human conditioning as a multi-ethnic, multi-cultural society, with myriads of religions, languages, castes, creeds, rituals and customs, faced the challenge of preserving her unity and nationhood while upholding the essential principles of democracy. It was not an easy process. There were many successes for India as well as some failures, and moments of glory as well as those of frustration. Despite some unsuccessful secessionist activity by a small segment of her population, India, to date, has politically remained an unified democratic entity. This record of success is in contrast to those of other multi-cultural, multi-ethnic or multi-religious societies, as in the Balkans, northern Ireland, Middle East or Africa which either split up, faced intense rivalry and violent conflict in their ranks, or were given over to autocracy or dictatorship of one kind or another. This success in India is despite the fact that there were, and still are, many social cleavages and factions within the Indian society, as well as questionable social customs and practices. Reform-minded Indian leaders such as by Raja Ram Mohan Roy, Ishwar Chandra Vidyasagar and Mahatma Gandhi, consistently fought against these impediments by calling attention to the pristine values of India, the people's *dharma*—the fundamental laws of existence, conscience, and sense of justice, succeeding in their mission more often than not. But, to begin with, there were certain underlying characteristics of the land and the people of India that made the experiment successful. These may be delineated as the socio-cultural diversity of the land, the assimilative *weltanschauung* of the largest segment of the population, for example, the Hindus, and the role of the Indian leadership.

### Concept: Nationality/nationhood

Before the perspective of the founding fathers is surveyed, it is expedient to refer to the concept of nationality/nationhood as it is being used here. Nationality or nationhood indicates a legal and/or political relationship, often accompanied by an emotional allegiance, on the part of an individual toward a state. Imagery of nationhood for a people may include, among others, a commonality of origin, ethnicity, customs, tradition, and language(s), as well as those who consider themselves as members of a nation-state or are capable of forming a nation-state. Although in most cases nation-states have defined geographical boundaries, there may exist extra-territorial aspirations on the part of some due to some actual or perceived unjust omissions or commissions of the past, as were the case with formerly colonised countries whose boundaries might have been established in terms of exigencies of conquest or some other political machination.

In the modern sense of the term, the idea of 'nationhood' is rather of recent origin, not in vogue prior to 1925 (for a detailed account of the evolution of the concept, see Hobsbawm 1992). Following a major theoretical statement by the political scientist, Paul R. Brass (1991), the concept of nationhood, like that of nationalism, is seen not as a 'given' but as a social and political construction (also see Nandi 1996: 178-79). This is particularly true for a colonised country that is in the midst of a struggle to throw off the yoke of oppression imposed by an alien ruler. In this sense, nationhood is not inherent in a group of people but rather is the result of a social, political and emotional interaction among people who consider themselves members of a given 'nation', the freedom and sovereignty of which is theirs to achieve, preserve and protect. As an eminent British historian (see Brown 1994: 155) comments on Indian nationhood:

> A sense of nationhood could not rest on geography, religion or language, as it so often seemed to in Europe. In India's circumstances it must be forged consciously out of a commitment to political liberalism which would unite Indians and transcend earlier divisions and loyalties.

## India—A Land of Veritable Diversity

> The singular thing about India is that you can only speak of it in the plural. This pluralism emerged from the very nature of the country; it was made inevitable by India's geography and affirmed by its history. There was simply too much of both to permit a single, exclusionist nationalism (Tharoor 1997:51).

India is, perhaps, one of the very few countries in the world, the other being theUnited States of America, that truly merits the label of a pluralistic society. The physical features of the country and her socio-cultural antecedents render a simple, monistic conception of truth, faith, dogma or world-view as an anathema. Truth in India is multifaceted and so are the various approaches to it. This characterisation of the country fits in well with the dualistic philosophical tradition of Eastern civilisations that abhors an absolute system of values (see Mehta 1978; Nandi 1980).

The pluralism referred to above is almost without bounds. Persuasions of every kind—political religious, philosophical, ideological—have co-existed in India since time immemorial. Being the birthplace of four major religions—Hinduism, Buddhism, Sikhism, and Jainism—a variety of philosophical and intellectual traditions developed and thrived in her hospitable soil. Add to this complex the impact of Islam and Christianity, and nearly two hundred years of colonial rule, and what one gets is a socio-cultural kaleidoscope in the shape of a country. Diversity is operative in its fullest exuberance. Tharoor (1997:9) quotes the noted British historian, E. P. Thompson, to underscore this diversity:

> All the convergent influences of the world run through this society: Hindu, Moslem, Christian, secular; Stalinist, liberal, Maoist, democratic socialist, Gandhian. There is not a thought in the West or East that is not active in some Indian mind.

Indian diversity defies formulations. Not only Hindus, who belong to numerous castes and sub-castes and worship different gods and goddesses, but also the Christians, Muslims and Sikhs of India are given to the diversity of orientations within their own religious ranks. For hundreds of years, these diverse groups have lived together, and in harmony. As Tharoor (1989: 133-34) notes:

> Until politics intervened Indians simply accepted that people were all sorts of different things–Brahmins and Thakurs and Marwaris and Nairs and Lingayats and Pariahs and countless other varieties of Hindu, as well as Roman Catholics and Syrian Christians, Anglo-Indians and Indian Anglicans, Jains and Jews, Keshadhari Sikhs and Mazhabi Sikhs, tribal animists and neo-Buddhists, all of whom flourished on Indian soil along with hundreds and thousands of other castes and sub-castes. Indian Muslims themselves were not

just Sunnis and Shias, but Moplahs and Bohras and Khojas, Ismailis and Qadianis and Ahmediyas and Kutchi Memons and Allah alone knew what else. These differences were simply a fact of Indian life, as incontestable and as innocuous as the different species of vegetation that sprout and flower across our land.

And these differences are functional. Every individual in India knows his/her distinctive place in society, and there is no danger of him/her being lost in the melting pot. As Tharoor (1989: 134) further notes:

> We Indians are open about our differences; we do not attempt to subsume ourselves in a homogeneous mass, we do not resort to the identity-disguising tricks of standardised names or uniform costumes or even a common national language. We are all different; as the French, that most Indian of European peoples, like to put it, albeit in another context, *vive la difference.*

**Unity based on diversity**

The leaders of yesteryear were realistic enough to appreciate that in a multi-ethnic, multi-religious society, such as India, it would not only be impossible but unnatural to expect 'perfect' unanimity. Their mission was not to eliminate diverse and pluralistic religious and cultural traditions but transform them into a functional consensus in regard to the national goal. This was aptly noted, for example, by Pherozshah Mehta (1845-1915), a Congress leader from the minority religious community of Parsis, who, while addressing the nation as the chairman of the Reception Committee of the Fifth Indian National Congress in Bombay, emphasized the need for recognition of the growth of national idea among the Indians 'not in spite of, but precisely on the basis of an infinite diversity of races and creeds' (see Rao 1969). As we can easily see, despite all internal divisions, India has succeeded in retaining her integrity.

**Key to integration**

Integration, in common parlance, constitutes the coming together of various segments into a unified cohesive whole (*Encyclopedia of Sociology* 1974: 141). A plurality such as a society may be said to have functional integration if its members carry on or engage in cooperative activity, and moral integration if they share some values and have some consensus (see Loomis 1970: 125). In this perspective, the key to integration is cooperation, and it is through this means that a society is sustained. Others have held, however, that whether the behaviour is in cooperation or in conflict is not all that important for a society to be an ongoing concern as long as people share a common culture that makes behaviour predictable. Rose (1962: 9-10), an eloquent interpreter of symbolic interaction, held that a society was only possible when people, through learning of a culture, were able to predict each other's behaviour most of the time and could gauge or adjust their own behaviour to the predicted behaviour of others. This proposition is especially true for a multi-ethnic, multi-lingual and multi-cultural society to be able to survive in all its diversity. The willingness of a native or dominant culture to be open to other influences, its sensitivity and sense of accommodation to truths and values as others see them, and the perspective of its elite are crucial in either facilitating or deterring promotion of such a context. Like nationalism, integration or the lack of it is not a 'given' but is the result of the socio-political context.

What is the key to the overall triumph of the forces of integration over those of disintegration in India? This paper takes the position that in large measure the answer can be found in the assimilative, all-encompassing and eclectic religious tradition in India which guided her throughout much of her long and checkered history. Liberalism, tolerance and acceptance of the 'others' were the hallmarks of this tradition. No religion was deemed small or insignificant. All were true. The humanistic liberalism underlying this spirit was, perhaps, best articulated by India's Swami Vivekananda (1863-1902) at Chicago's World Parliament of Religion in 1893. Scornful of religious bigotry and fanaticism, Vivekananda (see Pandit 1996) declared that all religions were equally worthy of respect:

> I am proud to belong to a religion which has taught the world both tolerance and universal acceptance. We believe not only in universal toleration, but we accept all religions as true. I am proud to belong to a nation which has sheltered the persecuted and the refugees of all religions and nations of the earth. I am proud to tell you that we have gathered in our bosom the purest remnant of the Israelites, who came to southern India and took refuge with us in the very year in which their holy temple was shattered to pieces by Roman tyranny. I am proud to belong to the religion which has sheltered and is still fostering the remnant of the grand Zoroastrian nation.

To underscore the spiritual oneness of mankind, Vivekananda, then, recited a few lines of a hymn which he, along with millions of others, repeated every day: 'As the different streams having their sources in different places all mingle their water in the sea, O Lord, the different paths which men take through different tendencies, various though they appear, crooked or straight, all lead to thee.'

It is this tradition which formed the core of the philosophy of the founding fathers of pre-independent modern India. It is also this tradition that led the pacesetters of India's freedom struggle to transcend the barriers of caste, region, language and religion. The common goal of attaining freedom generated, in all corners of the land, a nationalistic fervour that eschewed narrow parochialism. This liberal, all-encompassing fervour may be considered akin to the American anthropologist, Robert Redfield's (1955) concept of the 'grand tradition' of India.

The spirit of assimilation and brotherhood alluded to above is, perhaps, the result of the rich diversity of the Indian sub-continent itself—the snowbound Himalayas, rocky Deccan plateau, fertile Indo-Gangetic plain, mighty rivers criss-crossing throughout the land, tropical rain forests, arid deserts, lush coastal plains, and seas in the deep south—all of which have given birth to different lifestyles and cultures. Hordes of migrants and invaders throughout the last millennium who settled in India brought along their religion, culture, philosophy, lifestyle, language, technology, cuisine, art and architecture. The hospitable spirit of the land accepted them all and created a 'multi-dimensional tapestry of stunning richness and depth, as bewildering as it is compelling, as subtle as it is exuberant' (Nehru n.d.). Perhaps, the greatest tribute to India's eclectic catholicity was rendered by the Nobel laureate Bengali poet of India, Rabindranath Tagore (1861-1941), when he wrote in *Sanchayita* (see 1969: 506-507):

*Keho nahi jane kar ahobane kato manusher dhara*
*Doorbar shrote elo kotha hote, somudre holo hara*
*Hethai arjo, hetha anarjo, hethai dravid chin*
*Shok-hun-dal pathan moghul ek dehe holo leen*
*Paschime aaji khuliache dwar*
*Setha hothey sabey aane upahar*
*Dibe aar nibe, milabe milibe, jabe na phire*
*Aiyee bharater maha manaber sagar teere*

Roughly translated by the present author as follows:

No one knows at whose call
Arrived waves of humanity in tumultuous currents
And became absorbed in the ocean (of India).
Here are the Aryans, the un-Aryans, the Dravidians,

The Chinese, Sakas, Huns, Pathans, and Moghuls
All merging into one entity. ....
Giving, taking and sharing;
Getting together and assimilating
The gates in the West have opened
Wherefrom people bring gifts
No one turning away from the sea shores
Of the great humanity of India

It is suggested that the founding fathers of modern India as well as the freedom fighters were imbued with a liberal ideology that welcomes one and all to India as expressed by Tagore in this classic poem.

Rabindranath Tagore and Mohandas Gandhi (1869-1948), perhaps, more than anyone else, helped foster and rejuvenate India's ancient cultural heritage during the first half of the 20th century. Each in his own way raised the consciousness of generations of Indians, and shaped India as she is today; Tagore—with the beauty and sparkle of his literary masterpieces, music and art, and Gandhi—with his asceticism, religiosity and identification with the impoverished masses of India. As pointed out by Nehru (1946: 405):

> Tagore, the aristocratic artist, represented essentially the cultural tradition of India, the tradition of accepting life in the fullness thereof.... Gandhi, more a man of the people, almost the embodiment of the Indian peasant, represented the other ancient tradition of India, that of renunciation and asceticism...

Both Tagore and Gandhi, contemporaries as they were, became instrumental in revolutionising Indian thinking. They both shared the belief that India's shackles were homemade and, that only Indians could shatter them. In personal orientation and philosophy, however, Tagore and Gandhi were so very dissimilar. As Fischer (1950: 128-129) has noted:

> ...Gandhi was the wheat field and Tagore the rose garden, Gandhi was the working arm, Tagore the singing voice, Gandhi the general, Tagore the herald, Gandhi the emaciated ascetic with shaven head and face, Tagore the large, white-maned, white-bearded aristocrat-intellectual with a face of classic, patriarchal beauty. Gandhi exemplified stark renunciation; Tagore felt 'the embrace of freedom in a thousand bonds of delight'.

Despite their dissimilarity, both Tagore and Gandhi venerated each other. It was Tagore who conferred on Gandhi the title of Mahatma, and it was

Gandhi who called Tagore the great sentinel. Often, when despair struck Gandhi, he would sing a song composed by Tagore: 'If no one hears your call, then walk alone, walk alone.'

**Leadership's espousal of secularism**

Despite the numerous social cleavages intrinsic to India, a secularist ideology permeated the speeches and writings of the founding fathers and the freedom fighters of modern India from Mahadev Govind Ranade (1842-1901) to Jawaharlal Nehru (1889-1964).

This paper picks up, somewhat selectively, a group of Indian social and political luminaries who fought for India's freedom from the British. The ideology and rhetoric professed by them championed secular values, unity and brotherhood between different groups. Bipin Chandra Pal, a Bengali nationalist and one of the cohorts of the trio popularly known as Lal-Bal-Pal, that is, Lala Lajpat Rai, Bal Gangadhar Tilak and Bipin Chandra Pal, asked a question of seminal importance around the turn of the century: 'Can acute diversity, as in the matter of religion, be sublimated into a unity by the adoption of idealistic cosmopolitanism?' Writing a lead article in *Bande Mataram*, a Calcutta journal in 1903, Pal emphasised factors other than the purely spiritual, and saw an answer emerging from the growing awareness of the concepts of rationality, reality, spirituality and universality. The evolution of Indian unity, Pal thought, could be realised only through an intimate acquaintance with the character and spirit of the five great spiritual systems in India, that is, those of the Hindus, the Muslims, the Buddhists, the Christians, and the Zoroastrians. The unity of India, to Pal, was to be found in an intangible awareness experienced by her people, and was far more than a mere geographical expression (see Pal 1969: 35-37). In much the same vein Tagore exhorted his countrymen not only to achieve unity within the country but also to cultivate universal values wherein the East and the West might live together. Visionary as he was, the poet dreamed of a brotherhood of mankind, and alluded to the contributions of Ram Mohan Roy, M. G. Ranade and Swami Vivekananda whose genius lay in the realm of assimilation, harmony and creativity (Tagore 1909).

Given the diversity alluded to earlier, especially of religious belief, it was considered expedient that religion be given a minimal role in the development of national policies. The potentially divisive nature of religion was well understood, as also was the fact that religious conflicts could be the bloodiest. Once the political issues are addressed without alluding to religious differences, people, it was thought, would be free and uninhibited to pursue their religious beliefs, thus creating a rich, healthy and functional diversity.

**Hindus and Muslims: A commonality of interests**

Given the controversy generated today in India by terms such as 'Hindutva' and 'fundamentalism', it is of interest to note that Hindu leaders of yesteryear, some of whom were conservative and staunch, did not perceive the minority religious belief such as Islam as a threat to their own religion. M. G. Ranade (1842-1901), a western Indian Brahmin who served as a judge in Bombay, for example, held that it was wrong to regard Muslim rule in India as a period of humiliation and sorrow. Modern India, he thought, was the result of a joint human endeavour across religions, tribes and creeds. He believed that Muslim contact brought political strength, better administration and even greater solidarity to India.

> ...[the contact between Mohammedans and Hindus] brought about a fusion of thoughts and ideas which benefited both communities, making the Mohammedans less bigoted, and the Hindus more puritanic and more single-minded in their devotion.
>
> If the lessons of the past have any value, one thing is quite clear, viz., that in this vast country no progress is possible unless both Hindus and Mohammedans join hands together... (Ranade 1969).

In his presidential address at the Indian National Congress in 1909, Madan Mohan Malaviya (1861-1946) gave a clarion call for unity across religious beliefs and criticised both Hindus and Muslims who preached discord and disunity. The founder of the Banaras Hindu University and a staunch Hindu himself, Malaviya quoted Veda Vyasa wishing happiness on all: 'May all enjoy happiness; may all be the source of happiness to others; may all see auspicious days; may none suffer any injury.' From his high presidential pedestal, he proclaimed:

> That is the ideal which the Congress has placed before us all since the moment of its birth. I am a Hindu by faith, and I mean no disrespect to any other religion when I say that I will not change my faith for all the possessions of this world or of any other. But I shall be a false Hindu, and I shall deserve less to be called a Brahmin, if I desired that Hindus or Brahmins should have any advantage as such over Mohammedans, Christians, or any other community in India.
>
> ...How ennobling it is even to think of that high ideal of patriotism where Hindus, Mohammedans, Parsees and Christians stand shoulder to shoulder as brothers and work for the common good of all. ...we cannot build up in separation a national life such as would

> be worth living; we must rise and fall together (Malaviya, as quoted in Rao 1969: 38-41)

In *India Divided,* Rajendra Prasad (1946), the first President of the Indian Republic, brought out an articulated account of the impact of Muslim rule on India. Written when he was incarcerated by the British in an Indian jail, Prasad pointed out that the Muslim rule in India was not a history of continuous conflict and wars between Hindus on the one side and Muslims on the other. He noted that:

> Between 1193 and 1526, there sat on the throne of Delhi no less than 35 Sultans belonging to five dynasties. Each of these dynasties professed Islam and each was replaced in its turn by another Muslim dynasty. Of the 35 monarchs who sat on the throne, no less than 19 were killed or assassinated not by Hindus but by Mussalmans.

President Prasad discerned a history of cooperation between Hindus and Muslims. While Aurangzeb employed many Hindu generals, Shivaji, his Hindu rival, had a number of Muslim military officers who held important positions. Shivaji's navy had at least three Muslim admirals. Prasad noted further:

> I have mentioned these instances only to show that Muslims fought Muslims more than they fought Hindus and that it is a wrong and one-sided view of history to imagine, as has been done by some persons, that during the long period of over six hundred years, they were constantly engaged in wars against the Hindus whom they were oppressing all the time, leaving a legacy of hate and bitterness, the effects of which have not been and cannot be obliterated or forgotten.

On the concept of 'nationhood', Prasad quotes an eminent Muslim scholar, Sir Syed Ahmad Khan, who in a speech in 1885 spoke in the following manner:

> From the oldest times, the word Nation is applied to the inhabitants of one country, though they differ in some peculiarities which are characteristics of their own. Hindu and Muhammadan brethren, do you people any country other than Hindustan? Do you not inhabit the same land? Are you not burnt and buried in the same soil? Remember the words 'Hindu' and 'Muhammadan' are only meant

for religious distinction, otherwise all persons, whether Hindu, Muhammadan, or Christian, who reside in this country belong to one and the same nation.

Prasad was convinced that Hindus and Muslims shared common heritage and traditions. When outsiders came to India, they brought changes along with them, but they themselves got changed in the process. This was, indeed, a unique event in history. While retaining their religious identity, these different groups became part of a grand mosaic—more than what can be called a melting pot.

Cognisant of the antagonism between the Hindus and the Muslims in the late thirties and early forties in India, which he saw as largely being engineered by the British, Abul Kalam Azad, the President of the Indian National Congress in 1940 cautioned the country against undermining India's national solidarity. He saw so much in common between the two communities—Hindus and Muslims. In his presidential address of 1940, Azad (1959; see also 1969: 73-75) observed:

> Eleven hundred years of common history have enriched India with our common achievements. Our languages, our poetry, our literature, our culture, our art, our dress, our manners and customs, the innumerable happenings of our daily lives, everything bears the stamp of our joint endeavour. There is indeed no aspect of our life which has escaped this stamp.

Azad further cautioned both the communities:

> ...if there are any Hindus amongst us who desire to bring back the Hindu life of a thousand years ago and more, they dream, and such dreams are vain fantasies. So also, if there are any Muslims who wish to revive their past civilisation and culture which they brought a thousand years ago from Iran and Central Asia, they dream also and the sooner they wake up the better.

Azad had only one vision of the Indian nation—united and indivisible—which, in his judgment, neither fantasy nor scheming could separate and dismantle.

**Cultural unity**

It was, perhaps, left to Jawaharlal Nehru (1889-1964), the spiritual son of the father of the nation, Mahatma Gandhi, to articulate in rational terms the essence of Indian unity. The India of his dream was a synthesis of the spiritual values of India and advancement promised by science and technology. He traced Indian history from the days of the Indus Valley civilisation, citing innumerable peoples from outside, who brought along their language, religion, lifestyle and culture. All of these made a deep impact on India and, yet, India retained her own identity. Nehru (1938) pointed out:

> Like the ocean, she received the tribute of a thousand rivers, and though she was disturbed often enough and storms raged over the surface of her waters, the sea continued to be the sea. It is astonishing to note how India continued successfully this process of assimilation and adaptation. It could only have done so if the idea of a fundamental unity were so deep rooted as to be accepted even by the newcomer, and if her culture were flexible and adaptable to changing conditions.

The unity that Nehru referred to was based not on religion, but culture. And the culture was anything but exclusive. As Nehru further characterised the culture of India:

> That culture was not exclusive or intolerant to begin with; it was receptive and adaptable, and long ages of pre-eminence gave it deep roots and a solidarity which storms could not shake. It developed an aristocratic attitude which, secure in its own strength, could afford to be tolerant and broad-minded. This very toleration gave it greater strength and adaptability.

Going through history, Nehru recounted how Christianity came to India in the first century after Christ long before it came to Europe, and found a welcome. The Jews arrived next, followed by Zoroastrians who were driven out of Persia. Then came the Muslims who found full opportunities to propagate their faith on the soil of India. Nehru noted that there was no conflict except on the frontiers, and only when Muslims came as conquerers and raiders. Of course, during their colonial rule in India, the British tried to drive a wedge between the Hindus and Muslims by stressing those religious differences which brought them into conflict with one another.

No other Indian, perhaps, spoke and wrote as much as Mohandas Gandhi on the concept of India's unity. According to a leading educationist, D. S. Sarma (1956), 'He did far more than anyone had ever done before in Indian history to weld together, into one compact whole, the various sections of India's population—Hindus and Muslims, caste

Hindus and outcastes, and town-dwellers and the village folk.' Gandhi did not see introduction of other religions to India or, for that matter, outsiders settling in India as destructive to India's unity and integrity because he was convinced that India had always had a facility for assimilation. He forcefully asserted:

> Hindustan belongs to all those who are born and bred here and who have no other country to look to. Therefore, it belongs to Parsis, Ben Israels, to Indian Christians, Muslims and other non-Hindus as much as to Hindus. Free India will not be a Hindu raj; it will be [an] Indian raj—based not on the majority of any religious sect or community, but on the representatives of the whole people without distinction of religion....Religion is a personal matter which should have no place in politics (Gandhi in *Harijan,* quoted in Rao 1969: 50-53) .

Gandhi was a universalist who applied the same principles of ethics and morality across the board. He saw no distinction between one religion and another or between people and people, no matter what sect, community, religion or nation they belonged to. As he returned to India in 1914 from South Africa, he found an impoverished and stratified society being crushed under the heel of British colonialism. His sense of ethics called for a moral regeneration not only of India but also Britain. In order to fight the British, he wanted India to be strong and united. Through his speeches, writing and action, he campaigned against untouchability, caste and class antagonism, and conflict between Hindus and Muslims. He not only wanted to free India politically but also morally and socially.

**Truth in all religions**

The sub-heading of this section comes from one of the many of Gandhi's writings. He reinvigorated a unique feature of Hinduism by his pleading for universal brotherhood based on respect and regard for diverse religions (known in Sanskrit as *sarvadharmasamanatva*). This call for respect is based not just on goodwill but on moral principles. In a peaceful society, mutual respect for one another's religion is indispensable. The free impact of ideas, Gandhi held, was not possible under any other condition. Different religions to him were like beautiful flowers from the same garden. He spoke out openly against bigotry and lack of understanding of the true nature of religion:

> It is a travesty of true religion to consider one's own religion as superior and others' as inferior. All religions enjoin worship of the 'one God' who is all-pervasive. ...Various religions are like the leaves on a tree. No two leaves are alike, yet there is no antagonism between them or between the branches on which they grow (see Rao 1969: 143-150).

Belief in one God and seeking spiritual bonding with God is the quest of all who are religious. All faiths, Gandhi held, constituted a revelation of truth and he saw truth in all religions. However, these truths are received by mortals who are less than perfect. Hence, the question of the comparative merit of one religion over another does not arise. Thus, it is imperative for a religious person to be open and tolerant of others' religious truths.

## Conclusion

This essay highlights a belief in assimilation, adaptation and inclusiveness that characterised the orientation of a select group of Indian leaders who can be called both the founding fathers of modern India as well as leaders of India's struggle for freedom. It must be understood that the purpose of this paper was neither to analyse the success or failure of each of the notables referred to herein nor to evaluate their overall contribution to the freedom struggle. Rather it was to promote a sense of how they reacted to people, viewpoints, and religions unlike their own. The evidence suggests that among the Indian leadership, there existed an overwhelming support for opening the doors to incorporate the ideas brought home from outside or, at least, give them an opportunity for growth and development. Only a strong and secure culture can do this. India has provided ample testimony to being such a culture throughout the ages. This is all the more evident in view of the overall rejection by the people at large of any fundamentalistic type of belief system in India.

## References

American Mental Health Research Centre. 1996. 'Socio-political context of Sikh militancy in India.' *Journal of Asian and African Studies,* 31 (3-4): 178-90.

Azad, Abul Kalam. 1959. *India wins freedom—An autobiographical narrative*. Bombay: Orient Longman.

___________. 1969. 'The communal problem', in R. V. Ramachandrasekhara Rao (ed.). *Indian unity—A symposium*. pp. 73-75. New Delhi: Publications Division, Government of India.

Brass, Paul R. 1991. *Ethnicity and nationalism.* Newbury Park, CA: Sage Publications.

Brown, Judith M. 1994. *Modern India—The origins of an Asian democracy.* Oxford: Oxford University Press.

*Encyclopedia of Sociology*. 1974. Guilford, Conn.: The Dushkin Publishing Group, Inc.

Fischer, Louis. 1950. *The life of Mahatma Gandhi*. New York: Harper & Row.

Loomis, Charles P. 1970. 'In defense of integration: For one nation and for one world', *The Centennial Review,* 14 (2). Spring.

Mehta, Asoka.1978. *Perception of Asian personality*. Calcutta: S. Chand & Co.

Nandi, Proshanta K. 1980. *The quality of life of Asian Americans*. Chicago, Ill.: Pacific/Asian.

Nehru, Neena. n.d. *India—Continuity in change*. New Delhi: Ministry of External Affairs, Government of India.

Nehru, Jawaharlal. 1938. 'The unity of India.' *Foreign Affairs*.

____________. 1946. *The discovery of India*. Calcutta: Signet Press.

Pal, Bipin Chandra. 1969. 'The modern deal' in R. V. Ramachandrasekhara Rao (ed.), *Indian unity—A symposium*, pp. 35-37. New Delhi: Publications Division, Government of India.

Pandit, Bansi. 1996. *Hindu Dharma*. Glen Ellyn, IL.: B & V Enterprises, Inc.

Prasad, Rajendra. 1946. *India divided*. Bombay: Hind Kitab.

Ranade, M. G. 1969. 'Our common interests', in R. V. Ramachandrasekhara Rao (ed.), *Indian unity—A symposium*. pp. 93-98. New Delhi: Publications Division, Government of India.

Rao, R. V. Ramachandrasekhara. 1969. *Indian unity—A symposium*. New Delhi: Publications Division, Government of India.

Redfield, Robert. 1955. 'The social organisation of tradition,' *The Far Eastern Quarterly*, 15 (1), November.

Rose, Arnold M. 1962. *Human behavior and social processes*. Boston, Mass.: Houghton Mifflin Company.

Sarma, D. S. 1956. 'The father of the nation: The life and teachings of Mahatma Gandhi', reprinted in Martin Deming Lewis (ed.), *Gandhi—Maker of modern India?* pp. 9-14. Boston: D. C. Heath and Company, 1965 .

Tagore, Rabindranath. 1909. *A greater India*. Madras: Ganesh & Co. Pvt. Limited.

____________. 1969. *Sanchayita*. Calcutta: Vishwa Bharati Granthan Bibhag. 7th edition (first published in 1891).

Tharoor, Shashi. 1989. *The great Indian novel*. New Delhi: Penguin Books.

____________. 1997. *India—From midnight to the millennium*. New York: Harper-Perennial.

# 9

# Caste in and above History

*G. Aloysius*

Caste, in its double sense of an occupational-endogamous community as well as rank-ordered and ritually-legitimated varna, has come to be thought of in social science literature, as the one and unique social reality of the sub-continent: India is caste and caste is India.[1] Roland Inden in his seminal work has pointed out that 'Caste is conceptualised as the peculiar Indian essence that distinguishes the country from every other and particularly the Western', and again 'Caste has become essentialised and turned into the substantialised agent of history'. Essentialisation for Inden, 'is the idea that humans and human institutions, for example, the individual and the nation-state are governed by determinate natures that inhere in them in the same way that they are supposed to inhere in the entities of the natural world'. In other words essentialising caste means considering it as 'an unchanging ideal that precedes human history and stands outside it' (Inden 1990, Chap. 2).

A meta-historical caste would exhibit at least three characteristics: timelessness, all-pervasiveness and changelessness. First, since caste in India is recognised to have existed since Vedic times, it also has through sacred association become a time-immemorial entity; second, its operative nature is considered monolithical and co-extensive with the entire Bharatvarsh; third, the main elements of caste are supposed to have survived more or less unchanged down through history. Such an essentialised view of caste is held most often unconsciously, particularly when the term is used as a shorthand in academic discourse to describe social and group relations. It also runs parallel very often to more critical considerations of the subject. Sociological and historical studies of caste, starting off from either a single Sanskritic text or village-level micro-studies, do not hesitate to predicate generalised conclusions for the entire sub-continent. Curiously enough both those who attribute near total determinacy to caste as well as those who deny it in absolute terms subscribe to this same meta-historical vision. It does not require uncommon intelligence to point out that a reified caste is strikingly similar to the other, equally reified, referents of our discussion, namely, religion and nation. In a sense, caste has come to occupy the middle ground between the two in the sub-continent's transition from tradition to modernity; and the academic contribution to the construction and maintenance of this civil religion is certainly not insignificant.

The modest project here is, tentatively and in a limited way to de-essentialise the notion and historicise the reality by bringing together the sociological and historiographical insights generated in recent scholarship.[2] Such an exercise, it is hoped, would at the same time explain the ways in which caste has come to be implicated with nation and religion in modern India. The focus understandably will be on the colonial era: the commissions and omissions of both the imperialists and the nationalists as they bore on caste. However, a broad historico-sociological perspective on the sub-continent's social development in general and on the social formation of caste in pre-modern times in particular would serve as the appropriate take-off points.

## I

The Indian sub-continent today after millennia of known and continuous history encompasses multiple and relatively autonomous social formations of vastly varied levels and differential types of technological developments, labour-social organisations, linguistic-cultural achievements, religious beliefs and political control systems. This persistent and patterned diversity surviving from the pre-modern into the present times can and is increasingly being used as a heuristic tool to understand its past, ambiguously recorded in religio-literary texts and patchily revealed through archaeology (Allchin and Allchin 1996: 62 and ff)). Search into the pattern of this diversity has yielded two important starting points: geographical variability and ethno-linguistic multiplicity. As regards the former, it is understood that in the pre-modern context of low levels of food-production and transport-communication technology, geographical specificities such as the soil, vegetation, water, climate, terrain and the like must intervene and leave a definite impress upon the material and non-material cultures and social structures of the populations[3]; as for the latter, without going into the unsolved problems of race-language identity, locale of origin, among others, it can safely be asserted that language is not only an embodiment of kinship systems, and an expression of the material culture but also the dynamic repository of thought-affect systems, world views and politico-cultural values.[4]

Geographically the sub-continental land mass is characterised by a series of riverine valleys as distinct eco-zones–the Gangetic to begin with, but also, the Brahmaputra, the Sindhu, the Narmada, the Godavari, the Cauvery, and so on. Here the fertile soil, lush vegetation and above all assured availability of water for irrigation have contributed in transforming these valleys into high surplus-production areas and sufficient ground for the development of large-scale and highly stratified labour-social formations (Subbarao 1958, chap 1). If the valleys as eco-zones stand in clear contrast to the rest of the land mass taken together, it is still useful, to divide the latter into two categories; the plains and the hilly jungles (ibid.). The plains are a mediating type in which irrigation is carried through both rain water and artificially constructed tanks and lakes; here the economic level can be thought of generally as subsistence but with a perennial threat of food shortage due to drought, famine, war, pestilence; correspondingly the labour-social organisation is identified as smaller in size and the population less dense. The hilly jungles on the other hand, must have been as they are even today, under constant shortage of food, as whatever goes by the name of agriculture depended solely on the vagaries of the monsoon; continued and settled collective life here must have been conducted under difficult circumstances with sparse population and micro-level social units.[5]

Ethno-linguistically again three/four clear streams or substrata have been recognised among the modern Indian languages: the Indo-Aryan, the Dravidian, the Austric-Munda and Sino-Burman (the latter two could be together called the 'tribal'). The language-communities belonging to the different families generally occupy distinct geographical regions and these are more often than not contiguous.[6] Unlike that of geography, the role and importance of language in general and the impress, actual and potential, of its diversity in the formation and explanation of sub-continental societies, unfortunately are not given sufficient attention in social sciences. For understandable political reasons, language in the subcontinent is seen by scholars both foreign and native, merely as an instrument of communication in contrast to its supposedly encompassing role in the West (see, for example Khubchandani 1993; Washbrook 1991). However it needs to be remembered that just as geographical patterns have persisted down the millennia, the linguistic diversity has been continually affirming and asserting itself very much as a continuity since the ancient times and hence its explanatory value.

Along then, the lines of geographical and ethno-linguistic diversities, the peoples of the subcontinent, interacting on the one hand, with the natural environment, and among themselves on the other have given birth to not only diverse forms of speech and labour organisations, but also cultural beliefs and methods of political controls, and have formed themselves in small farming communities simultaneously in different parts of the country even during the pre-historic times as revealed in archaeological findings (Allchin and Allchin 1996: 33 ff). The processes of action and interaction among these diverse groups of communities continued into the historic period, first in semi-isolation from the great world movements of populations and later absorbing the incoming influences.[7] The result is a series of distinct yet interrelated societies in different regions, recorded though ambiguously and partially in the extant religious-literary sources. This over-arching process of mingling and fusing of scattered populations in the course of a long and continuous history exhibits certain definite characteristics. First, the civilisational mix is among communities placed unequally in terms of both geographical and historical advantages and disadvantages; this means that forces of dominance as well as resistance, of coercion as well as cooperation and of attraction as well as repulsion are to be identified within this process and problematised in order to explain the end product. In particular the extraordinary advantage that riverine valleys and its inhabitants enjoyed in terms of abundant and assured food supply and their consequent strength in comparison with the other zones need to be emphasised. It could safely be assumed that if the material prosperity of the valleys was an attraction, the non-material culture as the site of relational power was a source of equal repulsion. Second, the long-term trajectory of the process is certainly not the creation of a single monolith-Indian Society. Diversity in the sub-continent continually tends to reassert itself, without of course breaking the thin line of civilisational continuity. History is witness to the emergence of full-blown languages–script, grammar, literature and all; the formation of distinct and differential kinship systems; and the construction of region-based religious symbolisms. The societies embodying these, even overcoming the horizontal and other social cleavages, more often than not are found to be occupying contiguous territories. While the interrelatedness is certainly the undercurrent, the existential reality of the south Asian social formation clearly is diversity.[8] Third, is the incomplete nature of this process at all levels–local, regional and sub-continental. It is indeed remarkable that traits, simple and complex of both material and non-material cultures, identified as even millennia old, co-exist side by side with those relatively or contemporaneously modern. In other words, social development here has been in a radical sense uneven. Fourth, at the level of polity, the subcontinent has been the stage for multiple types of political incorporation among whom two types are significant: long periods of regional/ethno-linguistic multiple kingdoms, though often sub-divided in perennial rivalries, interspersed with short-term, often incomplete, and only partially successful meta-cultural empire formations mostly emanating from the valley regions of the north.[9] The salient point of distinction between the types is not the scale but the nature of incorporation itself. While the former is a symbol-based and vertical integration, the latter of necessity is lateral networking among the upper echelons of the different social structures.

## II

Within such a broad historical-sociological perspective, anchored in recent scholarship, the attempt here is to contextualise caste in all of its major dimensions–hereditary occupation, endogamous sexuality, ascriptive hierarchy and religious legitimation. The earliest period of Indian history to which the formation of caste-*varna* stratification is assigned by scholarly consensus is the second half of the first millennium B.C., the period of the Buddha (Sharma 1990: 90). And the location is the primary mid-Ganga valley. Understandably it is on this period and location that scholarship on Ancient India is concentrated; and the findings have definite influence in shaping our thinking on caste-varna in India. R.S. Sharma describes the process of varna-state formation in the context of the emergence of a complex agrarian society here.[10] The development of material culture such as the new agricultural tools, the availability of fertile soil and perennial water, boosted up the levels of food production leading to a significant surplus; with surplus in food and wealth emerges the social-political mechanism, the state-varna complex, to collect and redistribute the surplus unequally among the populace. The managing partnership in this process is the Brahmana-Kshatrya combine. The Priest/Brahmana legitimises the king through religion and ritual in general and the specific *Aswamedha* and other sacrifices in particular; the king/Kshatrya on his part reciprocates by granting primacy and privileges to the priest but also by upholding the foundations of the new order– the patriarchal family, private property and the varna form of social stratification. The process is identified to have taken place under the hegemony of the 'Vedic community' of the Aryans/Indo-European language speakers whose migration from the North-West, through the upper-Gangetic to the mid-Gangetic plains is clearly evidenced both by archaeology and Sanskritic texts. Certainly, the process encompassed and incorporated the already existing substrata of population *en route*. Varna here is not only a cognitive and volitional ideal or merely normative but also 'a stark reality'—actual divisions of society based on birth with discriminating rights and liabilities. Given the chronological priority of the process here and the migratory-expansionist nature of the Vedic groups, we are now clear as to the area, agency and method of the origin and spread of 'caste', both as concrete and cognitive reality in the sub-continent. Sharma's narrative, erudite as it is, appears to subscribe to a mono-model social-state formation for India, for he generalises, 'Ancient India's juridico-legal device for the distribution of the social surplus lay in the ritual-based varna just as that of Greece and Rome lay in the device of citizenship.'[11]

However, Sharma is not totally insensitive to the existence of alternative and competing models of social formations even here; only that he relegates them as 'tribal' and hence 'disappearing' or as post facto theorising. In comparison to his clearly Marxist-evolutionary model, Romila Thapar's study is more inclusive and nuanced, constructed on a larger data-base of Sanskrit and Pali sources (1984); she is aware that on several crucial issues the Sanskrit and Pali sources are in sharp contrast to each other. She also identifies the alternative and relatively autonomous gana-sangha model, delineates its contrasting features, particularly its resistance to the ritual-monarchical incorporation. Despite these and much more, Thapar evaluates the gana-sanghas as a passing or transitory phase to be located between the lineage (tribal) and the state formations.

Working largely through Buddhist-Pali sources, Uma Chakravarti on the other hand begins her study with an unambiguous affirmation of the parallel existence of two distinct types of social formations, their corresponding political or state forms and the presence of perennial tension between the two.[12] Monarchy and republic (gana-sangha) are the two state forms that presided over the two types of social formations that took shape during the most determining period of history within the dominant eco-zone of the subcontinent. The gana-sangha societies of the period were no less complex and stratified. However they were in sharp contrast to those developed under monarchy. Here the society is composed of a dominant community of gahapatis—the land owners/householders and supported by minor service groups such as Dasas, Kammakaras and Brahmins. Landholding was individual, unequal and the land was worked upon by the owner, as well as hired labour. While agriculture is the dominant economic activity here also, trade and crafts have begun to flourish under favourable material and ideological conditions, resulting in the proliferation of occupational groups/guilds of artisans and craftsmen. Social stratification tended to be polarised as the high and the low revolving around jati, kula, kamma and sippa. These referral points were neither rigid nor uniform everywhere. The gana-sangha was represented through a chief elected from among the gahapatis, the landholders, who as a collective retained effective power over the general mass. The chief owed his position in general to his physical prowess, skill at resource-mobilisation and other leadership qualities. There was no elaborate philosophico-ideological system justifying and thereby rigidifying the social order as within the varna system. Instead, the existential inequalities tended to be taken for what they were with certain ameliorative measures, thus providing space for a certain measure of fluidity and mobility of groups. The dominance, again was that of the land-owning gahapatis as opposed to the Brahmana-Kshatriya combine under monarchy. Above all the ritual-sacrificial legitimacy of the royalty and its corollary of royal upholding of the Brahminical social order was certainly missing.[13] When Buddhism appeared on the scene, it became the ideological banner of many of the gana-sanghas in their defensive struggle against the expansionist varna-state formation.[14] When the new religion eventually had to reckon with the 'king' or the 'emperor', it prescribed for him duties other than upholding the varna dharma–that of the establishment of just social order and a welfare state as a pre-condition for the dawn of the universal moral order. Chakravarti also indicates that the several gana-sanghas were situated in the interior region of hills and jungles, to remind us of the ecological base of this type of social-state structures (Chakravarty 1987, chapter 1).

Taken together and considered complementary, these historical studies lead to certain inferences, which, since they are from the earliest recorded social formations, have serious implications for our understanding of caste in subsequent history. First of all, varna-caste is primarily recognised as one kind of social formation in a single type of eco-zone–the riverine valleys of the sub-continent. Second, even here, the social formation in the primary Ganga valley was not only bifurcated but also of mutually antagonistic nature; in other words, the very origin of caste-varna in the sub-continent was tension-ridden and contained the seeds of its own negation, flagging off the very real possibility of historical development along either course–caste or non/anti-caste. Third, the apparent submergence and collapse of the relatively secular-flexible stratification of the gana-sanghas under the pressure of monarchy and its rigid-religious varna hierarchy was not a matter of course, of natural or internal evolution but a result of historical confrontation between the two and vanquishing of one formation by the other, after much contestation and resistance; the two distinct social formations along with their well-articulated and conflicting ideologies had advanced side by side too long to place them in sequence as inevitable and natural stages of a single evolutionary development. Fourth, the ritually-legitimated varna hierarchy, which was at once a concrete reality of social divisions as well as a cognitive ideal among the Vedic people, in its movement of conquest and encompassment had become merely a cognitive ideal, with its actualisation limited to and dependent upon actual power wielded on the ground; in other words the distinction between empirical castes and ideological varna became real; that is, when it was limited to its own original home varna division represented both the actual and the ideal; in its encompassment of wider reality however, Varna became more an aspiration than actuality. Fifth, the expansionist thrust of the primary valley and its inhabitants as a whole towards the other river valleys and the other eco-zones– the plains and hilly jungles, in itself has been double-edged, containing both caste and anti-caste. Wherever the caste virus is seen to germinate in a non-caste soil in any part of the subcontinent, antibodies of counter forces, and belief-ideologies also can be identified.[15]

The spreading/diffusion of caste in history through the contested and negotiated process of engulfment by the riverine valleys could be analysed in terms of the several important changes effected in the original phenomenon itself. First, as noted above, when varna as actual social division ventured forth to conquer it has had often to remain content with merely being a cognitive ideal very partially realised. Second, however varna does influence social relations, even when it could not change them to its own image: occupational groupings tend to become hereditary and or endogamous; smaller and scattered communities/tribes take on one or more characteristics of the varna divisions either in toto or in fragments. Third, varna itself becomes merely a general framework to accommodate and rank-order the existing and changing groups; such an accommodation of numerous 'new castes' are seen generally at the lowest shudra/ati-shudra levels. Fourth, in combination with the ethno-linguistic and ecological diversity, varna also becomes multiple, regional caste systems. Fifth, varna's alliance with the different state-forms is also to be noted: as the ethno-regional kingdoms are vertical and negotiated incorporation of the class with the mass within the ethno-culture, they result in the abatement of caste; but as the meta-cultural empires are basically a lateral and horizontal network of the valley elites, caste gets invigorated and valorised.[16] Sixth, this great process, as it moves along blurring the ecological and ethnic diversities tends to divide settlements and societies provoking disjuncted responses everywhere and also to create an overarching ideological and actual polarisation between caste versus anti-caste, orthodoxy versus heterodoxy, Brahminism versus Buddhism, and the like. In the event of uneven, incomplete and simultaneous social development of the pre-modern era, we thus find, vast areas of hilly jungles, inhabited by people whose economy ranges from primitive hunting-gathering to well settled and surplus producing, amidst whom stratification itself is in initial stages, not to speak of caste; in the intermediary plains we find the majority living in hereditary and or endogamous occupational groups called castes and communities, in several stages and types of acceptance or rejection of the primary hierarchical ranking and ritual legitimacy; and in the restricted area of different riverine valleys we have caste-varna being affirmed and negated in a contested manner.

This section could conclude with a summary note on the social situation of the pre-colonial years. Received wisdom has it that the century preceding the colonial take-over represents a dark age of Indian history marked by political fragmentation and social anarchy. From the point of view of traditional-classical empire and concomitant hierarchical-social ordering it perhaps was. However recent scholarship has begun to interpret the facts differently from the regionalist and non-dominant perspectives. In general the period is seen to have supported the emergence of the cultures, values and peoples of eco-zones other than the riverine valleys through the formations of regional economic zones, ethno-culture based polities and vernacular literatures.

The most remarkable phenomenon of the times was economic diversification. While irrigated agriculture continued to remain dominant, it ceased to be the single monopoly factor to determine and pattern social relations; increases in trade, manufacture, transportation, war-related crafts, soldiering, and so on, could be noticed everywhere requiring different kinds of skills and forms of social organisation of labour other than the ritual and literary. The tendency to be noted in these diversification processes is towards the regional rather than the subcontinental. The emerging economic configurations were multiple and differential; however their impact on the larger society was the same–boosting up the economic role of the non-valley populations and releasing the labouring groups from agrarian bondage in the valley zones. In general the 'plausibility structure' of the valley varna model of society was giving way to more pluralist and flexible forms of society. Formation of regional kingdoms in the concrete meant an increased dependence of the valley-dominant on the petty chiefdoms and other leadership of the plains and the hilly jungles for protection from the neighbours; soldiering as a profession became a possibility for many. While the new kings, at least several of them, did display classical-royal pretensions of priestly legitimation, in several other important ways they flouted the Brahminical notions of kingship; and they could in no way, and in fact did not, uphold the caste-varna social order. The late medieval period again is the time when the modern languages and literatures flourished, prose emerged and in general a movement away from the homogenising and uniforming effect of Sanskritism was registered. Bhakti movements arose in several parts of the country encompassing the general mass of the people in different regions, striking a middle path in religion and culture. These multiple processes at various levels of economy, society, politics and culture have been better researched, and documented in detail for peninsular India by a whole new generation of historians–Christopher Baker, David Ludden, Sanjay Subramanyam, Burton Stein, David Washbrook and others. The unifying thread of their findings, variegated as they are, is that caste while not disappearing was certainly abating, accommodating and becoming attenuated, with the balance of forces within society being tilted in favour of the generally lower classes and the fluid 'power' model of stratification of the drier eco-zones. Even if many fail to see the 'golden age' for the Paraiahs in the pre-colonial century, as suggested by Washbrook, it could easily be argued that the period was one in which hierarchical and uniforming forces emanating from the ritually stratified areas of the valleys were losing their edge over those of egalitarianism and diversity, the historical hallmarks of the people and culture of the plains and hilly jungles (for some important reading on this, see Stein 1969, Baker 1984, Washbrook 1993 and Pollock 1998).

## III

In this section our specific query is: what did British rule do to caste? As early as 1962 M.N. Srinivas correctly observed: 'It is my hunch that the varna model became more popular during the British period as a result of a variety of forces...' (1962: 16). What these many forces were and how their combined operation resulted in the popularisation of varna, Srinivas unfortunately did not explain. Roland Inden suggests that the imaginations and writings of Orientalist scholars and imperial bureaucrats have much to do with the construction/reconstruction of caste in modern India. Others similarly point to the caste enumeration of the census operations as being responsible: 'The enduring interest of the British in caste as a system which both divided and ranked their Indian subjects produced an extensive response among those subjects and also sometimes created new categories by statistical sleight of hand or administrative fiat' (Conlon 1981: 104). An extreme form of such a trend of analysis can be identified in several influential social scientists, when they are constrained to respond to the increasingly strident attacks by the oppressed castes on the traditionally caste-ridden Indian society: caste is a colonial construct! Colonialism in the sense of a collusive compact between the native and foreign elite indeed was responsible for essentialising caste. But those who point out to the Orientalist imagination and colonial inscriptions are not telling even half the story, for ideological imagination needs to be read in the context of the political economy of group relations of the period. What the British did to the caste in the singular cannot be, understood in isolation from what they did to the castes in the plural.[17]

The imperial unification and British bureaucratic rule were both a continuity as well as a break in the history of the subcontinent: on the one hand, as a pan-Indian empire the British were well within the same logic of the previous attempts at empire-building; on the other, they were a different phenomenon, that is, modern, meaning bringing in principles and practices of legitimation other than the traditional. As particularly pragmatic type of imperialists, the British were careful not to disturb the social order and this policy stood them well; however the very logic of imperialism necessitated, a serious internal transformation largely unintended, in the course of following their own objectives. Within the specific context of the pre-modern subcontinent as delineated above, both the conscious policy as well as unconscious consequences of this new empire resulted in bolstering up certain eco-zones, segments of population and socio-cultural forces and depressing the others; keeping with the general flow of Indian history, this last of the empires too had to bank on, stand by and promote the interests of the riverine valleys at the expense of the plains and hilly jungles. And here too, the imperial instinct for self-preservation did not falter. The Commissioner of Deccan, for example, in the course of administering justice 'argued that maintaining the hierarchical order would keep the subjects disunited and unable to combine against the British. An equalising policy would ultimately reduce British stability in his view' (Chakravarti 1998: 51). The caste-varna forces of the riverine valleys could not agree more. On this basic agreement the colonial bargain was struck.[18] Having decimated or neutralised the kings and chiefs, particularly of the plains and hilly jungles, the new rulers 'settled' with the socially powerful of the riverine valleys either as *zamindari* or *ryotwari*. The ending of the endemic wars, the increasing and unstable demand for land revenue and the linking of the local economy to that of the home country, all these had the devastating consequence of de-diversification and re-agrarianisation, albeit with a difference. 'A highly mobile and economically differentiated society rendered stationery and traditional by the processes of peasantisation implicit in the colonial project' is the conclusion of David Washbrook (1993: 68).

The colonial integration of the subcontinent was basically agrarian and this had to be on the already available and dominant and high-yielding riverine-valley model (Stein 1969). The valleys and their prosperous inhabitants easily acquired a sort of 'most favoured nation status' within this modern empire also. The constraints and opportunities presented by this nexus between the inhabitants of the river valleys and the immigrants of the sea-ports was the solid undergrid which effectively dictated and determined most of the colonial policies and practices well into the 19th century. While the British reigned in splendour and glory, it was the Brahmins and other upper castes, largely of the riverine valleys, who expanded, consolidated and were being trained through apprenticeship in the art of modern ruling (see, particularly, the conclusion by Frykenberg 1965).

For our purpose it was a colonial-modern process of riverine-valley-modelisation of the entire subcontinent with all its economic and cultural implications. The agriculture-based, relatively rigid and hierarchical labour-social organisation along with the attendant religio-cultural ideology-belief systems of these eco-zones was sought to be replicated everywhere, overcoming the earlier ecological and economic constraints certainly with differential success by those already trained in the traditional management of social hierarchies, that is, the upper-*dwija* castes lead by the Brahmins. This then is the most significant macro-process released and abetted under colonialism–the river-valley-modelisation of the economy and culture of the entire country. All others, even those running counter to this were only subsidiary and subordinate to this main process. An analysis of this unified and unifying mega-process into multiple sub-processes would at once clarify what the British did to caste during the major portion of their rule. Earlier, it was suggested that the British empire was both a continuity as well as a break in Indian history, seen as a successive and finally successful attempt at pan-Indian socio-political unification, originating generally from the riverine valleys of northern India. As a continuity, the British too largely followed the same logic of empire-building, first having done away with the petty rulers and then, unifying and consolidating the dominant either priestly-ritual or land-owning castes of the different riverine valleys. However, the instant case of pan-Indianisation was also different: it was effective-administrative and modern-legitimate. And this was crucial to the history of caste in the subcontinent.

Under colonialism, caste was not merely a feudal-agrarian-rural phenomenon on the verge of disappearance due to the development of a capitalist-industrial-urban society. On the contrary, the mutuality of export of surplus and support to traditional native order and the corresponding axis between the caste forces and imperialism was indeed the template on which modernity in India came to be constructed. Here, the social forces representing caste-perpetuation eventually determined much of the newly emergent civil spheres, notions of state and justice and how indeed the rule of law itself is to be realised in the concrete. In the words of Srinivas, 'The establishment of Pax Britannica has set the Caste free from the territorial limitation inherent in the pre-British political system' (1962: 16).

Once politically unified, the persisting diversities of the ecological zones and ethno-linguistic regions were viewed as obstacles and sought to be overcome and homogenised through the formation of uniform districts and construction of communication networks. The administration of these units was a joint responsibility of the British as well as the Indians, who usually were from the river valleys where educational institutions had developed early. Notions of hierarchy, order, right and wrong, custom, tradition and local law, among others, developed and practised over several centuries here thus came to be dovetailed into the imperial-bureaucratic rationality and administrative justice at different levels of the government. Through inter-district and inter-provincial consultations and communications, these sectarian notions became uniform and integrated with the state knowledge sources for policy purposes.

As early as 1776, a 'Gentoo-code' got formulated for application in the law courts. As a piece of colonial Shastraism the Gentoo-code needed to be interpreted and explained by the native expert–the Brahmin Pandit. The modern-colonial court, soon enough, was transformed not only into a vehicle to propagate Brahminical hierarchicalism but also to extend it over the entire country indiscriminately, including the areas and inhabitants of the plains and hilly jungles.

The skewed and sectarian growth of public education, mostly in the densely populated river valleys, with its emphasis on the classical and English rather than the technical and vernacular, priority to higher rather than the primary, empowering mostly the traditional religio-literary castes has been well documented as the rise of the middle classes in modern India. The most ideological sphere of the new civil society, education, from its inception was nearly monopolised by groups who were traditionally dominant and who did not have any reason to change their traditional notions of dominance (Ambedkar 1990, vol. V: 27-61).

The formation and re-formation of the traditional sector–agriculture–also unilaterally went in favour of the Brahminical and the allied land-owning castes; the attenuating aspects of pre-modern agrarian relations were done away with and tenurial rights were transformed into ownership of the revenue collectors. This gave birth to a number of new forms of social bondage in the valley zones and also extended the same pattern to other areas. Second, increasing demand for and dependence on land revenue turned the British into superior but silent recipients of the revenue and at the mercy of big land magnates–zamindars and mirasdars–who shaped and reshaped the agrarian ground-realities to suit their interests and conveniences. The speedy transformation of Britain from a buyer into a seller of manufactured product added to the miseries of the toiling and artisan castes by sending them all back into agriculture.

Examples of colonial valorisation and universalisation of caste through sectarian empowerment of certain castes and its implication for the emergent modernity could be multiplied. The story in each is a repetition with minimum variation of the same theme–the new lease of modernised life granted to the dominant and determining castes of the riverine valleys consistently at the cost of others of the same zone and extension and replication of the pattern to the other zones and regions. What in short is being argued through illustrative identification of various social processes under colonialism is that in the absence of large-scale or organised economic change (which certainly could not be a colonial agenda), the protagonists of caste-varna, enabled through their historical role of partnership with imperialism, went forth from their relative ecological isolation to all corners of the subcontinent as emissaries of the new state and civil society, dictating and determining their nature and contour everywhere, certainly with varying degrees of success. In other words, precisely because those who had been making a living and ruling out of caste and its alleged sanctity in the riverine valleys came to occupy largely all the positions of power and influence nearly as unbroken communities, they not only helped shape the emergent polity and society according to their interests in innumerable subtle ways but they also carried and consolidated the hitherto ecologically restricted, sectionally practised and perennially contested caste ideology and spirit, through their own communal identification with the state and society. Caste became the subconscious and subterranean foundation of all subsequent Indian modernity; caste and caste-like features and notions came to be a shadowy dimension of all the public life of the subcontinent.[19]

The issue that is likely to be contested in this formulation, would be not so much that empowerment under colonialism was differential or even sectarian but that the empowered communities did carry their caste along with them into the new civil society and that they should be described as castes at all. The generally accepted terms are the middle classes, the elite, the bourgeois and the like, indicating a definite break with tradition. However the point being made here is precisely the opposite: that there was no break but a strong continuity. The colonial compact had underwritten that. In the event of no transformatory economic change and of no serious contestation at the pan-Indian level, the caste-protagonists had no reason to give up caste in any significant sense except to adjust it to the exigencies of modern life-circumstances. That the caste-cluster that was fast taking over the reins of power and enriching themselves within the new-opportunity-structure, did not envisage the emergence of any new reality for the country as a whole was clearly evidenced in their consistent opposition to the attempts of the lower castes to gain entry within the same system. This opposition could be identified everywhere in the subcontinent, consistent with the social locale they had been enjoying, and founded on certain notions of social order which is best described as caste-varna. The opposition was there when the hitherto relegated communities made efforts to enter public school and education, market-places and public squares, public resources such as water, grazing land, religious services, particularly temples and above all government-public employment. Ambedkar has repeatedly drawn our attention to the nature of relationship among the castes constituting the varna order: 'an ascending scale of reverence/hatred and a descending scale of contempt'. The resistance of the twice-born communities everywhere to the emergence of the mass was based on apparently no reason other than that they were of low-birth, that is, belonging to certain castes and by implication they themselves were where they were, precisely because their entitlement also came by birth. The situation being so, identifying these groups as the elite, the classes, or the bourgeois is only to camouflage their real nature. The castes *qua* castes were being empowered within the new state and civil apparatus, and hence casteism came to percolate and pervade the new public arena. And this process is to be identified as the single most significant impact of colonial rule in India. And again, it is within this context that the Orientalist and imperialist imagination of India as a caste society is to be contextualised and its determining power understood.[20]

## IV

In the history of social formations of the subcontinent caste-varna along with its antithesis was identified first in mid-Ganga valley and subsequently in several other riverine valleys; the process of encompassment by the valley-culture was also found to be double-edged, polarising the multiple and scattered forces into caste and anti-caste formations and finally this process came to a head under colonialism. Validation and valorisation of the caste-forces by Imperialism had the disastrous, consequence of polarisation of subcontinental society by sub-alternising the other eco-zones in general and the lower castes and anti-caste forces in particular. These, far from being passive patients of the situation, were grasping the modern-egalitarian juridical framework of the state and on the basis of the limited and largely unintended empowerment of scattered groups and individuals, broke forth in multiple directions, to overcome the now colonially aggravated and universalised caste-subordination. M.N. Srinivas' estimation of the situation could hardly be improved upon: 'It was as though they were no longer inhabiting a prison' (1966: 91). And in the latter part of the century, when the British were compelled to take note of this countrywide restlessness of the generalised masses and with the sure instinct of self-preservation, began to make some half-hearted conciliatory moves, the larger scenario of colonialism itself suddenly changed. Nationalism erupted with the powerful unifying call of tradition/culture/religion/ nation being in danger.[21] And in this section we deal with how the nationalists and nationalism affected caste and the castes.

Any explanation of the genesis of nationalism in the subcontinent has to grapple with the crucial question of why the ritual-literary and landed-dominant communities everywhere, for whom the British-Imperial rule had been 'providential' so far, all of a sudden towards the end of the 19th century became 'satanic'. Within the above perspective the crucial change in the upper caste perception took place in the context of polarisation of and contestation between castes ranged differentially and poised antagonistically along the ideological line of perpetuation or abolition of caste. This actual divide and its ideological dimension found its expression in popular awareness as *dwija/ekaja, bhadralok/chotelok, dikku/adibasi, Ujjalalok/Kaliparaj, brahman/ Shudra, badajat/ Chotejat, melchati/Kizhchati*, and the like. Nationalism everywhere was identified with the leading partner of the combinations. Nationalism and anti-caste, in other words, the caste-reinforcing attitudes of the former and the caste-escaping aspiration of the latter came to be poised for confrontation at the very genesis of the new social formation–the nation. Here is the continuity of the history of caste in the subcontinent.

The agency of nationalism here from its inception to the very end continued to be more or less exclusively constituted not only by the same communities, accustomed to the wielding of power within the caste-varna mode, and now, under colonial auspices were fast becoming part of the state-structure, but also who were simultaneously rejecting and resisting similar aspirations and attempts of the mass of lower castes in the name of custom and tradition. The historical continuity from the riverine valley domination through sub-continental expansion under successive empires, to the articulation of nationalism towards sovereign hegemony, all these, as far as possible within the caste-varna mode, cannot be missed by any serious sociological analysis. Nehru for one did not miss this when he stated that 'it was natural for the old Brahmin faith to become the symbol again and again of nationalist revivals' (1956: 27). The nationalist organisation, far from integrating the now politically awakened other eco-zones and the subordinated castes and their leadership in comradeship of equality and fraternity, sought to exclusively and hegemonically represent the entire population.[22] When the traditional *noblesse oblige* and proxy presentation did not succeed and the same was rejected by the relegated castes in favour of relatively autonomous collective assertion, social antagonism, the hitherto hallmark of caste-relations now engulfed the political sphere also. The scores of equally subcontinent-wide attempts by the masses to escape caste-imposed liabilities–occupations and identities–were resisted and rejected as sabotage of age-old custom and tradition, caste-movements or imitation of and collusion with the British. The lower caste evaluation of nationalism on the other hand, was accurate enough as Brahmanic/upper casteist, although their rejection of it was attenuated in the context of their continued economic dependence. Every effort was made by the nationalists to ignore the existence of those who ought not to, according to tradition, venture into the public realm; when this was not possible their attempts at emergence was ridiculed as job-hunting or as tailor-parliamentarian and when this too would not suffice, their bid for power was confronted with plain violence (see particularly Aloysius 1997, chapter 5).

During the latter phase of nationalism, under the leadership of Gandhi, the hitherto largely undercurrent, mutual recrimination surged into an open, acrimonious debate, with his candid declaration in favour of the varna ideal. According to Gandhi, the varna system determining and dividing society into natural groups based on differential innate tendencies found in men is the priceless discovery of our ancient sages and the proper basis on which a harmonious society in contrast and contradistinction to the individualist, competitive and hence conflict-ridden Western society could be constructed. This formulation was to achieve simultaneously two things; one, to transform the hitherto defensive into an offensive war of nationalism vis-a-vis imperialism but more importantly it was a clear warning to the masses on what to expect when nationalism succeeded to state power. However, it was conceded that untouchability, defined most literally, was a distortion of tradition and should be removed forthwith. This concession too was not without its political implications of dividing the anti-caste forces into touchables and untouchables. Caste-varna a problem to the majority of those, though differentially located in the social structure, who suffered through various forms of disabilities was sought to be substituted by untouchability as a consensus problem of all. Ambedkar, who, by this time had become the spokesperson of the anti-caste forces at the pan-Indian level had to wage the war on multiple fronts: articulating an alternative vision of society in continuity with the heterodox-egalitarian dimension of Indian history, giving an enlarged and existential meaning to untouchability explaining its symbiotic link with caste-varna and as a bottom line providing minimal survival space for the 'untouchables'. History records that only on the last count some success was achieved, and the larger questions were settled mostly in favour of the caste-forces represented by Gandhi.

With the rise, consolidation and political success of the communities whose interests lay in the perpetuation of caste-varna the process of its identification with the emergent state and nation had also been guaranteed. In other words, the colonialism in the precise sense of conscious, consistent and continuous collaboration between the British and the ritual-land dominant of the river valleys had effectively laid the ground for essentialisation of caste in India if the imperialist dimension of colonialism could be held responsible for the universalisation (all pervasiveness) and uniforming of caste-varna through the unification of state, the nationalist had assured its sacredness (changeless and eternal) by identifying it with nation and religion. Orientalism has been rightly pointed out as the starting point of this latter process. As a colonial ideology Orientalism also needs to be understood as a joint project and it had a janus-like feature, both negative and affirmative. If through internalisation of the negative, the native dominance engrafted itself with the state, articulation of the affirmative enabled itself to engender the 'nation'. The simultaneously and mutually reinforcing nature of the processes requires to be emphasized. The cultural ensemble to be identified by the nationalists as the soul of the nation to be born had as its nucleus, caste as varna–the *Varnashrama Dharma* most often expressed simply as Dharma, with due regard to the antagonistic sensibilities of the masses, but meaning just the same. The extremist section of the nationalists glorified it openly, while the moderates tended to use more secular-sounding phrases such as 'civilisational synthesis', 'national legacy/heritage', and so on, though when contested it was pointed out that the ideal being apotheosized was very different from its current practice.

Gandhi time and again explained with remarkable candour that varna meant determination by birth of one's status and occupation in life, which precisely was the issue of contest since the time of the Buddha. Second, the construction, maintenance and projection of caste-varna in its minimal sense of superordination and subordination of communities around the notion of dharma, meaning differential duties, was a collaborative project of the entire range of newly empowered castes, which came to be called the 'middle classes'. Professional and political differences, though many and real did not interfere with this minimal consensus on dharma-varna as the ideal being the cultural nation. Politicians, professionals, journalists, writers, religionists and others, each in their respective sphere of activities, engraved and elaborated the ideal vision or the Golden Age of society in consonance with varna dharma and critiqued the actual society in dissonance from it. Third, this dharma was then easily identified as the natural and desirable development of all regions, in fact co-extensive with the colonially constructed state incorporating non-caste and anti-caste social and ecological formations. The presence and claims of other cultures, value systems and philosophico-religious streams, though not to be left out of the boundaries of the hegemonic nation-state in the name of diversity, ought not to be included in the newly sacralised sphere of the nation. Apparently the principle of inclusion and exclusion too operated in a hierarchical fashion.

'Dharma' as the ideal for society within Indian nationalism had two definite functions. For the nationalists in search of an effective ideological platform the notions of differential duties and a divided society provided the requisite opposition and contrast to that of the imperialists' notions of homogenised and universal rights as the organising principles; now a distinct national identity based on real difference, corresponding to very much the nationalists' own power-positions and interests has been invented. Following this, dichotomies such as east/west, spiritual/material, duties/rights, communitarian/individualist, religious/secular, imperialism/nationalism, and finally, we/they, have become perennial and persistent categories of all levels of dominant thought processes with the inbuilt evaluation of the good and the bad. Simultaneously however, the caste-varna traditions now shrouded and sacralised as the cultural-national became the master ideological weapon to contain and control the socio-politically restless mass–the generalised lower castes, and similarly placed other communities in the far-flung regions. If through association and articulation the caste-varna values became national and hence inviolable, through antagonistic dissociation anti-caste-varna values, beliefs ideologies and behaviour patterns, became anti-national and stood discredited; they represent the culture and values of the Other, imitation of the West and hence stand in serious need of correction.

Caste-varna traditions of the river valleys also became the kernel of the new 'religion' of the subcontinent–Hinduism–another Orientalist discovery. Variously labelled the Brahminic faith, Vedic religion, *sanatana dharma*–Hinduism, to the conjuring up of which much effort was expended by nationalist stalwarts from Raja Rammohun Roy down to Mohandas Karamchand Gandhi – was and has been invariably recognised by the masses in the absence of a specific set of beliefs, for what it actually is, an embodiment of a way of life, a form of social relationship, a pattern of organising society, not dissimilar to that of varna. Generally, in the wake of modernity and secularism, the rise of a civil religion has been noted in several parts of the globe, a sacralisation of the new and changed values surrounding egalitarian and fair-minded forms of socio-political relations and a contractual respect towards the public-civil spheres limited to and bounded by the particular culture or ethnie. In the subcontinental context, however, we have had the unique privilege of reifying-deifying through the accidents of history, what had hitherto been the sectional, sectarian and discriminatory practices of a particular set of people living in relatively isolated regions of this vast land mass. The traditional socio-religious practice of the dominant has reincarnated with no change in essentials as the new civil religion in modernity and secularism.

## V

Caste is a historical social formation peculiar to certain areas, particularly the river valleys in early India and its process of engulfment of the subcontinent has been double-edged in the sense of provoking its own antithesis. The process is far from complete. It was certainly possible, as Rhys-David points out that if Buddhism had persisted, today we would not have a caste-ridden India (referred to in Chakravarti 1987). We could have had other histories, and in fact we do, though submerged and fragmented. Nation and religion on the other hand derive their reality and salience precisely on their supposedly meta-historical and hence sacred nature. The deep enmeshing of the former with the latter under the historical accident of collusive colonialism in both its dimensions of imperialism and nationalism has made caste too in a real sense meta-historical, essentialist and quasi-sacred. Grasping this metamorphosis as the result not only of hegemonic imagination but also of the rise to state power of the dominant castes everywhere is the first step in its re-historicisation. Caste-varna, both as an existential reality and a cognitive ideal is another name for Brahminical social order or Brahminism in short, which as the socio-political ideology of modern India is inextricably entangled with the nation (India) and the religion (Hinduism). In a very real sense this trimurti is a colonial-collusive construct.[23] That is why any attempt to deconstruct or destruct caste has vital implications for nation and religion; and similarly any attempt to valorise either the nation or the religion has the unfortunate effect of sending the wrong signals to the masses who are victims of the caste-varna system and spirit, albeit at different levels.

## Notes

The author is grateful for discussions with Professors C.N. Venugopal and Uma Chakravarti.

1. ' a land... of the most inviolable organisation by birth' (Weber 1958: 3).
2. Having highlighted the issue Inden, however, is satisfied with merely suggesting that caste could be interpreted as an 'agency' instead of 'patiency', in the form of a citizenship though graded; see chapter 6 of Inden (1990:217-220).
3. A geographical view of the subcontinent is elaborated in O.H.K Spate et al. (1967); but see in particular B. Subbarao (1958).
4. The multiple relationship between language and society has been too well recognised in the social sciences to require specific documentation.
5. The actual eco-social classifications and their nomenclature vary from author to author. Subbarao (1958) speaks of the valley's isolated and the relatively isolated zones.
6. Though it is tempting to fit the three-fold geographical classification into the three-fold linguistic traditions, historically this cannot be validated.
7. Subbarao (1958: 5) notes the relative isolation of India from the main trans-continental trade routes of the world.
8. While popular as well as academic discourses insistently describe the subcontinent as unity in diversity, it is only the unity that is problematised and valorised for understandable political reasons. However, the knowledge that has resulted from this monotonous and mono-linear process is very meagre and often not significant.
9. H.K. Kulke (1995) has identified three state-forms–chiefdom, kingdom and empire–different from one another not only in scale, but also in other characteristics.
10. The following summary description is based on Sharma (1990, 1996).
11. Sharma's problem apparently is subsumption of varna-caste (1990: 15) under class as pointed out by Chakravarti (1987).
12. See Chakravarti (1987) and Chattopadhaya (1978, chap.3). To these must be added the non-caste/varna stratification as evidenced in the Sangam poetry of peninsular India.
13. Within the sociologically recognised types of social stratification, if caste-varna could be seen as based on 'status', this would be on 'power'. The south Indian variation of this latter is elaborated in Nicholas B. Dirks (1987).
14. While the resonance that Buddha and Buddhism have had down through history among non/anti-caste forces has been well recognised, the precise nature of Buddhist egalitarianism is debated. Perhaps D. Chattopadhya's (1978) evaluation is most accurate if we pardon him his Marxist bias: 'The Buddha alone of all the contemporary prophets, could offer to the people of his times the illusion of liberty,

equality and fraternity....' Typically the Marxist, the author regards the anti-varna democratic equality as an illusion (p. 467).

15. This expanding political horizon dominated by the varna-caste type of social stratification is well-captured in the changing nomenclature of the territory as Brahmanavarta, Aryavarta and Bharatvarsha.
16. There are also other reasons why caste forces become aggravated at the rise of empires–the need for administrative and clerical infrastructure requires the services of the traditionally literary and dominant castes; the language to be used at the level of the empire again is a distinct elite-classical one, requiring linguistic specialists from again the same ruling groups, thus expanding their role power.
17. The relation between ideology and political economy in determining social relations is explored in Abercrombie et al. (1980).
18. For a study of 'collaborative colonialism' see R. Robinson (1972:117-40).
19. An accurate, though somewhat propagandist summary of how colonialism empowered Brahminical castes could be had from one of the earlier social historians, Swami Dharma Teertha (1992: 159ff).
20. The argument is a much condensed version found in the the author's book (Aloysius 1997).
21. This and the following again is a sketchy argument, elaborated with extensive documentation in G. Aloysius (1997).
22. While sociology of movements in India has documented the stories of mobility and protests by the subalterns and historiography has recorded the political movement for independence by the elite, the mostly conflictual relation between the two is a child of no parents. Some attempts have been made to take care of this in G. Aloysius (1997).
23. P. Chatterjee (1986) spoke of nationalist thought in India as being derivative of colonialism. But he certainly did not explain it in this sense.

## References

Abercrombie et al. I980. *The dominant ideology thesis*. London: Allen & Unwin.

Ambedkar, B.R. 1990. *Collected writings and speeches*, Vol. 5. Bombay: Government of Maharashtra.

Allchin, Bridget and Raymond. 1996. *The rise of civilisation in India and Pakistan.* Cambridge: Cambridge University Press.

Aloysius, G. 1997. *Nationalism without a nation in India.* Delhi: Oxford University Press.

Baker, C. J. 1984. *An Indian rural economy.* Delhi: Oxford University Press.

Chakravarti, U. 1987. *The social dimensions of early Buddhism.* Delhi: Oxford University Press.

__________. 1998. *Rewriting history: The life and times of Pandita Ramabai.* New Delhi: Kali for Women.

Chatterjee, P. *Nationalist thought and the colonial world.* Delhi: Oxford University Press.

Chattopadhaya, D. 1978. *Lokayata: A study in ancient Indian materialism.* Delhi: Peoples' Publishing House.

Conlon, Frank, F. 1981. 'The census of India as a source for the historical study of religion and caste', in N.G. Barrier (ed.). *The census in British India.* Delhi: Manohar.

Dirks, N. B. 1987. *Hollow crown.* Cambridge: Cambridge University Press.

Frykenberg, R. E. 1965. *Guntur district (1788-1848): A history of local influence and central authority in South India.* Oxford: Clarendon Press.

Inden, R. 1990. *Imagining India.* Oxford: Basil Blackwell.

Khubchandani, Lachman. 1993. 'India as a sociolinguistic area', in A. Ahmed (ed.), *Social structure and regional development.* Jaipur: Rawat Publications.

Kulke, H.K. 1995. *The state in India 1000-1700.* Delhi: Oxford University Press

Nehru, Jawaharlal. 1956. *The discovery of India.* London: Meridian Books Ltd.

Pollock, S. 1998. 'The cosmopolitan vernacular', *The Journal of Asian Studies,* 57(1): 6-37.

Robinson, R. 1972. 'Non-European foundations of European imperialism', in R. Owen and B. Sutcliffe (eds), *Studies in the theory of imperialism.* London.

Sharma, R. S. 1990. *Material culture and social formation in ancient India.* Delhi: Macmillan.

__________. 1996. *The state and varna formation in the mid-Ganga plains.* Delhi: Manohar

Spate, O.H.K. and A.I.A. Learmont. 1967. *India and Pakistan: A general and regional geography.* London: Methuen & Co.

Srinivas, M. N. 1962. *Caste in modern India and other essays.* Bombay: Asia Publishing House,

__________. 1966. *Social change in modern India.* Hyderabad: Orient Longman.

Stein, Burton. 1969. 'Integration of the agrarian system of south India', in R.E. Frykenberg (ed.), *Land control and social structure in Indian history,* pp. 175-216. Madison: The University of Wisconsin Press.

Subbarao, B. 1958. *The personality of India.* Baroda: M.S. University.

Thapar, R. 1984. *From lineage to state.* Delhi: Oxford University Press

Theertha, Swami Dharma. 1992. *History of Hindu imperialism.* Madras: Dalit Educational Literature Centre.

Washbrook, D. 1991. 'To each a language of his own: Language, culture and society in colonial India', in P. J. Corfield (ed.), *Language, history and class,* pp. 179-203. Oxford: Basil Blackwell.

__________. 1993. 'Land and labour in late 18th century south India: The golden age of the pariah?' in P. Robb (ed.), *Dalit movements and the meanings of labour in India.* Delhi: Oxford University Press.

Weber, M. 1958. *The religion of India. The sociology of Hinduism and Buddhism.* Illinois: Glencoe.

# 10

# Religion and Language in the Formation of Nationhood in Pakistan and Bangladesh

*Tanveer Fazal*

In the wake of decolonisation, the newly liberated states of Pakistan and Bangladesh faced a precarious situation. While most of the colonies, owing to a variety of historical factors, had retained their 'multi-national character', the accepted maxim in the West on which they aspired to model their polity was 'one nation-one state'. Following the collapse of the monarchy and with it divinity as the sole legitimiser of authority, cultural homogeneity or the isomorphism between state and society became the bedrock on which the sustenance of the former was believed to be guaranteed. Hence, the term nation-state came into vogue despite the fact that the 'nation-state was only an aspiration', which could never be 'realised even in Western Europe' (Oommen 1997: 136). While the 'nation' was a cultural concept, the state was an embodiment of rational-political institutions.[1] And behind this thin veneer was hidden the project of drawing people's sentiments to the state so as to ensure their loyalties—lone and terminal.

The narrative of the triumph of the West European 'nation-states'—colonisation and industrialisation—was quite enticing for the decolonised and peripheral states in the non-Western world. The Western model offered them a state for their nascent 'nationalism', an idea they had already imbibed during their struggle for independence. It promised political coherence for the polyglot states, only if they could transcend traditional group loyalties in favour of an abstract sense of community called the nation. The received model sought to reconcile the centrifugal pulls of ethnic and primordial collectivities by instilling an idea of nationhood. Where the nation and the state were not coterminous, the push was towards constructing such coterminality. In other words 'project homogenisation', a term Oommen uses quite pejoratively, was unleashed through a state-patronised and sponsored nationalism (1997: 135-37). For many, enthused by the Deutschian thesis of social mobilisation, this could most impressively be achieved through a solvent like modernisation. But as Sheth points out, 'the politics of social mobilisation, instead of being shaped by the state's modernising project proceeds from the existing relationships of power within the society' (1989: 626). This only strengthened the domination of the numerically dominant and politically entrenched over the structures of power. In their effort to create an appropriate phantasmagoria, the cultural moorings of the 'nation' came to be defined in terms of the symbols and ethos of the dominant group. This led to the 'ethnification' of weak and marginal national and ethnic groups.

Pakistan, comprising the territories of erstwhile British India, had at its shoulder the claim of separate nationhood by the Muslims of the subcontinent. The Muslim homeland itself underwent ruptures as its eastern half, catapulting on a linguistic nationalism, shunned all its association with a religion-defined 'national identity'. Despite a near religious homogeneity in Pakistan, and a linguistic unity in Bangladesh, both the South Asian states have had a turbulent exercise in 'nation-building'. If religion in Pakistan has failed to subsume various bases of peoples' identifications, language in Bangladesh has created its own insiders and outsiders. A pertinent question that troubles social cognition then is, how should nation be conceived and comprehended ? Our effort in the following pages would be guided towards bringing forth the state's agenda of 'nation-building' and its cultural-ideological proclivities in the particular context of Pakistan and Bangladesh. In contraposition to the state-defined national agenda, the endeavour shall also be towards explicating the alternative notions of nation and its attributes, which will go a long way in interrogating the state defined-categories.

## Pakistan: The state and its ideology

As the theory of 'two nations' culminated in the creation of the sovereign Muslim state, the same became the ideology in the nascent state for the purpose of legitimising political authority. 'Muslim nationalism', the raison d'etre of Pakistan, was defined abhorring territorial nationalism, an antithesis to the 'universal community of faith' as idealised in the sacred texts. The notion of an all-encompassing 'Indian nation', embracing the entirety of the peoples and territories comprising British India, was repudiated. The 'Muslim nationalists', perceiving the threat of an imminent Hindu hegemony, popularised the notion of a distinct Muslim personality—universalistic in orientation and indistinguishable despite cultural, linguistic or territorial ties with those outside the faith. Iqbal, to whom is owed the ideological foundation of 'Muslim nationalism', while presenting the Indian Muslim personality specifically governed by Islamic ideals, was actually contesting the West and its exhortation of the binary opposition between the spiritual and the temporal. It was for this reason that Iqbal was derisive of 'western nationalism' for it prioritised peoples' loyalty to their fatherland over and above all other identifications.

> It is not the unity of language or country or the identity of economic interests that constitutes the basic principle of our nationality. It is because we all believe in a certain view of the universe...that we are members of the society founded by the Prophet of Islam. Islam abhors all material limitations, and bases its nationality on a purely abstract idea objectified in a potentially expansive group of concrete personalities . . . In its essence it is non-temporal, non-spatial (cited in Syed 1979: 80-1).

Yet in its application to the political context, the ideological or spiritual nationhood of Iqbal was concretely linked to the claim over a separate homeland. And Jinnah, in his presidential address to the Lahore session of the League (1940), put it succinctly: 'Mussalmans are a nation . . . and they must have their homeland, their territory and their state' (1960: 57).

Pakistan as it emerged, post-Partition, was a state sui generis. The people inhabiting the newly carved out territories belonged to multiple speech communities and, ensconced in their respective customs and traditions, were even living in geographically non-contiguous territories. Pakistan had for its frontiers two isolated regions, situated at the far corners of the subcontinent with an intervening stretch of almost 1,500 kms of Indian territory. In terms of its ethnic or national composition it had Bengalis comprising the bulk of the eastern wing, with Punjabis, Sindhis, Pashtuns and Baluchs placed in its western part. In retrospect, the demand for Pakistan was raised on behalf of the Indian Muslims in their entirety. Yet the creation of Pakistan foreclosed any neat equation between the demand and the reality. Well after Partition, millions of Hindus still lived in Pakistan and the 1951 Census recorded their numbers at as high as around 14 per cent, with the largest chunk residing in East Pakistan (Gankovsky 1964: 97).

It was not that the architects of Pakistan missed the reality. The dilemmas that confronted the new state were delineated in an article written by a successive president of Pakistan:

> [Pakistani nationalism was] based more on an idea than any territorial definition. Till then ideologically we were Muslims, territorially we happened to be Indians and parochially we were conglomeration of at least eleven smaller provincial loyalties. But then Pakistan emerged as a reality, (we) were faced with the task of

> transforming all our traditional territorial and political loyalties into one great loyalty for the new State of Pakistan (Ayub Khan, cited in Wilcox 1969: 347).

The decades following the establishment of Pakistan were marked by intense debates within the intelligentsia and amongst the political actors, so as to find a viable basis for the consolidation of the state and its people. Discerning the tension inherent in Pakistan's geographical and ideological frontiers, the pragmatist in Jinnah did a volte face invoking secularism and common citizenship rights as principles guiding state policy:

> You are free; you are free to go to your temples, you are free to go to your mosques or to any other place of worship in this state of Pakistan. You may belong to any religion or caste or creed–that has nothing to do with the business of the state (Jinnah n.d: 8-9).

Notwithstanding the founder's inclination for a secular polity, conflicting views came to the fore once the incipient state undertook the task of drafting its future Constitution. The initial controversy began on the question of Islam's centrality, reminiscent of the old tension between the traditionalists and the modernists. Interestingly, barring a few secularists, the majority of the political leadership of the new state agreed that the morals and traditions of Islam should find some reflection in its laws and institutions. This consensus, however, faced a crisis once Islam's relationship with the modern state and its institutions came to be put in practice. The traditionalists, including the fundamentalists, negated any role to the 'human will' or 'human legislation', in favour of the discretion of the divine. The 'supreme sovereignty', it was held, rested in God alone; the 'state' could at most, 'administer the country as His agent' ( Maududi, cited in Binder 1961: 102-3). The modernist version, on the other hand, was an apologist one, which stood for an ideal balance between divine restrictions and human freedom.

In the final analysis, none emerged victorious. The objectives-resolution incorporating the principle on which the future Constitution was to be fashioned, was in effect a compromise accommodating both the contentions. It accepted the traditionalist position that the 'sovereignty over the entire universe belongs to God Almighty alone, and the authority which He has delegated to the state of Pakistan through its people for being exercised within the limits prescribed by Him is a sacred trust'. But in its assurance that 'the principles of democracy, freedom, equality, tolerance and social justice, as enunciated by Islam shall be fully observed', the resolution also contained the modernist underpinnings (reproduced in Ahmad 1991: 219). The ambiguous wording of the resolution has remained a bone of contention down to the present day, thereby subjecting the Constitution to a continuous process of re-writing.

Issues of national identification continued to sharpen diversities of opinion in Pakistan. Linked to different worldviews they impinged on different modes of conceptualising the nation and its cognates. In a survey conducted in the late sixties, Nasim Javed categorises his respondents under three heads: the 'Islamic nationalists', solely or prevalently identified with the confessional faith which was seen as the only real collective bond of the Muslims of Pakistan and elsewhere; diametrically opposed to them were the 'secular nationalists'; occupying the middle ground were 'Pak-Islamists' who reconciled the competing identities of 'territory' and religion (Javed 1974:19-25). It was the latter formulation around which the Pakistani national identity came to be grounded. Consequently, Islam acquired the centrality that alone could fortify the state, at the same time making the nation an ineluctable part of the *millat* (religious community). As a prominent Pakistani politician argued, 'The spirit of Pakistan is Islam or if you prefer it, Muslim. That spirit has to be preserved. You can only cherish and safeguard it if . . . vehicles for the operation of the *millat* within the *qaum* (nation) are afforded and preserved' (cited in Wilcox 1969: 347).

The 'official nationalism' attempted to fix and objectify an essentialised sense of 'Muslim identity'. The ideology of the state found its most ardent advocates in Punjabis who enjoyed monopoly over structures of state power, so much so that, the Punjabi identity fused into the identity of Pakistan. In this hegemonic project, the Muhajirs[2] joined as junior partners. Being a people uprooted from their native land, the theory of Muslim nationhood could alone provide the rationale for their continued existence in the new state. While the Muhajirs filled in the bureaucracy along with the Punjabis, the Punjabi domination in the military—a colonial legacy—remained unperturbed. Approximately 80 per cent of the army and 55 per cent of the federal bureaucracy were from the Punjab. The Muhajirs--3.5 per cent of the population—had a share of 21 per cent in the Pakistan Civil Services (Samad 1995: 28). Power, as inhered in the state, came to be monopolised between these two ethnic groups resulting in a highly centralised structure. It manifested itself through the domination of a military-bureaucratic oligarchy over the civilian-political authority.

Their domination in the field of culture was most evident when Urdu, historically the language of the Muslim nobility and, in Pakistan synonymous with Muhajir culture, was chosen to become the language of the state. Given the diversities in the linguistic and cultural association of the inhabitants, Urdu alone, it was believed, could realise a 'monolithic nation'. Notably, merely 2.4 million inhabitants spoke Urdu, yet the rationale was the rhetoric of Islam. As the state's first governor-general sought to emphasise:

> The State language, therefore, must obviously be Urdu, a language that has been nurtured by a hundred million Muslims of the sub-continent, a language...which, more than any other provincial language, embodies the best that is in Islamic culture and Muslim tradition and is nearest to the language used in other Islamic countries (Jinnah n.d.: 90)

Interestingly, those arguing for the pre-eminence of a supra-national Islamic identity argued in favour of Arabic, for it was the 'language of Islam' which alone could bring in 'lingual unification of Muslims' as an 'integral part of their overall unification' (Matin 1954).

The triumphalist approach, while essentialising Islam as the sole determinant of a Muslim's predilections, simultaneously projected and reified a monolingual Islam. Scriptural Islam was idealised, at the cost of other social practices. President Ayub Khan's observations on Bengali Muslims' cultural practices smacks of such contempt: 'East Bengalis, who constitute the bulk of the population, probably belong to the very original Indian races...they have been and still are under considerable Hindu cultural and linguistic influence. As such they have all the inhibitions of downtrodden races' (1967: 187).

The ideology of the state was de facto a hegemonic project—an universal ideological enterprise that could conceal class and ethnic conflict. As Gramsci, clarifying the concept of hegemony, had noted, the supremacy of a social group manifests itself in two ways, as 'domination' and as 'intellectual and moral leadership'. While domination is actualised through the coercive machinery of the state, hegemony of ideas is objectified in and mainly exercised through civil society, the ensemble of educational, religious and associated institutions (1973: 242, 259-65).[3] The state-aligned intellectual activity, through school text books and historical projects, have particularly concentrated on moulding cognitive structures.[4] Consequently, history is the biggest casualty as attempts are made to situate the yearning for Muslim nationhood in the medieval past. A Radio Pakistan broadcast thus declared:

> The foundations of Pakistan were laid with the arrival of the first Muslim in the subcontinent. Pakistan has at its back the historical heritage of a thousand years. The strength of Pakistan lies in the political, cultural and religious supremacy of the Muslims...The people of Pakistan are firm in their belief in Islamic principles (cited in Nayyar 1972: 147).

Islam, in this sense, came to be deployed as an ideological apparatus so as to legitimise political authority. For the ruling clique, a flirtation with the idea of the Islamic state remained, primarily, an effort to superimpose an essential 'Muslimness' on its populace. This alone, it came to be believed, could sustain the Pakistani nation.

### Contesting hegemony: Rise of Bengali nationalism

No sooner was the new state established, than the ambiguously conceived 'Muslim nationalism' lost its contextual significance. Whereas the Muslims in British India carried with themselves myriad layers of identification—religious, linguistic, class—each historically contingent, it was a misconception on the part of the ideologues of Pakistan to assume a perpetually stable 'religious identity'. At the height of 'Muslim nationalism', the other bases of association had merged or were temporarily suspended so as to absolutise an overwhelming 'Muslimness' in their identity. This interface between religion and politics was not to remain the same in an obverse socio-political context. This was augmented by the Punjabi-Muhajir détente and its consequent concentration of power and essentialisation of culture. The severest jolt to the state's ideological enterprise was the emergence of nationality movements, particularly Bengali, where nation came to be conjured on the edifice of cultural-specificity, linguistic identity and a claim over the ethnically associated homeland.

In the case of the Bengali Muslims it marked a significant departure, as prior to Partition a large majority of them had been active campaigners in the League's acceptance of Islam as the sole definer of their personality. With the rise of a vernacular-oriented non-*ashraf* (noble by birth) intelligentsia, a new search for an identity had begun. This shift had shown strong undercurrents as early as in 1955, when Mujibur Rahman, in a speech in the Constituent Assembly, gave vent to his anxiety:

> Sir you will see that they want to place the word 'East Pakistan' instead of 'East Bengal'. We have demanded so many times that you should make it Bengal (Pakistan). The word 'Bengal' has a

history, has a tradition of its own. You can change it only after the people have been consulted (*Seminar*, June 1971: 24).

With their roots in the eclectic culture of Bengal, the emerging intelligentsia came out against the hegemonic language of the state. As against the idiom of Islam invoked in favour of the imposition of Urdu, the language movement, which shaped the formative phase of Bangla nationalism, questioned its validity: 'We refuse to believe that any language under heaven can be Islamic or Christian or Heathen' (cited in Murshid 1995: 303). Spearheaded by the students and the intelligentsia, the movement demanded parity of Bangla with that of Urdu as the language of the state. Though the demand was conceded, the fervour that it generated refused to die down.

The contest, however, was not confined to the arena of culture alone. Besides their subjective association with the Bangla language and culture, Bengali nationalism contained actual material ramifications for the Bengali speech community. While questioning the pre-eminence that Urdu enjoyed, they were, in effect, struggling against the imminent closure of power and opportunity that such a measure would inevitably have brought (Phadnis 1989: 168). In the context of the highly centralised garrison state structure of Pakistan, Bengali protagonists questioned internal colonialism, dominant-subordinate relationship and inequity in the distribution of power within the society. Following Hechter, who sees 'internal colonialism'[5] as a situation in which 'the core' seeks 'to dominate the periphery politically and to exploit it materially' (1975: 9); the eastern wing could well qualify as a periphery colonised by the western wing. Though the imbalance between the two wings was a legacy inherited by the Pakistani state, the new regime could do little to set it right. Despite being a numerical majority (56 per cent), Bengali representation in the military elite remained a miniscule 5 per cent whereas they could form only 30 per cent of the civil-bureaucratic elite (Jahan 1972: 24-26). Mujib's six-point demand named *Amader bachar dabi* (Our Right to Live), therefore, concentrated on measures such as regional autonomy, land reform, nationalisation of industries, to correct the unevenness embedded in Pakistani social and political structure.

Centred on language, Bangla nationalism inevitably came into conflict with the religion-specific Muslim/Pakistani identity. Until the mid-1960s, as a survey concludes, Bengali Muslims faced no fundamental conflict in their identification as Bengalis and simultaneously as Pakistanis (Schuman 1973). This tension between the pulls of religion and language is evident in the reflections of Abul

Mansur Ahmad, a prominent politician of Pakistan. Contrary to the single-symbol thrust in Bengali nationalism, he laid stress on multi-symbol congruence–language and religion–in determining their national identity. His enthusiasm for Bengali had a strange slant–he favoured Pak-Bangla, with heavy doses of Persian, to serve as the distinct language of Bengal Muslims (Murshid 1995: 295).

This ambiguity dissipated as Bengali discontent culminated in mass Bengali nationalism leading to the emergence of Bangladesh in 1971. 'Bengali' acquired a secular connotation emphasising the cultural dimension of identity. 'Pakistani', on the other hand, implied a continuing belief in the oppressive two-nation theory and in giving primacy to religion, subsuming all other identities. The works of Nazrul Islam and Rabindranath Tagore came to be celebrated. And in place of *'Pakistan Zindabad'*, *'Jai Bangla'* became the nationalist outcry (Phadnis 1989: 169).

### Post-1971 quest for identity in Pakistan

The secession of the eastern wing had truncated Pakistan of a sizeable territory and reduced its population to about half its size. More so, the 'new Pakistan' that had remained was hardly an ethnically coherent formation. The insurmountable loss, however, was to the ideological edifice on which national identity was conceived. The Muslimness of their identity, which many among them, for so long, had zealously guarded, lay shattered in history. 'The two-nation theory, formulated in the middle class living rooms of Uttar Pradesh, was buried in the Bengali countryside' (Ali 1983: 96). An event setting forth to a gradual realisation, as we shall see in the following pages, of bases of association, other than that informed by their religion. The situation purported to what Gramsci had called, the 'crisis of hegemony', meaning whereby 'the ruling class has lost its consensus . . . i.e., . . . the great masses have become detached from their traditional ideologies, and no longer believe what they used to believe previously' (1973: 275-6). Consequently, post-dismemberment Pakistan was witness to a quest for ideological coherence and a 'national identity' which could fuse the contending trends. The crisis, as many began to feel, could only be averted by a renewed commitment to Islam, the cornerstone of Pakistan. Pakistan of post-1971, was witness to a fervour in favour of Islamic idiom and symbols (Richter 1979). The group of leading Pakistani historians who had met in Islamabad to explore the 'quest for identity' arrived at the same conclusion:

> ...the wish to see the kingdom of God established in a Muslim territory...was the moving idea behind the demand for Pakistan, the cornerstone of the movement, the ideology of the people, and the raison d'etre of the new nation-state...If we let go the ideology of Islam, we

> cannot hold together as a nation by any other means…If the Arabs, the Turks, the Iranians, God forbid, give up Islam, the Arabs yet remain Arabs, the Turks remain Turks, the Iranians remain Iranians, but what do we remain if we give up Islam? (cited in Richter 1979: 549)

Subsequently, Islam retained the pre-eminence in the state-defined 'national identity'. Ironically, what could have provided a basis to realise the futility of deploying religious symbols, instead came to be interpreted as implying that a digression from Islamic ideals and principles had been instrumental in bringing Pakistan to such a pass. Islam, we would argue, again acquired the status of ideology that, for the statists, could alone provide legitimate authority. This functional attribute of Islam was handy for both the regimes with modernist orientations as well as those with avowed commitment to the Islamic state.

Zulfikar Ali Bhutto, the leader of Pakistan People's Party that had swept the polls in West Pakistan in the 1970 elections, had his political discourse anchored in socialism, decentralisation and restoration of democracy. While analysing the political developments leading to the cataclysmic events in the eastern wing, Bhutto had remained steadfast in his ideas blaming overarching centralisation and 'cold blooded exploitation' of the people : 'The tragedy of Pakistan lies in the fact that…[it] has been a federation in name only…The spirit of federalism and the rules of co-existence were sacrificed at the altar of ambition. In the name of "strong centres" the power of the provinces were weakened to the point of being extinguished' (Syed 1992: 18). Despite his modernist inclinations, Bhutto continued to make liberal usage of Islamic idioms to draw a popular base for his political goals. Islamic socialism, the thrust in his political vocabulary was a curious admixture of Islam with populist slogans of *roti, kapda aur makan*. With his ascendance to power, the dissonance between theory and practice became explicit. As disillusionment with his populist rhetoric aggravated, he increasingly reverted back to Islam.

Islamisation of the state and society became a professed aim as Zia-ul-Haq staged a successful coup d'etat. The theory of two-nations, the fulcrum on which Pakistan was realised, now needed to be coterminous with a theocratic state—an issue successfully avoided by the previous regimes. 'Pakistan', as Zia held, 'was created in the name of Islam' and would 'continue to survive only if it sticks to Islam' (Richter 1979: 555). The unprecedented Islamisation that followed to establish the ideal *Nizam-i-Mustafa* (the ideal governance delineated by the Prophet), was all-encompassing, covering the totality of Pakistani life. As Pakistan proceeded to become a confessional state, nationhood came to be defined in terms of religious affiliations. All other cultural or ethnic ties had to be surrendered in favour of Islam, and thereof, to the state, failing which, disintegration would be the fait accompli. Zia tried to make this point by drawing an analogy from the Zionist state, Israel:

> Other than Israel, Pakistan is the only state created on religious grounds. We were created on the basis of Islam. Look at Israel : its religion and its ideology are the main sources of its strength. We in Pakistan have lost sight of the importance of these things. And without them you're like straw being thrown about in the ocean. You're a Sindhi, a Baluch, a Punjabi, a Pathan. Pakistan's binding force has always been Islam. Without it Pakistan would fall (cited in Wilder 1995: 67).

Consistent with this, Arabic, claimed as the language of the *ummah* (community of believers) by the Islamists, became obligatory along with Koranic and Islamic studies. Laws were enacted making jurisprudence consistent with the Shariah (Islamic law). The enforcement of *zakat, ushr* and *riba*—traditional Islamic taxation and trading norms—sought to make the Islamisation of human behaviour complete.

Notwithstanding the fact that the inconsistency of such an ideological offensive strikes the modern mind, the Islam which the state and its hegemonic apparatus sought to project suffered from contradictions from within the Islamic discourse. The 'scriptural Islam' of the state either remained oblivious to other trends or such trends were declared antithetical to Islamic observances—the Ahmediyas[6] providing the glaring instance. In such a construction of national identity, the non-Muslims were definitely not to find a place, as was attempted through the system of separate electorates. The minorities have instead argued for a composite Pakistani nationhood based on their equal claim to the homeland. As one Pakistani Christian laments, 'Is Pakistan not a nation ?—Then why separate electorates?...we do not consider ourselves to be a separate people from Pakistanis just because of religion?' (cited in Richter 1982: 147).

### The criticality of language and territory in Pakistan

Sociological insights in the study of nations, their formation and political articulation confirm the criticality of both language and territory as their objective foundations. Since nations are essentially cultural concepts, language is seen as the nucleus of culture. The speakers of the same language develop an immense common bond and with such an attachment they go back to a 'common store of social memories'. Joshua Fishman has expressed this view strongly: '...the essence of nationality is its spirit, its individuality, its soul.

This soul is not only reflected and protected by the mother tongue but, in a sense, the mother tongue is itself an aspect of the soul, a part of the soul made manifest' (cited in Karna 1998). Moreover, for the nation to articulate and express itself, it has to be residing in a common territory often claimed as its ancestral homeland. The crucial significance of territory is illustrated by the fact that the 'loss of homeland invariably results in the loss of one's mother tongue' (Oommen 1997: 194).

Both language and its association with a distinct homeland gained salience as different ethnic groups—the Sindhis, the Pashtuns, the Baluchs and more recently, even the Muhajirs—came to contest the state-defined national identity. The defection of the Bengalis, rather than containing, exacerbated the ethnic tensions in Pakistan. And part of the reason, as we would argue, was the underestimation on the part of the ruling elite of the 'festering contradiction that lay beneath the surface of Pakistan's political structures' (Ali 1983: 112). Despite the centrality of Islam in the official enterprise to provide ideological foundations for the state, the assertion of these units as nations-in-themselves, contests the 'theory of two-nations'. Wali Khan, the doyen of Pashtun nationalism, articulating the tangible markers of Pashtuns' cultural distinctiveness, discounted any attempt to subsume them within the overarching identity of 'Muslimness'. On being asked whether he was 'a Muslim, a Pakistani, or a Pashtun first', he emphasized that he was a 'six-thousand-year-old Pashtun, a thousand-year-old Muslim and a-27-year-old Pakistani' (cited in Harrison 1987: 285).

The 'ethno-nationalists' have remained resilient to any effort at subsumption in any larger collectivity. With their cultural affiliations anchored in language and territory, their narratives refute any validity to the state defined categories. Pakistan, Islam, Urdu and Punjab are seen enmeshed in each other and designed to obliterate their cultural specificities. This invariably leads to derision of the deterministic role of religion. G. M. Syed, the 'grand old man of Sindhi nationalism', was candid in putting forth his views:

> Sindh has always been there, Pakistan is a passing show. Sindh is a fact, Pakistan is a fiction. Sindhis are a nation, but Muslims are not a nation. Sindhi language is 2000 years old, Urdu is only 250 years old. Sindhi has 52 letters, Urdu has only 26. The enslavement of Sindh by the Punjab in the name of 'Pakistan' and 'Islam' is a fraud …The Sindhis have long been fooled in the name of Islam (reproduced in Malkani 1984 : 134).

Pakistan is not seen as a 'nation' but, with a subtle inflection of meaning, it is transmuted into a 'state' or a 'country'. The territories of Pakistan, therefore, are the abodes of multiple-nations some of which, particularly the Pashtuns, retain extra-territorial ties with their co-nationals in neighbouring states. The duality in their identity and subsequently their loyalty is sought to be reconciled by ethno-nationalists by demanding recognition of this multiplicity by the state. The Pakistan National Party (PNP) and its leader Ghaus Baksh Bizenjo, have been propagating the theory of four nationalities, that is, the Sindhi, Punjabi, Baluchi and Pashtun, each situated in their national homelands, should form a federation of Pakistan, which would ensure iron-cast guarantees against the violation and usurpation of the rights of federating nationalities (Bahadur 1986: 141).

Seemingly accommodative, the theory of four nationalities suffers from its own inadequacy, particularly on the question of Muhajirs. In the emerging ethnic situation and reformulation of national identity, the Muhajirs as an ethnic category provide by far the most adequate illustration for sociological cognition. In the inceptual phase of Pakistan, the Muhajirs along with the Punjabis came to monopolise the structure of authority and decision-making. Muhajir domination was most pronounced in the arena of culture, wherein, their inclination towards scriptural Islam and the language, Urdu, came to determine the ideological parameters of the state. So much so that, the two-nation theory and Islamic fundamentalism remained the dominant ideological-political current among the Urdu-speakers. Post-Bangladesh, Muhajir political identity came to be redefined. With the rise of the Muhajir Qaumi Movement (MQM), Muhajirs have increasingly shunned their association with the broader Muslim-Pakistani identity in favour of a particularistic-ethnic identity. Claiming that the Muhajirs constitute the 'fifth nationality' of Pakistan, the MQM has increasingly dissociated itself from the two-nation theory:

> Those who have become flag-bearers and self styled champions of the Two Nation Theory do not even know its fundamentals. If believers in this theory were alive today 250,000 believers would not have been living a life of misery and deprivation in Bangaladesh; the Indian Muslims would not have been paying a levy for creating Pakistan by living at the mercy of Hindus; nor would believing Muhajirs had been worse than animals in Pakistan (MQM Document 1972: 1).

Though the MQM ostensibly claims to retain a fledgling link with the theory of 'Muslim nation', the claim of separate national status by the Muhajirs effectively amounts to its repudiation by the very actors in whom the agency for its realisation was restored. The reformulation of

Muhajir identity was accompanied by two significant developments—each impinging on the former. One was the 'relative deprivation', as Farhat Haq has argued (1995: 991-3), in the Muhajir political and economic status. and b) the political repercussions that followed the Bangla secession. The upheaval that followed seriously questioned the validity of the two-nation theory, which had been the sole justification for the Muhajir's presence in Pakistan. If even the pre-eminence to Islam had proved insufficient in holding Pakistan, then what else would? The threat gathered strength with the rise of Sindh national movement, and the Muhajirs were faced with the possibility of their extermination from the Sindh province (Ahmed 1988: 38). The course left to the Muhajirs was then the claim of a 'national status' in association with the territories which they inhabited.

Significantly, in the contending ethnic scenario in Pakistan, Punjabis remain the only national group that has not claimed cultural distinctiveness. Even more striking is the fact that while Muhajirs in the pre-Bangladesh phase of Pakistani politics found no fundamental dissociation between their self-identity and that of the state-defined national identity, the same came into conflict in the later phase. This invariably brings us to our larger concern, the interface between power and culture and the situational compulsions in which ethnic nationalisms increasingly adopt a distinctive path.

Power as defined by Weber is 'the chance of a man or a number of men to realise their own will in a social action even against the resistance of others who are participating in the action' (Weber 1978: 26). Though power is ubiquitous and manifests itself in different interactive situations between groups and individuals, our reference here is to the location of power within the state and its institutions. In Pakistan, Punjabi domination through military-bureaucratic oligarchy, the ruling clique, has fused Punjabi interest with the interest of the state. This is to the extent that in the eyes of the marginalised nations, 'Pakistan has become Punjabistan' (G.M. Syed, cited in Malkani 1984: 31). It is then a group's proximity to power that determines its political trajectory. Exclusion results in the politicisation of the identity. Muhajirs provide the most apt illustration of groups whose earlier association with the state made them the most vociferous campaigners of Pakistan's ideology. Their exclusion, thereof, has led to identity based mobilisation. It is this disjuncture between culture and power that has led the Sindhis, the Baluchs and the Pashtuns to assert their distinctiveness demanding the distribution of power over cultures.

## The 'Other' in the Pakistani discourse

With the vivisection of the state, considerable engagement of sociologists and social scientists has been directed towards comprehending the ethnic mosaic in Pakistan, its social composition and political implications. While the multi-ethnic and multi-national composition has been explicated, in retrospect, they have also bemoaned the lack of a unified Pakistani nation owing to the 'shallow roots of the Pakistan Movement' and the absence of a 'sense of a shared national culture and symbols and long historical memory that binds people into a nation' (Alavi 1991: 153). Stretching this argument, some such as Tariq Ali have seen it as an 'irrationality' whose 'interior was diseased from birth', thus suggesting an eventual dismemberment of the state (1983: 145). Almost three decades since the Bangla-breakaway, Pakistan as a polity survives. An upsurge in nationality movements notwithstanding, the state in Pakistan has resisted any balkanisation. It is not that the state has been able to politically contain the festering contradictions leading to the evolution of any monolith of opinion or identity of interests. For one, unlike the case of the Bengalis, the different nations in Pakistan are territorially contiguous making secessionism a difficult possibility. Second, and much more significant is the extraneous source on which Pakistan's integrity finds its foundations—the construction of an 'external other'. For social groups, the awareness of the 'other', distinct from the self, invariably assumes the existence of an unambiguous collective self-identity. Where the 'other' is nebulous, an effort is made to construct one (Oommen 1994). In Pakistani social and political discourse, therefore, India appears as the 'external other'—vilified and demonised. The theory of 'Muslim nationalism' in British India had gained salience in the context of the fear of an imminent Hindu hegemony. The same, in relation to India and Pakistan, assumes geo-political dimensions, wherein India appears as the abode of a Hindu nation eternally at odds with Muslim Pakistan.

Pakistan's engagement in Kashmir, therefore, has significant ideological connotations, besides its strategic pertinence. Kashmir, for its Muslim majority and geographical contiguity with Pakistan, is viewed as an unfinished agenda of the 'two-nation' theory. Since 'K' in the acronym PAKSTAN stands for Kashmir, Pakistan is as seen incomplete without Kashmir having acceded to it (Varshney 1991: 999-1001). Illuminating the Pakistani commonsense on Kashmir, Iftikhar Malik writes:

> Kashmir emphatically manifests a cross-sectional, inter-regional, ideological unanimity within Pakistan and is more than a territorial issue. The mass based revolt in the Kashmir Valley and the Indian atrocities are reminders to the Pakistanis that a growing Hinduised India is unable to reconcile to an assertive Muslim factor in South Asia politics. Kashmir, to an ordinary

> Pakistani, is…a constant challenge to their nationhood. (Malik 1996: 5-6).

By constantly engaging peoples' priorities vis-à-vis Kashmir and thereof, India, the aim is to define and solidify the 'nation-state' itself. For ordinary Pakistanis possessing layers of identities, their identification with the state or with their particular national/ethnic group usually operates in different contexts. An inclusive Pakistani identity gains pre-eminence when confronted with a 'Hindu India'. When it concerns the allocation of resources, their particularistic association as a Punjabi, Sindhi, Baluchi or as a Pashtun asserts itself (Islam 1981: 69-70). Pakistan as a state partly draws its sustenance through a manipulation of the above identities.

**Bangladesh: Competing trends of language and religion**

In the course of their long-drawn liberation struggle, the Bengali nationalist identity came to be structured around a strong sense of association with the peculiarities of their language and culture. The ideological hegemony of the Pakistani state, built on Islam, was thus countered giving pre-eminence to ties supposedly un-Islamic. A secular state distancing itself from religion and a nationalism anchored in the Bangla language was, for the *Bangobandhu* Sheikh Mujib and his party—the Awami League—the logical corollary. The preamble to the new Constitution (1972) pledged on the 'high ideals of nationalism, socialism, democracy and secularism' and the national edifice of the new state was defined as:

> The unity and solidity of the Bangalee nation, which, deriving its identity from the language and culture, attained sovereign and independent Bangladesh through a united and determined struggle in the war of independence shall be the basis of Bangalee nationalism (Article 9).

Consistent with it, the Constitution termed the citizens of Bangladesh '*Bangalees*' and adopted *Amar Sonar Bangla* as the national anthem of the republic (Article 6 & 4 [1] ).

Since the rupture from the Pakistani state had to be complete, both politically and ideologically, the secular Bangladesh state epitomised the rejection of all that the Muslim state had stood for—the separate electorates, two nation theory, and flirtation with the idea of a theological state. A secular polity, however, was not coterminous with promoting irreligiousness in the social and cultural moorings of the people. Aware of the religiosity of the people, Mujib himself felt the compulsion to re-assure them against any misgivings regarding the principle:

> Secularism does not mean the absence of religion. You are a Mussalman, you perform your religious rites. There is no irreligiousness on the soil of Bangladesh but there is secularism. This sentence has a meaning and that meaning is that none would be allowed to exploit the people in the name of religion.... No communal politics will be allowed in the country.

Seemingly accommodative, the 'Bangalee nationalism' of Mujib still suffered from serious lacunae. The Bangladesh that had emerged was far more homogeneous than its predecessor. An overwhelming majority (99 per cent) constituted the Bengali speech community of which nearly 86 per cent were the followers of Islam. The remaining, a miniscule one per cent who were not part of the Bengali speech community, comprised the tribals inhabiting the hill tracts and the Biharis, the descendants of the Urdu-speaking immigrants (Phadnis 1989: 39). A religion-neutral Bangalee national identity would be able to include all the Bengalis irrespective of their religious beliefs but, for the ethnic minorities, assimilation alone into the mainstream could guarantee their continued existence. Further, Bengali nationalism suffered from its own contradictions. Historically, the popular form of Islam in Bengal had facilitated the growth of a peculiarly Bengali syncretist tradition. This, however, did not completely obliterate the Hindu-Muslim distinctions or lead to any fusion of identities. Murshid notes that up till the arrival of the British, the Bengalis were identified as Hindus and the Muslims as immigrants. This distance was maintained by giving a subtle variation in the Bangla language with *Do-bhasha*, containing dozens of Persian and Arabic words being particularly popular in the Muslim majority East Bengal (Murshid 1993). Besides, during their 20-25 years long association with the Pakistani state, the Muslims of Bengal were subject to the indoctrination that being Muslims they were a nation-in-themselves. In their struggle against Pakistani hegemony, though they had shunned the primacy of Muslim identity, the sovereign Bangladesh still had groups and individuals who had found this hard to digest. The 'Bangalee nationalism' of Mujib was primarily contested by two social and political groupings, the thoughts of each emanating from their own life conditions.

The ethnic minorities comprising a cluster of tribal groupings and inhabiting the Chittagong Hill Tracts had for long preserved their specific culture and tribal solidarity. In contrast to the overwhelming

Muslim-majority in Bangladesh, the tribals were adherents of different religions—Buddhism, Christianity, animism and so on, and spoke a variety of Tibeto-Burmese languages. The 'Bangalee nationalism' espoused by the Bangladesh state wherein all the citizens were to be called Bengali, necessarily pre-supposed either the extermination of non-Bengalis or their submergence in the larger collectivity. Thus, the Chakma leader, Manabendra Narayan Larma, refused to be identified with the Bengali nation : 'Under no definition or logic a Chakma can be a Bengalee or a Bengalee can be a Chakma.... As citizens of Bangladesh we are all Bangladeshis but we also have a separate ethnic identity, which unfortunately the Awami League leaders do not want to understand' (cited in Hussain 1986: 201).

A refusal to submerge in the dominant nationality led to the extermination of Urdu-speaking ethnic groups, the Biharis, from the state. The Biharis, instead, have identified themselves with the 'Pakistani' state. With the Muhajirs in Pakistan still seen as alien by the local populace, the Biharis' continued allegiance with Pakistan provides a strange case. A spokesman of the 'stranded Pakistanis' expressed this tension while speaking about their plight : 'The plight of Pakistanis stranded in Bangladesh for more than 23 years presents a very strange situation ... We are refugees in Bangladesh and eat our heart out for our country which is Pakistan' (Nasim Khan's statement in *Muslim India* 1995:45).

The second category of political actors vehement in their denunciation of the 'linguistic nationalism' were, if broadly termed, the traditionalists or 'Islamic nationalists'. They consisted of the ulamas and political formations such as the Jamaat-i-Islami, the Muslim League and others. Being the bearers of scriptural Islam, they regarded the importation of Bengali language and cultural observances as contrary to Islamic consciousness. Envisaging a pan-Islamic solidarity, they had remained scornful of the liberation-struggle. Some of them, such as the Jamaat-i-Islami of East Pakistan had actively collaborated with the Pakistani army against their co-nationals (Ahmad 1993: 501).

A conscious decimation of the Islamic identity and adoption of secularism as state policy compelled the Islamic traditionalists, in the post-liberation phase, to launch a campaign for 'Muslim Bengal'. Retaining a vague association with the original two-nation theory, they argued for only Muslims in Bengal to be declared nationals. Quite oblivious to the verdict of history, they nursed the vision of a united Pakistan. Owing to the lack of organisational base and popular support, the 'Muslim Bengal' movement gradually dissipated. The secular oriented 'Bangalee nationalism' as it had evolved in the liberation struggle remained a strong ideological current among the Bengali populace particularly so in the inceptual phase. As Trevor Ling, writing as early as in 1972, observed:

> There is, in fact,... a greater community of interest between Muslims and Hindus than might be expected. The division between the two no longer corresponds with a difference in economic function. The real lines of cleavage, as recent events have demonstrated, are more between Bengali and non-Bengali than along religious communal lines .... There is thus likely to be a reasonable degree of convergence between the expectations of the leadership with regard to the new state, as secular, democratic and socialist, and, of the people (1972: 227).

The above observation of Ling receives further confirmation through an empirical study of Nasim Javed, done in more or less the same period. The study, conducted among middle-class professionals, found greater incidence of those who described their nationality in terms of their country or ethnic group (60 per cent) over those who defined their nationhood in terms of the Islamic faith. Significantly, a substantial proportion (24 per cent) identified with Islam as well as the Bengali nation, finding the two identifications perfectly compatible (1974: 38-9, 47-8).

The 'Bangalee nationalism' of Mujib, defined in terms of a single-symbol thrust—the language—could barely distinguish itself from the sixty million Bengali Hindus in the neighbouring West Bengal. The above orientation of the state took a retreat following the military coup, whereby Zia-ur-Rahman took over the reins of power. And as was witnessed in the case of Zia's Pakistan, Zia-ur-Rahman turned increasingly towards Islam to legitimise his military junta. One of the foremost actions in this regard was the insertion of the invocation 'Bismillah-ir-Rahman-ir-Rahim' (In the name of Allah, the Beneficient, the Merciful) in the preamble to the Constitution. Article 8 (1) which had declared secularism as the cardinal principle was amended to read, 'absolute trust and faith in the Almighty Allah'. Similarly, a new clause was included which declared the intentions of the state towards 'stabilising, preserving and strengthening fraternal ties with the Muslim states on the basis of Islamic solidarity' ( Ahmad and Nazneen 1990: 796). In the process, the national identity also came to be remoulded. The 'Bangalee nationalism' was replaced by 'Bangladeshi' in the amended Constitution, and Zia himself gave a comprehensive explanation of the new connotation:

> Bangladeshi nationalism means, we are Bangladeshis. We have a different history. Our country has been through a different process. Our traditions and culture are different. Our language is different, we are moulding it in our own way—we are modernising it. We have different prose and poetry; we have different arts and thoughts. Our geographical position is different, our rivers and soils are different. Our people are different. We are completely free and sovereign...And, today a consciousness has grown among our people, which is different from that of the people of our neighbouring country and other countries of the region (cited in Huq 1984: 58).

Apparently identical, the 'Bangalee nationalism' of the Awami League and the 'Bangladeshi nationalism' associated with the BNP (the Bangladeshi national party), differed markedly in terms of emphasis on language and culture, inclusion and exclusion of 'nationals' and 'aliens'. While the former appreciated the territorial and political separateness from the Indian Bengal but accepted the entire heritage of the Bengali language and culture as its own, the latter highlighted the cultural differences between the two regions by bringing in religion as the defining marker of 'Bangladeshi nation' along with language. The change was significant, as Urmila Phadnis has pointed out:

> ... instead of the earlier single symbol thrust (Bengali) for the identity of its people, the inclusion of Islamic provisions (connoting a religious symbol) coupled with the change from 'Bengalis' to 'Bangladeshis' (emphasising territorial homeland symbol) provided a multi-symbol congruence in the Bangladesh nation in differentiating it from India just as language differentiates it from Pakistan (1989: 107).

The anxiety to invoke a 'national personality' free of the cultural association with the neighbouring Bengal, drove Zia towards adopting certain hegemonic measures. Endeavours were made to remould the language, history and culture of Bangladesh, particularly so in language, where efforts were made to infest the Bengali language with words from Persian and Arabic vocabulary—measures to revive the now obsolete *Do-bhasha* or the artificial measures to create *Pak-Bangla*. Thus, the slogan *'Jai Bangla'*— linguistically of Bengali origin was replaced with the more Persianised *'Bangladesh Zindabad'*. The de-emphasisation of Bengali language was carried further by referring to Bangladesh Betar as 'Radio Bangladesh'(Murshid 1993: 70-2).

Sociologically, the new concept of 'Bangladeshi nation' invoked by Zia was essentially teleological as it impinged on the formation of the state. The nation here is defined then in terms of the political unit and the political community to which it caters; while historically, nations have preceded states. Moreover, the possibility of the same nation residing in the realms of different states has remained a theoretical as well as an empirical viability; for instance, the pre-unification Germans, and among the Muslims, the Arabs. The 'Bangalee nationalism' of the Awami League has effectively addressed this ambiguity:

> In terms of statehood and citizenship we are Bangladeshis but in terms of nationality we are Bangalees ... Bangladesh has been created through a bloody liberation war based on the symbol of Bangalee nationality. Bangalee is the national identity of the people of this Bangladesh. This identity is hundreds of years old. It has not been possible to wipe out this identity despite all out efforts during the Pakistan period. Nor will it be possible to do so in the future (cited in Huq 1984: 63).

## Conclusion

The coceptualisation of nation and national identity in the state-societies of Pakistan and Bangladesh have been contingent to the vicissitudes of history. More often than not, it is the exigency of power and politics that have been deterministic in drawing its parameters and boundaries, terms of inclusion and exclusion. Given the flux in the political context itself, a constant reshaping of the attributes of nation often reveals contradictions. Muhajirs provide an interesting illustration. When in alliance with Punjabis, they remained the principal bearers of Muslim/Pakistani nation. Devoid of power and patronage, the Muhajirs, more recently, have claimed themselves as the 'fifth nation' of Pakistan. Similarly, among Muslims of Bengal, language-centric Bengali nationalism remained the dominant trend vis-à-vis the religious nationalism espoused by the Pakistani state. Post-liberation, religion has reappeared to define the nationhood of the populace.

Such flexibility in conceiving 'nation' receives validity from theoretical formulations where the 'subjective will' of the political actors remains the only viable attribute of nation. Consistent with this, an incessant drive in the South Asian states of Pakistan and Bangladesh has been to conflate state and nation. Designed towards obfuscating the reality, their implications—social and political—have been far and wide, one of the professed objectives being to define the terminality of loyalty, so as to hierarchise the bases of association with which people identify themselves (Oommen 1997). Nation tends to be constructed in terms of the 'will of the dominant', thus making 'national mainstream' an euphemism for the cultural proclivities and material interests of the former. Punjabi domination in Pakistan and Bengali Muslim hegemony in Bangladesh represent such an appropriation of nation leading to the ethnification or extermination of marginal groups.

Since concepts in social science emerge out of particular historical experience, yet without transcending their immediate empirical context, they remain of limited utility (Oommen 1997 : 23); a plausible way out would be to conceive nation as an objective social reality rather than as an appendage, or a construct. The task is to find out tangible factors—language, culture and territory—critical in conceiving and defining nation. Seen thus, Pakistan is an abode of multiple nations—Punjabi, Baluch, Pashtun and Sindhi. A near homogeneity of Bengali-speakers in Bangladesh still restricts it from qualifying as a 'nation-state' owing to the presence of non-Bengali tribal groups in the Chittagong Hill Tracts. For the state and their ideologues, this amounts to a recognition of the plurality of identifications, not necessarily detrimental to the political association with the state. This implies the recovery of concepts like nation and nationhood from artificially contrived statist discourses and institutionalisation of multi-cultural co-existence within the confines of the same polity. A pluralist perspective of the kind derides attempts to define any cultural/national mainstream through coercive measures like assimilation or annihilation. In contrast, the orientation is towards accepting and accommodating differences.

## Notes

1. The idea that the 'nation' and 'state' are conceptually distinct and may not appear coterminous has had a long career. However, in most contributions on the theme, nation is seen as a prerequisite for state formation. Nation is seen either coinciding with state, or as state-seeking. This leads to considerable interchangeability in the usage of the two terms. More recently, Oommen (1997), has emphasized the importance of maintaining a distinction between the two. The existence of the multi-national ethnic states is therefore not only a theoretical possibility, but also an objective fact of history.
2. Muhajirs comprise largely the Urdu-speaking immigrants from the erstwhile Muslim minority provinces of British India. The Muhajirs arrived in Pakistan as proud champions of the 'Muslim nation'. Interestingly, not all the Partition-induced immigrants acquired this connotation. A vast majority of the nearly seven million Muslims who crossed the frontiers consisted of Punjabi speakers from eastern Punjab, who, on account of the commonalty of language and culture, readily assimilated with the ethos of the West Punjab. The term Muhajir came to be associated only with the latter section of the Urdu-speaking Muslim migrants who filled urban Sindh, replacing the migrating Sindhi Hindus. Resenting their being referred to by the natives as Pahangirs or Hindustanis, they conferred on themselves

the nominative Muhajir, owing to its association with the prophetic tradition of *hijrat,* or emigration due to religious motives (Ahmed 1988: 33-4). For the migrating Punjabis, it was at the most a shift from one part of their homeland to another. The Muhajir case, on the other, is typical of social groups de-nationalised from their native land, and who have failed to re-nationalise in the adopted homeland. They thus qualify as an interest group or an ethnic category in Pakistan.

3. Whereas others have seen civil society in opposition to the state, Gramsci (1973) did not perceive it to be completely autonomous. Since the institutions of civil society are subject to the control of the state, the hegemony of ideas necessary for the sustenance of the state is actualised only through civil society and its institutions.
4. This is of course not to suggest that Pakistan has been solely a consensual state where force is not resorted to. In fact, politics everywhere and particularly so in Pakistan, has rested upon a mix of consent and coercion, both being omnipresent. When consent is absent, coercion shows its face, usually in the form of the application of military power.
5. The model of internal colonialism put forth by Hechter (1975) contrasts with the diffusion model of nation-building espoused by the theorists of political development and modernisation. According to Hechter, rather than levelling cultures as the latter claim, economic development institutionalises inequality creating conditions of internal colonialism and crystallisation of cultural markers. During the regime of Ayub Khan, Pakistan took to economic development and industrialisation hoping that the modernising impulses would diffuse tensions. Contrarily, the state's agenda failed to arrest the discontent since the fruits of development were cornered by Punjab in particular.
6. The Ahmediyas, followers of Mirza Ghulam Ahmad of Quadian (Punjab), have been regarded as heretics by the orthodoxy due to their rejection of the finality of Mohammad's prophethood. Soon after the formation of Pakistan, anti-Ahmediya riots, actively abetted by the traditionalists, broke out in Pakistani Punjab. In the early 1970s, Ahmediyas were declared non-Muslims as a beleaguered Bhutto government took recourse to Islam. The measure, carried out with vehemence during Zia's regime, confirmed the ethnification of the Ahmediyas in their own land.

## References


Ahmad, Emajuddin and D.R.J.A. Nazneen. 1990. 'Islam in Bangladesh: Revivalism or politics', *Asian Survey,* 30(8): 795-808.

Ahmad, Ishtiaq. 1991. *The concept of an Islamic state in Pakistan: An analysis of ideological controversies.* Lahore: Vanguard.

Ahmad, Mumtaz. 1993. 'Islamic fundamentalism in South Asia: The Jamaat-I-Islami and the Tablighi Jamaat in South Asia', in M.E. Marty and R.S. Appleby (eds). *Fundamentalism and the state: Remaking parties, economies and militance,* pp. 457-530. Chicago: Chicago University Press.

Ahmed, Feroz. 1988. 'Ethnicity and politics: The rise of Muhajir separatism', *South Asia Bulletin,* 8: 33-45.

Alavi, Hamza. 1991. 'Nationhood and communal violence in Pakistan', *Journal of Contemporary Asia,* 21(2): 152-78.

Ali, Tariq 1983. *Can Pakistan survive? The death of a state.* Harmondsworth: Penguin.

Bahadur, Kalim. 1986. 'Islam and national question in Pakistan', in K. Bahadur (ed.). *South Asia in transition: Conflicts and tensions,* pp. 133-47. Delhi: Patriot.

Binder, Leonard. 1961. *Religion and politics in Pakistan.* Berkeley and Los Angeles: University of California Press.

*Constitution of the Peoples' Republic of Bangladesh, The.* 1972. Dhaka.

Gankovsky, Y.V. and L. R. Polanskaya. 1964. *A history of Pakistan.* Moscow: Nauka

Gramsci, Antonio. 1973. *Selections from the prison notebooks.* New York: International Publications.

Haq, Farhat. 1995. 'Rise of MQM in Pakistan', *Asian Survey,* 25(11): 990-1016.

Harrison, Selig. 1987. 'Ethnicity and political stalemate in Pakistan', in A.Banuazizi and M. Weiner (eds), *The state, religion and ethnic politics: Pakistan, Iran and Afghanistan,* pp. 267-98. Lahore: Vanguard.

Hechter, Michael. 1975. *Internal colonialism: The Celtic fringe in British national development, 1536-1966.* London: Routledge and Kegan Paul

Huq, Abul F. 1984. 'The problem of national identity in Bangladesh', *Journal of Social Studies,* 24: 47-73.

Hussain, Hayat. 1986. 'Problem of national integration in Bangladesh', in S.R. Chakravarty and V. Narain (eds), *Bangladesh.* Vol. 1: *History and culture,* pp. 196-211. Delhi: South Asian.

Islam, Nasir. 1981. 'Islam and national identity: The case of Pakistan and Bangladesh', *International Journal of Middle-East Studies,* 13(5): 55-72.

Jahan, Rounaq. 1972. *Pakistan: Failure in national integration.* New York and London: Columbia University Press.

Javed, Nasim A. 1974. 'Islam and political attitudes in Pakistan and Bangladesh: A thematic and quantitative approach.' Ph.D Dissertation in fascimile, Los Angeles: University of California.

Jinnah, M. A. 1960. *Speeches and writings.* Vol. 1, ed. Jamiluddin Ahmed. Lahore: Ashraf.

____________. n.d. *Speeches as Governor-General of Pakistan 1947-48.* Karachi: Pakistan Publications.

Karna, M. N. 1998. 'Language region and national identity.' Paper presented in XXV All-India Sociological Conference, Aligarh Muslim University (AMU), Aligarh.

Khan, Ayub. 1967. *Friends not masters: A political autobiography.* Karachi: Oxford University Press (OUP).

Ling, Trevor. 1972. 'Creating a new state: The Bengalis of Bangladesh', *South Asia Review,* 5(3): 221-30

Malik, Iftikhar H. 1996. 'Kashmir and Pakistan: Politics of mutualities and denied opportunities', *Strategic Studies,* 18(4): 5-47.

Malkani, K. R. 1984. *The Sindh story.* Delhi: Allied.

Matin, H. M. 1954. *National language of Pakistan.* Karachi: Marsh

*MQM Document.* 1972, 'Mr. Altaf Hussain stands by his views on the two nation theory', July.

Murshid, Tazeen M. 1993. 'Bangladesh: The challenge of democracy—Language, culture and political identity', *Contemporary South Asia,* 2(1): 67-73.

____________ 1995. *Sacred and the secular: Bengal Muslim discourses, 1871-1977.* Calcutta: OUP.

*Muslim India.* January 1995, 145: 45.

Nayyar, K. K. 1972. 'Pakistan's experience of two nation theory', *Secular Democracy,* 5(8): 147-53.

Oommen, T. K. 1994. 'The changing trajectory of constructing the "Other": West Europe and South Asia'. *Sociological Bulletin,* 43(1): 161-76.

____________ 1997. *Citizenship, nationality and ethnicity: Reconciling competing identities.* Cambridge: Polity.

Phadnis, Urmila. 1989. *Ethnicity and nation-building in South Asia.* Delhi: Sage Publications.

Richter, William L. 1979. 'The political dynamics of ethnic resurgence in Pakistan', *Asian Survey,* 19(6): 547-57.

__________ 1982. 'Pakistan', in M. Ayoob (ed.). *The politics of Islamic reassertion,* pp. 141-61. Delhi: Vikas.

Samad, Yunas. 1995. 'Pakistan or Punjabistan: Crisis of national identity', *International Journal of Punjab Studies,* 2(1): 23-42.

Schuman, Howard . 1973. 'Note on the rapid rise of mass Bengali nationalism in east Pakistan', *American Journal of Sociology,* 78(2): 291-8.

*Seminar*. 1971. 'Symposium on Bangladesh'. Vol. 142. June.

Sheth, D.L. 1989. 'State, nation and ethnicity: Experience of Third World countries', *Economic and Political Weekly,* 24(12): 615-26.

Syed, Anwar H. 1979. 'Iqbal and Jinnah on issues of nationhood and nationalism' in C. M. Naim (ed.). *Iqbal, Jinnah and the two-nation theory: The vision and the reality,* pp. 77-106. Syracuse: University Press.

__________ 1992. *The discourse and politics of Zulfikar Ali Bhutto.* London: Macmillan.

Varshney, Ashutosh. 1991. 'India, Pakistan and Kashmir: Antinomies of nationalism', *Asian Survey,* 31(11): 997-1019.

Weber, Max. 1978. *Economy and society: An outline of interpretative sociology.* Berkeley: University of California.

Wilcox, Wayne. 1969. 'Ideological dilemmas in Pakistan's political culture', in D. E. Smith (ed.). *South Asian politics and religion,* pp. 339-51. Princeton: University Press.

Wilder, Andrew. 1995. 'Islam and political legitimacy in Pakistan' in M.A. Syed (ed.). *Islam and democracy in Pakistan,* pp. 31-87. Islamabad: NICHR.

# 11

# Caste, Ethnicity and Problems of National Identity in Sri Lanka

*Kalinga Tudor Silva*

Much of the literature on nationalism and its divisive and violent tendencies focuses on problems posed by ethnicity. Ethnic divisions in each country are products of historical processes operating in their respective settings. In the US where ethnicity in its modern form was first discovered by social scientists, ethnic differences in the sense of culturally-defined group identities, which refused to get blended into one American culture in the way anticipated by architects of modern American society, were by and large produced by waves of population movement from various parts of the world (Gordon 1964). Similarly, ethnicity in modern South Asia must be understood in the light of its own historical developments and cultural setting. What this paper seeks to illustrate is the relationship between caste and ethnicity in the South Asian context with a focus on Sri Lanka where ethnic polarisation has intensified to an unprecedented level in the post-independence era. What appears to be happening in parts of South Asia is that the basis of the explicit primary identity of individuals is shifting from caste to ethnicity. This, in turn, has multiple implications for problems of nation building and problems of evolving higher order citizenship ideals.

In a recent essay, 'Race, caste and ethnic identity', Beteille (1997) argues that while both caste and ethnicity give expression to cultural rather than racial differences among people, in a caste system differences among people are always perceived within a socially and culturally defined *hierarchical framework* whereas ethnic groups need not be arranged in a similar fashion. Insofar as ethnicity creates unity and common sentiment among diverse peoples and ethno-nationalism gives rise to 'a deep horizontal comradeship' among people 'imagined' to be of one kind, as claimed by Anderson (1983), ethnicity may come in conflict with the hierarchical idiom of caste. Further, since ethnicity evolves as a higher order social differentiation, whereas caste has primarily to do with who is superior to whom at the community or at most the subregional level, the rise of ethnic sentiments and politicisation of ethnicity at the higher level is bound to undermine some of these aspects of caste which highlight internal differences and status distinctions *within* an ethnic group. However, there is no evidence that with social change caste simply gives way to ethnicity; nor is it evident that the rise of ethnicity necessarily implies a weakening of caste. It is this dialectical interaction between ethnicity and caste and its implications for problems of nation building in South Asia that forms the primary focus of this brief paper.

As in any interaction, there is a two-way relationship between caste and ethnicity in the South Asian context. First, we must look at the ways in which caste dynamics impacted on the formation and rise of ethnic sentiments. We have some evidence on the caste and class background of people who gave leadership to militant ethno-nationalist movements in the region. Why would certain people in certain circumstances want to renounce or at least undervalue their caste identity and replace it with a higher order ethnic identity? Second, once ethnic polarisation reaches a critical stage what impact does it have on more parochial identities of caste? Does it make caste less important or does it merely make caste less visible and more of a *doxa* ('taken for granted reality') in Bourdieu's terms (1977: 166)? In view of its ethnonationalist developments and more manageable size, contemporary Sri Lankan society provides an ideal setting for investigating both types of issues.

## Caste and the Rise of Militant Ethno-Nationalism

The rise in ethnic sentiments in contemporary South Asia dates back to the colonial period. Ethno-nationalist movements evolved as part of anti-colonial struggles for affirming the cultural roots and heritage of indigenous groups interacting with each other and with the colonial masters.

The literature on nationalist movements typically sees these as social movements capturing the imagination of new social forces (for instance, the indigenous middle classes) created under colonialism (Anderson 1983; Chatterjee 1993). As evident from the expanding literature on the subject (De Silva 1986; Kapferer 1988; Hellmann-Rajanayagam 1992; Tambiah 1992), this analysis is broadly applicable to both Sinhala Buddhist and Tamil nationalist movements which evolved in British Ceylon. These movements, which were largely cultural-revivalist in character, had more or less receded by the time of the political independence of Sri Lanka in 1948. What is of particular relevance to the current study is the resurgence of nationalist discourse in the post-independence era in the form of militant ethno-nationalisms driven by grassroots-level organisations engaged in socio-political reform and ethnic activism within a framework of competitive struggle for access to state power. In particular we will examine the extent to which and the mechanisms whereby a shift from caste to ethnicity occurred in regard to the primary social identities of individuals.

In one of the early works dealing with the precursors of the Tamil separatist movement in Sri Lanka, Pfaffenberger (1990), examined the 1968 temple entry crisis in Jaffna. He argued that challenges to the Vellalar domination in Jaffna first evolved in the ritual arena where the untouchable castes sought entry to the famous Maviddapuram temple. The Vellalar landlords crushed this challenge with physical violence. Efforts on the part of the Colombo government to mediate in this dispute angered the conservative Tamil leadership, which viewed it as 'interference in private matters of caste relations and temple worship'. According to Pfaffenberger, this in turn encouraged the conservative Tamil political leadership to formulate a '*defensive nationalism*' in order to unify the Tamil community and promote common ethnic sentiments as a defense against divisive caste skirmishes.

Even though the temple entry crisis was an internal conflict within the Tamil community it paved the way for a broad-based and more militant struggle inspired by radical ethnic sentiments and led by non-Vellalar elements in time to come. While it is possible that the temple entry crisis led to a rise in caste consciousness at least in the short run, it also represented a weakening of consensus regarding the respective ritual positions of the Vellalars and their traditional service providers, as well as an overall demise of the organic solidarity model of interdependence and mutual concern among castes. It appears that a degree of relaxation of intercaste practices built around rigid notions of pollution inevitably resulted from the temple entry crisis and the subsequent effort to unify Jaffna community along ethnic lines.

The exact composition of the Liberation Tigers of Tamil Eelam (LTTE) cadres and their social background are not known. However, the broad parameters of the movement indicate that its leadership is largely drawn from frustrated elements among upwardly mobile caste groups (immediately below the dominant Vellalar caste in Jaffna society) and that the movement perhaps has a higher participation of traditionally disadvantaged groups (including women and those from depressed caste backgrounds) in the northern and eastern parts of Sri Lanka (Hellmann-Rajanayagam 1994; Shalk 1994; Swamy 1994). According to available evidence, the organisation has 'outlawed' the caste system, and banned the dowry system and other such repressive aspects of traditional Jaffna society. Adela Ann has noted that the LTTE is simultaneously engaged in two struggles, one for changing Tamil society from within (meaning demolition of the oppressive structure of caste and gender) and the other for the liberation of the Tamil homeland from the repressive Sinhala state (1993, 1994). While the origin of the militant ethno-nationalism of LTTE cannot be attributed to grievances within one section of Tamil society alone, there is considerable evidence that perhaps the most ardent support for the movement comes from the less privileged sections of Tamil society. Many outside observers see this as a major cause of the uncompromisingly radical stand of the movement (Schalk 1994).

It is important to note that in formulating its militant nationalist ideology the Tamil separatist movement has drawn much inspiration from elements within Tamil culture common to Tamilnadu and northern Sri Lanka. Roberts (1996) brings out the extent to which the Tigers' cult of martyrdom and readiness for self-sacrifice are rooted in the popular Cankam and *bhakti* traditions. Of particular interest is the highly emotive practice among the Tamil liberation fighters of applying an '*iraththa tilangam*' (application of a blood spot on one's own forehead or on the forehead of a Tiger hero by instantly and publicly slashing one's finger), at funerals of martyrs and other emotional occasions as an expression of deep commitment to the liberation struggle, of the determination to take revenge on the enemies, and to express the common identity of the militants. This, in turn, signifies that notions of common identity, derived from shared common blood stemming from caste ideology, continue in the Tamil liberation movement, creating an image of Tamil society as made of common blood as well as of common culture.

The evidence examined here indicates that certain changes in the caste system preceded the rise of ethnicity among northern Tamils in Sri Lanka. The changes in the caste system signified by the temple entry crisis are two-fold. On the one hand, the mobilisation of people along caste lines over the issue of temple entry indicates, to a certain extent, the continuation of caste dynamics and the ability of the dominant caste to reinforce its position despite the formidable challenges from the downtrodden. The resulting tensions between the dominant caste and the menial service castes on the other hand indicate an inevitable weakening of the organic solidarity model, in which each caste looks to several other castes for obtaining required goods and services offered within an assured hierarchical framework (Leach 1960; Dumont 1966). According to Leach, within the organic solidarity model even low castes had a sense of inalienable rights and certain privileges which were unique to them, and their willingness to respect the privileges of the higher castes rested firmly on the shared understanding of those rights and privileges. As the cement that holds the castes together (organic solidarity) begins to crack, the need arises for an alternative means of ensuring Tamil solidarity. Hence the 'defensive nationalism' and the resulting mobilisation of ethnic consciousness as a defence against possible fragmentation of Jaffna society.

Similarly, a degree of weakening of the hierarchical ideology was perhaps necessary for a strong ethnic ideology to evolve within a multi-caste society. This is because one could not visualise 'a deep horizontal comradeship' of the type typically associated with ethno-nationalism (Anderson 1983) where hierarchy remained intact. While it would be too idealistic to expect that the LTTE has rooted out all forms of hierarchy in Jaffna society, the rise of ethnic sentiment has proceeded hand in hand with a perception of a fundamental cultural and socio-political unity of the Tamil people conceptualised within the notion of '*eelam*' (a Tamil homeland devoid of caste, class and other forms of inequality). Finally, for ethnic sentiments to take root there must be a critical mass of people who wish to perceive their commonality and identity in ways other than in conventional caste terms.

The Tamil separatist movement and Tamil ethnicity in Sri Lanka in general cannot be discussed in isolation from the Sinhala-Buddhist nationalism of the majority ethnic group, against whose hegemony the Tamil separatist movement is in revolt. Unlike Tamil nationalism in Sri Lanka, the Sinhala-Buddhist nationalism of the majority ethnic group has had both hegemonic and anti-hegemonic forms. Sinhala-Buddhist nationalism was formulated by nationalist leaders drawn from the indigenous middle classes within the context of a relatively mild anti-colonial campaign started in Ceylon during the 19th century. Anagarika Dharmapala, the founder of the movement, who came from a Goigama-caste business family in Colombo, laid the framework for a Buddhist lay ethic which he identified as morally superior to Western values. Even though in the writings of Dharmapala minority commercial interests were identified as exploitative, sapping the vitality and wealth of Sinhala peasants, in its early stage Sinhala-Buddhist nationalism did not necessarily come in conflict with the interests of the minority ethnic groups. In addition, in the colonial era several of the upwardly mobile caste groups in the western coastal belt sought to improve their caste position through processes analogous to Sanskritisation. In his analysis of the rise of the Karawa elite in Sri Lanka, Roberts (1982) has illustrated the working of these processes among one of the caste groups among the Sinhalas.

Having kindled the ethnic sentiments of the Sinhala-Buddhists, excluding those sections of the ruling elite which were highly anglicised, the movement gradually lost its vigour until it was resurrected by the populist Mahajana Eksath Peramuna (People's United Front), led by S.W.R.D. Bandaranayake, in 1956 as a part of a political campaign to oust the Westernised ruling elite. Even though this politicised version of Sinhala-Buddhist nationalism adopted an anti-hegemonic stance in its attempt to challenge the ruling elite at the time and although it represented the interests of the 'common man' vis-a-vis the ruling elite, once elected to power, Sinhala-Buddhist nationalism made a hegemonic turn in its ideology by shaping discriminatory policies and programmes of the state represented by the 'Sinhala only' official language policy. In the run-up to the 1956 elections and in the subsequent eras Sinhala nationalism became more radicalised largely due to the participation of persons representing lower but upwardly mobile layers of Sinhala society, often referred to as the rural middle classes. The more militant forms of Sinhala nationalism were often associated with those coming from oppressed backgrounds, whether in caste or strictly socio-economic terms, who were unhappy with the status quo and who wished to improve both their economic position and social status (Chandraprema 1991; Moore 1993). For instance, some of the more ardent Sinhala nationalist politicians of both the Sri Lanka Freedom Party (SLFP) and the United National Party (UNP), the two leading political parties primarily representing the majority ethnic group, came from the upwardly mobile layers of the more marginal caste groups emerging from generations of feudal or semi-feudal oppression. The 1956 political change was associated with a disruption of traditional inter-caste relations in rural Sinhala society culminating in the passing of the Paddy Lands Act of 1958, which in turn led to conflict between landlords and tenants who typically came from high and low caste backgrounds respectively.

In more recent times the anti-hegemonic trends in Sinhala-Buddhist nationalism were manifested through the Janatha Vimukti Peramuna (JVP) which resorted to armed insurrection against the state in 1971 and again in 1987-89, largely with the participation of educated Sinhala rural youth from underprivileged backgrounds. It utilised a militant blend of nationalist and leftist ideologies to attract the rural youth who were economically frustrated, socially rootless and psychologically vulnerable. Referring to their social background and attitudes, Jiggins reported that:

> socialism and welfarism has ameliorated their situation but has not changed it greatly: the closer the young have come to a decent standard of life, to emancipation through education, to participation in public affairs through the radical politics of the established left-wing parties, the greater has been their frustration that the real fruits

have been reserved for the continuing traditional elites, and the real power pre-empted by a restricted caucus of Goigama families (1979: 132).

In essence the social background of JVP activists was in many ways similar to those of the LTTE activists except for the fact that the former came from the majority ethnic group. Education has raised their aspirations but the opportunity structure was no way in keeping with their aspirations. To add insult to injury, many of them also experienced social disabilities in that they had insufficient contacts with those wielding power and had low dignity because of their social origin. To them socialism and ethno-nationalism provided meaningful and complementary explanations of their plight and means of overcoming their problems. The JVP consciously mobilised Sinhala youth from selected 'depressed low-caste communities' in rural areas. The traditional upper caste leaders at the village level were one of the common targets of JVP attacks during 1987-89 period. On the whole, grievances arising from the caste system played an important role in the inner workings of the JVP movement (Chandraprema 1991).

The Sinhala-Buddhist nationalist agenda of the JVP was reflected in various ways. The JVP looked up to popular grassroots level national heroes of the past such as Weera Puran Appu. 'Motherland or death' was a popular slogan of the JVP. The JVP always identified itself as '*deshapremi*' (lit., lover of the homeland) and labeled its opponents as '*deshadrohi*' (lit., traitors to the cause of the homeland). The latter were popular targets of JVP attacks. The leader of the JVP adopted the name Rohana Wijeweera to signify his origin in southern Sri Lanka and his continuity with previous national heroes like Dutugamunu, who reportedly started his military campaign against the Tamil king Elara from a southern base. The leader of the military arm of the JVP of 1987-89 was known as Kirthi Wijebahu, reminiscent of a popular Sinhala king who successfully expanded his territory against invading Tamil kings between AD 1059-1114. Thus the JVP clearly represented the anti-hegemonic elements of Sinhala-Buddhist nationalism.

Ethnicity in the Sri Lankan context must be seen in part as a response to and, at the same time, a reaction against grievances arising from the caste system. This is clearly reflected in the fact that the Sinhalas use the same term *jati* to describe both caste and ethnicity. The different meaning of the term is conveyed by the context in which it is used and in the slight modification of the term depending on the context. For instance, the adjectival form *jatika*, which figures mostly in the mass media and public discourses, typically refers to ethnicity and ethnic nationalism. It may also point to a perception of some affinity between caste and ethnicity. The term jati literally means 'stemming from birth' or 'of one kind'. Both in the case of caste and in the case of ethnicity the term indicates 'primordial oneness of those identified as members of a group'. Similarly, phrases such as 'our people' (*ape minissu*) could mean people of the same caste or people of one's own ethnic group depending on the context. This suggests that ethnicity in the South Asian context perhaps involves a reformulation of ideas derived from the caste system. While caste hierarchy within an ethnic group is rejected or more commonly ignored, the primordial oneness within a single caste group, usually understood in terms of shared bio-genetic substances such as common blood, is applied to the whole ethnic group. Hierarchical notions may be applied to relations among ethnic groups rather than relations among different caste groups within a single ethnic group. This in turn raises the question: what happens to caste when ethnic consciousness is on the rise?

## Ethnic Consciousness: Its Rise and Impact on Caste Ideology

Once ethnic consciousness takes precedence over caste consciousness and hierarchical thought comes in conflict with egalitarian thought, at least at the ideological level, it is likely that social formations are conceptualised more in ethnic rather than caste terms. It may be expected that with the development of a stronger ethnic identity, lower order identities become less tenable. The extent to which such processes actually take place can be examined by considering some recent trends of ethnic polarisation in Sri Lanka.

The Sinhalas, the majority ethnic group in Sri Lanka, were traditionally divided into Kandyan Sinhalas and Low Country Sinhalas who in turn were divided into numerous caste groups which were endogamous. Roughly 50 per cent of the Sinhalas belong to the Goigama caste, which occupies the highest position in the Sinhala caste hierarchy, with the remaining Sinhala population divided into roughly 15 caste groups some of whom are geographically concentrated in certain areas in the country. The distinction between the Kandyans and Low Country Sinhalas have more or less disappeared in recent decades due to a variety of population movements between the so-called Low Country and Kandyan areas as well as due to intermarriage. Despite various demographic shifts in the country, caste distinctions have been maintained through the continuation of endogamy, particularly in rural areas, a degree of continuation in caste specific family names and political exploitation of caste identities and sentiments particularly during elections.

Names of Sinhala persons, however, have been undergoing radical changes since the colonial era. Traditionally, both family and personal names of individuals were caste specific with family names indicating either place of origin or occupational and cultural heritage of the people concerned. Place names, and occupational as well as cultural identities served to specify caste status within the hierarchical social space operating in local areas. Similarly personal names of individuals too tended to specify respectability, merit and relative position of each caste.

**Table 11.1**

**A Sample of Customary Names of Individuals in a Kandyan Village**

| Caste | Occupation | Family Name | Personal Name |
|---|---|---|---|
| Patti | Official/ Landlord | Wijethilaka Wasala Mudianselage | Tikiri Banda |
| Galladu | Smiths | Hangidi Gedera | Abarana Appu |
| Hena | Dhoby | Kuda Henayalage Gedera | Mutuwa |
| Nakathi | Drummers | Berakara Gedera | Pina |

*Source*: Silva 1986

Each of the names given in Table 11.1 was caste specific. The family names specified rank (for instance, Wijethilaka Wasala Mudianselage meant a descendant of a respected palace official) or caste occupation (for instance, Hangidi, Hena, Berakara all indicated respective caste occupations). Where place names were included as part of the family names they too indicated caste status as hamlets were caste-segregated in several areas in Sri Lanka. Personal names too were caste-specific in that honorifics or symbols applicable to respective caste statuses were often part of the personal names. In the personal names listed in Table 1. Tikiri Banda conveys authority, Abarana Appu conveys occupation ('Abarana' referring to jewellery and 'Appu' referring to service); Mutuwa (lit., 'like a pearl') conveys skill in washing cloths, Pina (lit., 'one who is given to merit-making') conveys the readiness and capacity of the drummer caste people to serve in temples and earn merit in the process. The names conveying caste identities had been maintained through administrative machineries dating back to the Kandyan kingdom with a vested interest in maintaining local caste hierarchies as well as through culturally-inscribed notions of the evil impact *(vas)* of any moves to adopt inappropriate names. The ability of even the low castes to perceive irreducible rights and a sense of special privilege within the caste system as illustrated by Leach (1960) may also have contributed to the perpetuation of caste identity through name usage.

Nowadays, caste-specific personal names have completely disappeared except in the case of surviving members of older generations, and caste specific family names too are generally on the decline. With rising educational levels, population movement and diffusion of egalitarian ideals, efforts have been made to adopt more fashionable names, particularly on the part of those from deprived caste backgrounds. Broadly speaking, two phases of name changes became evident. In the colonial era, middle level castes in the maritime provinces were the first to adopt anglicised family names of Portuguese origin, such as Perera, Silva, Soyza, De Alwis. The popularity of Westernised family and personal names declined in the 1930s and indigenous names resembling the names of national heroes and other popular local figures gained in popularity. In part due to the impact of Sinhala Buddhist nationalist movement and propaganda by nationalist leaders such as Anagarika Dharmapala, names from Buddhist canon classical literature such as Piyadasa, Dharmasena and Buddhadasa as well as names from Sinhala folklore and nationalist historiography such as Gaminie, Wijebahu and Parakrama have been increasingly adopted as personal names in place of both caste specific names and anglicised names of the previous eras. While in actual practice a complex intermingling of names can be seen, the broad process is one where any names conveying a low status in the traditional hierarchy are replaced by names conveying ethno-nationalist identities and sentiments.[1] Thus names and personal identities of individuals have been redefined in nationalist rather than caste terms signifying shifting personal identities in the modern era. There has been a corresponding redesignation of place names along nationalist lines particularly under new settlement programmes driven by nationalist agendas rather than pure developmental or technocratic considerations (Tennakoon 1988). Here we must also note that the name of the country itself was transformed from 'Ceylon' to 'Sri Lanka' in 1972.

In the emerging ethno-nationalist conceptualisations, all Sinhala-speaking people, irrespective of their caste and social status, are increasingly projected as members of *an extended kin group*. In offices all workers of similar or nearly similar ranks address each other as older brother (*ayya*) or younger brother *(malli)* and older sister (*akka*) or younger sister (*nangi)* depending on their gender and age. A similar trend is evident among school children and university students who always talk to those in senior classes as older brothers and older sisters and those in junior classes as younger siblings.This widespread notion of brotherhood\sisterhood within the majority ethnic group is a relatively recent development that occurred over the past two decades. Perhaps this practice disseminated throughout Sinhala society from the Sarvodaya Movement engaged in a crusade against moral decay. It became an accepted practice among the Sarvodaya workers to address each other as brother and sister, conceptualising the entire movement as 'one happy family'. The image of Sinhala society as one happy family is also repeatedly conveyed in popular Sinhala songs as evident from a verse in a popular song of Victor Ratnayake.

*Api okkoma rajavaru*
*Okkoma vasiyo*
*Tun Sinhalayama nadayo*

(All of us are rulers, and all of us citizens too; all of us who descended from the great Sinhala kingdoms of Ruhunu, Maya and Pihiti are kinsfolk.)

The practicc of addressing each other using selected kin terms in day-to-day social interaction is mainly found in select sections within the majority ethnic group. Occasionally this notion may be extended to known members of minority ethnic groups as well. Therefore, it cannot be seen purely as a manifestation of a feeling of ethnic solidarity. However, it signifies the diffusion of a broad-based but somewhat diluted kinship ideology as a moral bond linking known people of similar rank irrespective of their caste backgrounds. It is likely that those who share such a perception of 'a deep horizontal comradeship' typically come from one's own ethnic/linguistic community.

Given the social distance that characterised interaction among those of different castes in the past as expressed in highly formalised terms of address, differential seating arrangements for those of different castes and the deference and demeanour that those of lower castes were expected to display in their interaction with those of superior status, this new development must be seen as the extension of an anti-caste egalitarian idiom in place of the traditional hierarchical one within spheres of day-to day social interaction. It must be noted here that in rural Sinhala society local people within each caste group addressed each other using appropriate kinship terms irrespective of whether they are actual kin or not, indicating the culturally inscribed possibility of extending kinship within one's own caste group and conforming to the principle of caste endogamy. The new practice implies that at least in the realm of ideas the kinship ideology is now being stretched to cover the entire Sinhala ethnic group.

We must hasten to add, however, that the ethno-nationalist conceptualisation of 'a deep horizontal comradeship' among the Sinhala, conveyed in popular forms of address, remains highly inconsistent with the actual reality of deep-seated animosities and hostilities evident among people of the same ethnic group as well as between people of different ethnic groups in work places, neighbourhoods and communities of all types. In support of this assertion one can note that in recent years Sri Lanka has earned the dubious distinction of having one of the highest suicide rates in the world, besides being involved in a ruthless civil war (Silva and Pushpakumara 1996). If suicide can be seen as an index of inner stresses within each ethnic group, the practice of addressing fellow members of the ethnic group in kinship terms merely conceals the extent of turmoil within each ethnic community. Similarly, among the university students in Sri Lanka ragging,[2] the very process expected to generate equality and comradeship among students, has led to several casualties including unfortunate deaths of certain ragging victims, thereby indicating the serious gulf between ideology of comradeship and social practice (Silva et al. 1998).

One of the outcomes of the apparent popularisation of an egalitarian ethos within the majority ethnic group has been the increased tendency to conceal caste identities and look down upon any open expression of caste distinctions. The name changes discussed earlier clearly reflect this tendency to hide caste identities and replace them with ethno-nationalist identities where change of name is possible through personal choice. However, this does not necessarily mean a decreased importance of caste in critical issues like marriage and community activities. In effect people have become less comfortable about recognising or even mentioning caste in public discourses. There is no public debate about caste or any serious interventions on the part of the state or civil society to minimise caste inequality to the extent such interventions are evident in India. Caste continues to be important not only in private matters, such as selection of marriage partners, but also in certain public matters, such as voting in elections. In the theoretically anonymous settings such as new settlements and public institutions people practice the guessing game of caste, sometimes using euphemisms and indirect English usages, such as 'G caste', 'K people', 'person coming from a good family', when people have to refer to someone's caste position in public. This indicates an overall tendency to conceal objective social inequality as well as a subjective recognition of it in ways that adds to social unrest (Chandraprema 1991; Moore 1993). As Ortner (1998) has recently reported for class in the

US, caste in Sri Lanka increasingly forms a 'hidden identity'. On the other hand, resistance against caste and other social oppressions surface, from time to time in explosive outbreaks of violence such as the JVP uprisings in 1971 and 1987-89. This in turn suggests that despite its manifest egalitarianism as regards intra-ethnic social relations, ethno-nationalism tends to conceal rather than eliminate social inequality. More importantly, ethnic nationalism can often inhibit perception of and even justify inequality where it benefits one's own ethnic group usually at the expense of other groups.

## Conclusion

There is an apparent contradiction between caste and ethnicity at the ideological level. According to Dumont (1966), hierarchy is the operative principle of caste. This involves open and ritualised recognition of inequality among people of different castes in day-to-day social behaviour as well as in the conceptualisation of society itself. In contrast, ethno-nationalism, particularly in its more militant form, seeks to foster 'a deep horizontal comradeship' among the members of an ethnic group. It follows that ethnicity can only progress at the expense of caste. The political agendas of youthful organisations like JVP and LTTE may be superficially understood as signifying the transition from caste to ethnicity. Several of the political and social movements in South Asia may be seen as initiatives on the part of those from marginal caste backgrounds to redefine their identity in ethnic and ethno-nationalist terms.

The contradiction between caste and ethnicity, however, may be more apparent than real. To the extent ethnicity represents conceptualisation of a primordial oneness of a human collectivity possessing an assumed common cultural heritage and belonging to an assumed common stock, it tends to have some continuity with caste ideology. Hierarchy may easily shift from a model shaping inter-caste relations to a model shaping inter-ethnic relations. Chatterjee (1993) was perhaps right when he stated that 'the unifying concept of nation' has replaced the 'unifying force of dharma'. But we must realise that there are many forms of mutual accommodation, mutual reinforcement as well as inherent contradictions between caste and nationalist ideologies in the South Asian context. The Sri Lankan case on the other hand suggests that while ethnicity and ethno-nationalism thrive in the public domains of the mass media and national politics, caste consciousness devoid of practices leading to organic solidarity can continue in some fashion in the private domains of family and marriage. In contrast to ethnic identity, caste identity is muted but it does not necessarily make the latter less real. In such a situation, while ethnicity constitutes a contested terrain (field of discourse as evident from rival ethno-nationalisms), caste forms a field of doxa where the social order is seen as natural and, therefore, not amenable to change (Bourdieu 1977, 1990). Even though militant ethno-nationalism may involve some efforts to suppress caste, as is evident in the case of LTTE, it may merely conceal the reality of caste and thereby make it secretive, shameful and potentially more explosive. To the extent grievances generated by caste and other forms of inequality are the underlying causes of militant ethno-nationalism, one can even talk of a mutual reinforcement between caste and ethnicity. Similarly ethnicity and caste share a common ideology in that concern for purity of stock and exclusiveness is common to both.

Since ethnicity in parts of South Asia may have some continuity with the traditional caste system, it may be qualitatively different from ethnicity in the rest of the world. If 'caste attaches to the body and not to the soul' (Chatterjee 1993: 194), a parallel emphasis on purity of blood as reflected, for instance, in notions of Aryan or Dravidian origin may be more significant in South Asian ethnicity. This view needs to be explored further in future research on ethnicity and nationalism in the region. While caste represented an organic model within which differences were recognised and accommodated within a non-egalitarian framework, in its more militant forms ethno-nationalism can provide limited basis for accommodating socio-cultural diversity within a framework acceptable to all ethnic groups. In this regard ethnicity in the South Asian context can be closer to racism where differences between people are 'conceived as proceeding from somatic characteristics' (Dumont 1966: 16). In this sense ethnicity can pose a more serious challenge to nation building in South Asia.

## Notes

1. Names of Tamil liberation fighters too indicate a similar trend. Popular names of liberation fighters such as Thamil Chelvam, Chandrahasan and Pottu Amman may be cited as examples of this trend.

2. Ragging refers to the practice of subjecting annual newcomers to the student community to forms of verbal and physical abuse by the senior students as a mechanism for initiating the new students to the subculture of the student community.

## References

Anderson, Benedict. 1983. *Imagined communities*. London: Verso.

Ann, Adela. 1993. *Women fighters of liberation tigers*. Jaffna: Thasan Printers

____________.1994. *Unbroken chains: Explorations into the Jaffna dowry system.* Jaffna: Malathi Press.

Beteille, Andre. 1997. *Society and politics in India: Essays in comparative perspective.* Delhi: Oxford University Press.

Bourdieu, P. 1977. *Outline of a theory of practice.* Cambridge: Cambridge University Press.

____________. 1990. *The logic of practice.* Cambridge: Polity.

Chandraprema, C.A. 1991. *Sri Lanka: The years of terror; the JVP insurrection 1987-89.* Colombo: Lake House.

Chatterjee, Partha. 1993. *The nation and its fragments: Colonial and postcolonial histories.* Princeton, N.J.: Princeton University Press.

De Silva, K.M. 1986. *Managing ethnic tensions in multi-ethnic societies: Sri Lanka 1880-1985.* Lanham, MD: University Press of America.

Dumont, L. 1966. *Homo Hierarchicus: The caste system and its implications.* Chicago: University of Chicago Press.

Gordon, M. M. 1964. *Assimilation in American life.* New York: Oxford University Press.

Hellmann-Rajanayagam, D. 1992. 'Ethnicity and nationalism—The Sri Lanka Tamils in the late nineteenth century: Some theoretical questions', in D. Wiedemann, (ed.). *Ethnicity and political developments in South Asia.* pp. 25-49. New Delhi: Manohar.

____________. 1994. *The Tamil Tigers: Armed struggle for identity.* Stuttgart: Fraz Steiner Verlagi.

Jiggins, Janice. 1979. *Caste and family in the politics of the Sinhalese.* Cambridge: Cambridge University Press.

Kapferer, B. 1988. *Legends of people, myths of state.* Washington: Smithsonian Institute Press.

Leach, E.R. 1960. 'Introduction: What should we mean by caste', in E.R Leach (ed.). *Aspects of caste in south India, Ceylon and northwest Pakistan,* pp. 1-10. Cambridge: Cambridge University Press.

Moore, M.P. 1993. 'Thoroughly modern revolutionaries: The JVP in Sri Lanka', *Modern Asian Studies,* 27 (3): 593-642.

Ortner, S.B. 1998. 'Identities: The hidden life of class', *Journal of Anthropological Research,* 54 (1): 1-17.

Pfaffenberger, B. 1990. 'The political construction of defensive nationalism: The 1968 temple entry crisis in Northern Sri Lanka', *Journal of Asian Studies,* 49(1): 78-96.

Roberts, M. 1982. *Caste conflict and elite formation: The rise of the Karawa elite in Sri Lanka 1500-1931.* Cambridge: Cambridge University Press.

____________. 1996. 'Filial devotion in Tamil culture and the Tiger cult of martyrdom', *Contributions to Indian Sociology,* 31 (2): 245-72.

Schalk, P. 1994. 'Women fighters of liberation tigers in Tamil Ilam: The martial feminism of Atel Palacinkam', *South Asia Research,* 14 (2): 163-83.

Silva, Kalinga Tudor. 1986. 'Names of individuals in a Kandyan village: A socio-linguistic enquiry', *Nawa Samsriti* , 1 (1): 11-39.

Silva, K.T. and W.D.N.R Pushpakumara.1996. 'Love, hate and the upsurge in youth suicide in Sri Lanka: Suicide trends in a Mahaweli new settlement', *Sri Lanka Journal of Social Sciences,* 19 (1&2): 73-92.

Silva, K.T., C. Sivayoganathan and P. Ratnayake. 1998. 'Social class, gender and attitudes of senior undergraduates towards ragging', in *Confronting complexities: Gender perceptions and values*, pp. 69-83. Colombo: CENWOR.

Swamy, M.R.N. 1994. *Tigers of Lanka: from boys to guerrillas.* New Delhi: Konark.

Tambiah, S.J. 1992. *Buddhism betrayed? Buddhism, politics and violence in Sri Lanka.* Chicago: University of Chicago Press.

Tennekoon, Serena N. 1988. 'Rituals of development: The accelerated Mahaweli development program of Sri Lanka', *American Ethnologist,* 15 (2): 294-310.

# Contributors

G. ALOYSIUS is Professor, Centre for Social Studies, Surat.

MAITRAYEE CHAUDHURI is Associate Professor, Centre for the Study of Social Systems, School of Social Sciences, Jawaharlal Nehru University, New Delhi.

TANVEER FAZAL is a Research Scholar at the Centre for the Study of Social Systems, Jawaharlal Nehru University, New Delhi.

DIPANKAR GUPTA is Professor, Centre for the Study of Social Systems, School of Social Sciences, Jawaharlal Nehru University, New Delhi.

M.N. KARNA is Professor, Department of Sociology, North-Eastern Hill University, Shillong.

PROSHANTA NANDI is Professor at the University of Illinois, Springfield (Ill), USA.

T.K. OOMMEN is Professor, Centre for the Study of Social Systems, School of Social Sciences, Jawaharlal Nehru University, New Delhi.

VIKASH N. PANDEY is Reader, Tata Institute of Social Sciences, Mumbai.

JAGANATH PATHY is Professor, Department of Sociology, South Gujarat University, Surat.

M.L. SHARMA retired as Professor, Department of Sociology, Punjab University, Chandigarh. He is Managing Editor of the *Sociological Bulletin.*

KALINGA TUDOR SILVA is Professor, Department of Sociology, University of Peradeniya, Sri Lanka.

J.P.S. UBEROI retired as Professor, Department of Sociology, Delhi School of Economics, University of Delhi.

# Index